Essentials of ...

Everything you need to know to administ[...]

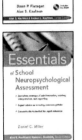

I'd like to order the follo..... Essentials of Psychological Assessment:

- ❑ WAIS®-IV Assessment (w/CD-ROM) / 978-0-471-73846-6 • $48.95
- ❑ WJ III™ Cognitive Abilities Assessment, Second Edition / 978-0-470-56664-0 • $38.95
- ❑ Cross-Battery Assessment, Second Edition (w/CD-ROM) / 978-0-471-75771-9 • $48.95
- ❑ Nonverbal Assessment / 978-0-471-38318-5 • $38.95
- ❑ PAI® Assessment / 978-0-471-08463-1 • $38.95
- ❑ CAS Assessment / 978-0-471-29015-5 • $38.95
- ❑ MMPI®-2 Assessment, Second Edition / 978-0-470-92323-8 • $38.95
- ❑ Myers-Briggs Type Indicator® Assessment, Second Edition / 978-0-470-34390-6 • $38.95
- ❑ Rorschach® Assessment / 978-0-471-33146-9 • $38.95
- ❑ Millon™ Inventories Assessment, Third Edition / 978-0-470-16862-2 • $38.95
- ❑ TAT and Other Storytelling Assessments, Second Edition / 978-0-470-28192-5 • $38.95
- ❑ MMPI-A™ Assessment / 978-0-471-39815-8 • $38.95
- ❑ NEPSY®-II Assessment / 978-0-470-43691-2 • $38.95
- ❑ Neuropsychological Assessment, Second Edition / 978-0-470-43747-6 • $38.95
- ❑ WJ III™ Tests of Achievement Assessment / 978-0-471-33059-2 • $38.95
- ❑ Evidence-Based Academic Interventions / 978-0-470-20632-4 • $38.95
- ❑ WRAML2 and TOMAL-2 Assessment / 978-0-470-17911-6 • $38.95
- ❑ WMS®-IV Assessment / 978-0-470-62196-7 • $38.95
- ❑ Behavioral Assessment / 978-0-471-35367-6 • $38.95
- ❑ Forensic Psychological Assessment, Second Edition / 978-0-470-55168-4 • $38.95
- ❑ Bayley Scales of Infant Development II Assessment / 978-0-471-32651-9 • $38.95
- ❑ Career Interest Assessment / 978-0-471-35365-2 • $38.95
- ❑ WPPSI™-III Assessment / 978-0-471-28895-4 • $38.95
- ❑ 16PF® Assessment / 978-0-471-23424-1 • $38.95
- ❑ Assessment Report Writing / 978-0-471-39487-7 • $38.95
- ❑ Stanford-Binet Intelligence Scales (SB5) Assessment / 978-0-471-22404-4 • $38.95
- ❑ WISC®-IV Assessment, Second Edition (w/CD-ROM) / 978-0-470-18915-3 • $48.95
- ❑ KABC-II Assessment / 978-0-471-66733-9 • $38.95
- ❑ WIAT®-III and KTEA-II Assessment (w/CD-ROM) / 978-0-470-55169-1 • $48.95
- ❑ Processing Assessment / 978-0-471-71925-0 • $38.95
- ❑ School Neuropsychological Assessment / 978-0-471-78372-5 • $38.95
- ❑ Cognitive Assessment with KAIT & Other Kaufman Measures / 978-0-471-38317-8 • $38.95
- ❑ Assessment with Brief Intelligence Tests / 978-0-471-26412-5 • $38.95
- ❑ Creativity Assessment / 978-0-470-13742-0 • $38.95
- ❑ WNV™ Assessment / 978-0-470-28467-4 • $38.95
- ❑ DAS-II® Assessment (w/CD-ROM) / 978-0-470-22520-2 • $48.95
- ❑ Executive Function Assessment (w/CD-ROM) / 978-0-470-42202-1 • $48.95
- ❑ Conners Behavior Assessments™ / 978-0-470-34633-4 • $38.95
- ❑ Temperament Assessment / 978-0-470-44447-4 • $38.95
- ❑ Response to Intervention / 978-0-470-56663-3 • $38.95
- ❑ Specific Learning Disability Identification / 978-0-470-58760-7 • $38.95
- ❑ IDEA for Assessment Professionals (w/CD-ROM) / 978-0-470-87392-2 • $48.95
- ❑ Dyslexia Assessment and Intervention / 978-0-470-92760-1 • $38.95
- ❑ Autism Spectrum Disorders Evaluation and Assessment / 978-0-470-62194-3 • $38.95

Please complete the order form on the back.
To order by phone, call toll free 1-877-762-2974
To order online: www.wiley.com/essentials
To order by mail: refer to order form on next page

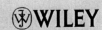

Essentials

of **Psychological Assessment** Series

ORDER FORM

Please send this order form with your payment (credit card or check) to:
John Wiley & Sons, Attn: J. Knott, 111 River Street, Hoboken, NJ 07030-5774

QUANTITY	TITLE	ISBN	PRICE

Shipping Charges:	Surface	2-Day	1-Day
First item	$5.00	$10.50	$17.50
Each additional item	$3.00	$3.00	$4.00

For orders greater than 15 items,
please contact Customer Care at 1-877-762-2974.

ORDER AMOUNT _____

SHIPPING CHARGES _____

SALES TAX _____

TOTAL ENCLOSED _____

NAME_____

AFFILIATION_____

ADDRESS_____

CITY/STATE/ZIP _____

TELEPHONE _____

EMAIL_____

❑ Please add me to your e-mailing list

PAYMENT METHOD:

❑ Check/Money Order   ❑ Visa   ❑ Mastercard   ❑ AmEx

Card Number _____ Exp. Date _____

Cardholder Name *(Please print)* _____

Signature _____

*Make checks payable to **John Wiley & Sons.** Credit card orders invalid if not signed.*
All orders subject to credit approval. • Prices subject to change.

To order by phone, call toll free **1-877-762-2974**
To order online: **www.wiley.com/essentials**

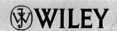

Essentials of
WMS®-IV Assessment

Essentials of Psychological Assessment Series
Series Editors, Alan S. Kaufman and Nadeen L. Kaufman

Essentials

of WMS®-IV
Assessment

Lisa Whipple Drozdick

James A. Holdnack

Robin C. Hilsabeck

John Wiley & Sons, Inc.

Published by John Wiley & Sons, Inc., Hoboken, New Jersey.
Published simultaneously in Canada.

This publication is designed to provide accurate and authoritative information in regard to the subject matter covered. It is sold with the understanding that the publisher is not engaged in rendering professional services. If legal, accounting, medical, psychological or any other expert assistance is required, the services of a competent professional person should be sought.

Designations used by companies to distinguish their products are often claimed as trademarks. In all instances where John Wiley & Sons, Inc. is aware of a claim, the product names appear in initial capital or all capital letters. Readers, however, should contact the appropriate companies for more complete information regarding trademarks and registration.

For general information on our other products and services please contact our Customer Care Department within the United States at (800) 762-2974, outside the United States at (317) 572-3993 or fax (317) 572-4002.

Wiley also publishes its books in a variety of electronic formats. Some content that appears in print may not be available in electronic books. For more information about Wiley products, visit our website at www.wiley.com.

Library of Congress Cataloging-in-Publication Data:
Drozdick, Lisa Whipple.
  Essentials of WMS-IV assessment / Lisa Whipple Drozdick, James A. Holdnack, Robin C. Hilsabeck.
    p. cm. – (Essentials of psychological assessment series)
  Includes bibliographical references and index.
  ISBN: 978-0-470-62196-7 (paper); 978-0-470-94643-5 (ePDF); 978-0-470-94644-2 (eMobi); 978-0-470-94645-9 (ePub)
  1. Wechsler Memory Scale.   2. Memory–Testing.   I. Holdnack, James A.   II. Hilsabeck, Robin C.   III. Title.
  BF375.5.W43D76 2011
  153.1'20287 – dc22
                                                            2010039796

10 9 8 7 6 5 4 3 2 1

To Keller, Hayley, and Aidan
LWD

To Tina, Julia, and Adam
JAH

To Tyler
RCH

Contents

Series Preface

I n the *Essentials of Psychological Assessment* series, we have attempted to provide the reader with books that will deliver key practical information in the most efficient and accessible style. The series features instruments in a variety of domains, such as cognition, personality, education, and neuropsychology. For the experienced clinician, books in the series will offer a concise yet thorough way to master utilization of the continuously evolving supply of new and revised instruments, as well as a convenient method for keeping up to date on the tried-and-true measures. The novice will find here a prioritized assembly of all the information and techniques that must be at one's fingertips to begin the complicated process of individual psychological diagnosis.

Wherever feasible, visual shortcuts to highlight key points are utilized alongside systematic, step-by-step guidelines. Chapters are focused and succinct. Topics are targeted for an easy understanding of the essentials of administration, scoring, interpretation, and clinical application. Theory and research are continually woven into the fabric of each book, but always to enhance clinical inference, never to sidetrack or overwhelm. We have long been advocates of "intelligent" testing—the notion that a profile of test scores is meaningless unless it is brought to life by the clinical observations and astute detective work of knowledgeable examiners. Test profiles must be used to make a difference in the child's or adult's life, or why bother to test? We want this series to help our readers become the best intelligent testers they can be.

The *Essentials of WMS-IV Assessment* continues the tradition of the *Essentials* series. The exceptionally qualified authors have provided a thorough introduction to the administration, scoring, and interpretation of the Wechsler Memory Scale– Fourth Edition. This major revision of the popular scale includes new subtests, new indexes, and a new type of score, all of which are described in detail. The interpretation information includes detailed case examples that illustrate various levels of interpretation, and an overview of the current clinical literature involving the WMS-IV as well as highlights from the WMS-III literature. This volume provides the examiner with the tools needed to administer and interpret results specific to the individual needs of a particular client. *Essentials of WMS-IV Assessment* is a valuable addition to the growing literature on the comprehensive memory assessment of individuals from late adolescence through old age. Because the WMS-IV was normed alongside the Wechsler Adult Intelligence Scale—Fourth Edition (WAIS-IV), and is commonly administered to individuals who are referred for evaluation on the WAIS-IV, this new *Essentials* book is a specially good companion for Lichtenberger and Kaufman's *Essentials of WAIS-IV Assessment*.

Alan S. Kaufman, PhD, and Nadeen L. Kaufman, EdD, Series Editors
Yale University School of Medicine

Acknowledgments

The authors would like to thank Justin B. Miller for providing data from his dissertation and Drs. Tammy Hietpas-Wilson and Russell Pella for assistance with illustrative cases. In addition, the work and assistance of André C. Lane, MA, Jayme Lyon, MA, and Elsa Tijerina, MA, was instrumental in the development of the WMS-IV and checklist of behaviors in Appendix A. The authors would also like to thank Drs. Tom Cayton and Larry Weiss for their support.

Essentials of
WMS®-IV Assessment

Chapter One

OVERVIEW

INTRODUCTION

Memory is a fundamental aspect of cognition, and characterization of memory functioning is an essential component of clinical and neuropsychological evaluation. A thorough assessment of the various aspects of memory is particularly important in individuals with known or suspected cognitive impairment. Many neurological and psychiatric disorders involve disruption or impairment of memory processes (e.g., dementia, traumatic brain injury). In normally aging older adults, decline in some aspects of memory functioning is common (Rockey, 1997; Smith & Rush, 2006). However, memory disorders are more prevalent in older adults, and complaints of memory decline are a frequent reason for referral in this population. Therefore, comprehensive evaluation of memory ability is needed to differentiate normally aging individuals from those experiencing more pathological memory loss.

The Wechsler Memory Scale–Fourth Edition (WMS-IV; Wechsler, 2009) is the most recent revision of one of the most popular memory assessment instruments (Rabin, Barr, & Burton, 2005). This book provides an easy-to-use reference for individuals learning the essentials of administration, scoring, and interpretation of the WMS-IV. It maintains the direct, systematic approach to presenting material that is characteristic of the *Essentials* series. In addition, administrative and interpretive guidelines are provided for those who administer complete or partial WMS-IV batteries and want to integrate the results with other tests, such as the Wechsler Adult Intelligence Scale–Fourth Edition (WAIS-IV; Wechsler, 2008) and Advanced Clinical Solutions for the WAIS-IV and WMS-IV (ACS; Pearson, 2009). Throughout this book, the latest research on the WMS-IV and on memory processes is provided to assist in applying results obtained with the WMS-IV.

Essentials of WMS-IV Assessment covers topics that emphasize the appropriate administration, scoring, interpretation, and application of the WMS-IV. Each chapter includes several "Rapid Reference," "Caution," or "Don't Forget" boxes to highlight important points for easy reference and clarification. At the end of each chapter, a short "Test Yourself" quiz is provided to help readers solidify what they have read. The information in this book is provided to help clinicians understand the nuances of the WMS-IV and become proficient users.

HISTORY AND DEVELOPMENT

The concept of memory and the assessment of memory ability have been widely researched. Early approaches viewed memory as a global skill, with emphasis in assessment placed on the ability to recall information, with scores generally reflecting overall memory ability. As research progressed, memory was broken down into subcomponents; short-term and long-term memory emerged as key concepts along with right- and left-hemisphere lateralization theories of memory. More recent conceptualizations of memory suggest even more memory components, as well as describe the influence of other cognitive abilities on memory functioning. The evolution of the Wechsler Memory Scale reflects this changing view of memory. Current research and theories on memory, as well as research on previous editions of the Wechsler Memory Scale, were utilized in the conceptualization and development of the WMS-IV. Therefore, it is important to review the previous editions to place the WMS-IV in context. Previous editions include the original Wechsler Memory Scale (WMS; Wechsler, 1945), Russell's adaptations of the WMS (Russell, 1975, 1988), Wechsler Memory Scale–Revised (WMS-R; Wechsler, 1987), Wechsler Memory Scale–Third Edition (WMS-III; Wechsler, 1997b), and Wechsler Memory Scale–Third Edition Abbreviated (WMS-IIIA; Wechsler, 2002b). Each of the editions reflects the knowledge and theories of memory at the time of its development. This section provides a brief history of the content and standardization of the Wechsler Memory Scales, while later chapters provide a review of the literature related to memory and research completed with the Wechsler Memory Scales.

VARIOUS EDITIONS OF THE WECHSLER MEMORY SCALE

The Original Wechsler Memory Scale (1945)

The Wechsler Memory Scale (WMS) was a brief survey of immediate memory skills. WMS included seven subtests: Personal and Current Information, Orientation, Mental Control, Digits Forward and Backward, Logical Memory, Associate Learning, and Visual Reproduction. For each subtest, the examinee recalled information immediately; no delayed conditions were included. This immediate recall only approach allowed for a quick 15- to 30-minute administration. A single composite score, the Memory Quotient (MQ), was derived and converted to a standard score metric that could be directly compared to a Full Scale IQ derived on the Wechsler

Adult Intelligence Scale (WAIS; Wechsler, 1955). The MQ reflected the examinee's overall memory performance. Although information was collected in visual and verbal modalities, no index level scores or comparisons were provided. Two forms were developed, allowing for an alternate form at retest; however, norms were developed only for Form I, so most research utilized Form I (Mitrushina, Boone, Razani, & D'Elia, 2005). Norms were based on 200 patients, ages 25 to 50, at Bellevue Hospital in New York; norms for younger and older individuals were extrapolated from this patient sample. Despite its problems, the WMS was widely used in practice and research (Erickson & Scott, 1977; Russell, 1981) and translations were developed and normed in five countries (Mitrushina et al., 2005).

Russell's Wechsler Memory Scale (1975, 1988)

In an attempt to improve the utility of the WMS, Russell adapted and renormed the scale. He administered the Logical Memory and Visual Reproduction subtests with a recall condition immediately after presentation *and* after a 30-minute delay filled with interference activities. His scale allowed for left (verbal)/right (visual) hemisphere and immediate and delayed memory comparisons. Russell's version gained some popularity and was utilized in several research studies (e.g., Brinkman, Largen, Gerganoff, & Pomara, 1983; Chlopan, Hagen, & Russell, 1990). He titled his revision the WMS-R, the same name given the later revision by the publisher. Although Russell's WMS-R improved upon the content coverage of the WMS, problems were noted with the normative sample and psychometric properties of the scale (Crosson, Hughes, Roth, & Monkowski, 1984; Curry, Logue, & Butler, 1986; Haaland, Linn, Hunt, & Goodwin, 1983).

Wechsler Memory Scale–Revised (1987)

The first revision of the test by the publisher, the Wechsler Memory Scale–Revised (WMS-R), expanded the original normative sample down to age 16 and up to age 74, added measures of delayed recall, and introduced a new visual memory task, Visual Paired Associates. The assessment of attention and concentration was also expanded in the WMS-R with the inclusion of Spatial Span. Eight subtests were included in the WMS-R: Information and Orientation, Mental Control, Digit Span, Visual Memory Span, Logical Memory, Verbal Paired Associates, Visual Reproduction, and Visual Paired Associates. The subtest scores were combined to form five index standard scores: Verbal Memory, Visual Memory, General Memory, Attention/Concentration, and Delayed Recall. The General Memory Index was comprised of the immediate recall conditions of both the verbal and visual memory subtests.

The WMS-R was a significant improvement over the original WMS, particularly with its larger normative sample (N = 316). It provided nine normative age groups, although norms for three of the age groups were interpolated from adjacent sampled groups. The normative sample for the WMS-R was also more diverse, reflecting the 1980 census. In addition, extensive reliability and validity data were collected. Similar to Russell's revision, the WMS-R allowed for evaluation of different aspects of memory through the new index scores, which were scaled on the same metric and thus were directly comparable. Finally, scoring procedures were improved through the provision of detailed scoring criteria, increasing reliability across examiners.

Despite these improvements, several problems were observed including low subtest and index reliability, floor and ceiling effects on several index scores, lack of an integrated theoretical foundation, a small normative sample and interpolated norms for three age groups, and lack of consistent factor analytic support for the index structure. In addition, the new visual memory tasks required other cognitive abilities beyond visual memory; one measured attention along with visual memory and one contained visual stimuli that were easily verbalized, confounding the visual memory task with verbal memory. Finally, the WMS-R did not include recognition memory tasks.

Wechsler Memory Scale–Third Edition (1997)

The WMS-III was developed with guidance from an advisory board of prominent memory researchers and neuropsychologists to address many of the criticisms of the WMS-R. A large representative sample of the population was collected to update the norms, and the age range was expanded to include ages 16 to 89. Each of the 13 normative age groups was sampled so no norms required interpolation, although weighting was used to increase the standardization sample from 1,032 actual test cases to the 1,250 cases used for norming. The WMS-III was conormed with the Wechsler Adult Intelligence Scale–Third Edition (WAIS-III; Wechsler, 1997a) and the Wechsler Test of Adult Reading (Wechsler, 2001). This conorming enabled the derivation of comparative statistics across the instruments.

In terms of content, delayed recognition trials were added for some of the subtests to assess for encoding versus retrieval deficits, the working memory tasks were updated, additional comparative scores were developed, and two new visual memory tasks (Faces and Family Pictures) were introduced. Also, several process scores were developed to examine individual skills utilized in subtest performance. For example, a copy condition was added to the Visual Reproduction subtest to enable clinicians to rule out psychomotor problems as a cause of impaired performance. Finally, scoring procedures and reliability were improved, and an upgrade to the scoring software provided demographic adjustments for the norms.

The WMS-III consisted of 11 subtests, six primary subtests required to derive index scores (Logical Memory, Verbal Paired Associates, Letter–Number Sequencing, Spatial Span, Faces, and Family Pictures) and five optional subtests that expanded the content areas assessed (Information and Orientation, Mental Control, Digit Span, Word Lists, and Visual Reproduction). The six primary subtests required an average of 42 minutes to administer (Axelrod, 2001) and were used to derive eight primary index scores (Auditory Immediate, Visual Immediate, Immediate Memory, Auditory Delayed, Auditory Recognition Delayed, Visual Delayed, Working Memory, and General Memory) and four auditory process composites (Single-Trial Learning, Learning Slope, Retention, and Retrieval). The General Memory Index was comprised of the auditory and visual delayed recall tasks and auditory recognition tasks. If all 11 subtests were administered, administration time increased to 100 minutes (Lichtenberger, Kaufman, & Lai, 2002).

The WMS-III resolved many of the problems observed in the earlier versions. However, several limitations were noted including:

- Increased length of testing (particularly for older adults)
- Inclusion of many more subtests in the standardized version compared to the final published version leading to questions about the effect of fatigue on the normative data (Doss, Chelune, & Naugle, 2000; Zhu & Tulsky, 2000)
- Poor quality of materials (e.g., the Visual Reproduction response booklet was produced on thin paper that was easily seen through)
- Lack of factor analytic support for the proposed index structure, particularly for the visual memory index (Burton, Ryan, Axelrod, Schellenberger, & Richards, 2003; Millis, Malina, Bowers, & Ricker, 1999; Price, Tulsky, Millis, & Weiss, 2002; Wechsler, 2002a; Wilde et al., 2003)
- Shared content between the WMS-III and WAIS-III, which created confusion when interpreting the two Working Memory Indexes as they were comprised of overlapping as well as distinct subtests
- Inclusion of potentially undiagnosed predementia cases in the normative sample, which may have reduced sensitivity in older adults in comparison to other memory measures
- Lack of clinical sensitivity in some subtests, particularly Faces and Word Lists (Glassmire et al., 2003; McDowell, Bayless, Moser, Meyers, & Paulsen, 2004)
- Problems with subtest score ranges, floors, or ceilings (Flanagan, McGrew, & Ortiz, 2000; Holdnack & Delis, 2004)
- Examiner difficulty tracking responses accurately on Spatial Span

- Excessive time required to score Visual Reproduction (Lichtenberger et al., 2002)
- Confounding of the Visual Memory Index as Family Pictures was easily verbally encoded
- Influence of guessing on scores on Faces (Levy, 2006)
- Failure to provide subtest recognition scores for primary subtests, in addition to the combined Auditory Recognition Delayed Index
- Inclusion of recognition memory in the General Memory Index, which affected the distribution of scores and interpretation of this index
- Lower reliability of supplemental index scores
- Lack of supplemental index scores for the visual domain
- Inclusion of only delayed memory tasks in the General Memory Index and therefore not representing global memory functioning

Wechsler Memory Scale–Third Edition Abbreviated (2002)

The WMS-IIIA was introduced as a screener for memory functioning, allowing a quick estimate of memory ability. It included the Logical Memory and Family Pictures subtests from the WMS-III, allowing assessment of both auditory and visual modalities. To maintain the brevity of the instrument, no recognition tasks were included. It took approximately 15–20 minutes to administer, although a 25- to 35-minute delay was required between the immediate and delayed conditions. Three composite scores were available, Immediate Memory, Delayed Memory, and Total Memory, and age- and education-corrected norms were available. The Total Memory Index included both immediate and delayed recall. Although the screener greatly reduced testing time, the content was directly lifted from the WMS-III. Thus, several of the problems with the WMS-III discussed previously also apply to the WMS-IIIA.

OVERVIEW AND ORGANIZATION OF THE WMS-IV

The development of the WMS-IV incorporated reviews of the psychometric properties of each WMS-III subtest and index to evaluate cultural and gender bias, reliability and stability, score range and distribution for floor and ceiling problems, and clinical utility. In addition, the content was reviewed to ensure appropriateness, thoroughness, and usability. Moreover, customer service data and research on the WMS-III were reviewed, surveys of WMS-III users were conducted, and a panel of prominent researchers and experts on memory and assessment was formed to provide feedback on the user's experiences with the WMS-III and potential areas for improvement. Detailed information on the modifications and improvements to the content, psychometric properties, and clinical utility are described in the *WMS-IV Technical and Interpretive Manual* (Wechsler, 2009). An overview of the changes is provided in Rapid Reference 1.1.

The WMS-IV includes seven subtests, utilized in two different batteries: Brief Cognitive Status Exam, Logical Memory, Verbal Paired Associates, Designs, Visual Reproduction, Spatial Addition, and Symbol Span (see Figure 1.1). The Adult

≡ *Rapid Reference 1.1*

Modifications from the WMS-III to the WMS-IV

Introduced two separate batteries for adults and older adults.

Norms reflect standardized version because the final battery was the same as the standardization battery.

Administration time for each battery is shorter than administration time for the entire WMS-III; the Adult battery has a longer administration time than the WMS-III primary subtests.

No overlap between WMS-IV and WAIS-IV.

Index structure simplified with supplemental indexes moved to ACS; General Memory Index dropped; and recognition memory removed from Delayed Memory Index.

Increased sample size from 1,250 to 1,400.

Fully sampled each age group (100 cases collected per age group), no weighting as was used in WMS-III.

Each normative age band had a mean WAIS-IV General Ability Index (GAI) score of 100.

Sample screened for cognitive impairment and effort.

Improved internal validity.

Improved subtest range, floors and ceilings.

Reduced impact of guessing on subtest and index scores.

Working Memory in visual modality only.

Modified and developed visual memory subtests to more accurately measure visual memory; Visual Reproduction scoring reflects memory ability.

California Verbal Learning Test–Second Edition (CVLT-II) score substitution developed.

Dropped supplemental subtests and cross-modality subtests: Family Pictures, Faces, Information and Orientation, Spatial Span, Word List, Letter–Number Sequencing, and Mental Control dropped.

Introduced contrast scaled scores.

Figure 1.1 WMS-IV Structure, by Battery

Domain Measured	Adult Battery	Older Adult Battery
Cognitive Status	Brief Cognitive Status Exam	Brief Cognitive Status Exam
Auditory Memory	Logical Memory I and II	Logical Memory I and II
	Verbal Paired Associates I and II	Verbal Paired Associates I and II
Visual Memory	Designs I and II	Visual Reproduction I and II
	Visual Reproduction I and II	
Visual Working Memory	Spatial Addition	Symbol Span
	Symbol Span	

battery is comprised of all seven subtests and is administered to individuals ages 16–69. The Older Adult battery contains five subtests (Designs and Spatial Addition are not included) and is administered to individuals ages 65–90. For individuals ages 65–69, examiners may administer either battery, depending on the needs of the individual being assessed. In addition to the different subtest composition, the content of Logical Memory and Verbal Paired Associates differs between the two batteries. Rapid Reference 1.2 lists the differences between the Adult and Older Adult batteries.

Three subtests were retained with modifications from the WMS-III (Logical Memory, Visual Reproduction, and Verbal Paired Associates), and four new subtests were added (Brief Cognitive Status Exam, Designs, Symbol Span, and Spatial Addition). Logical Memory, Verbal Paired Associates, Designs, and Visual Reproduction

≡ Rapid Reference 1.2

....

Differences Between Adult and Older Adult Battery

Adult Battery

7 subtests

5 indexes

14 items in VPA

Story B and C in Logical Memory

Older Adult battery

5 subtests

4 indexes

10 items in VPA

Story A and B in Logical Memory

have both immediate and delayed conditions. Delayed conditions are administered 20–30 minutes after the immediate condition and include optional recognition tasks. Seven WMS-III subtests were dropped from the WMS-IV: Word List, Faces, Family Pictures, Letter–Number Sequencing, Spatial Span, Mental Control, and Information and Orientation. Detailed information on the new and retained subtests and rationale for dropping subtests is provided in the *WMS-IV Administration and Scoring Manual* and the *WMS-IV Technical and Interpretive Manual.* Of the seven subtests, only the Brief Cognitive Status Exam (BCSE) is considered optional. All other subtests are primary and required to obtain the index level scores, although not all conditions within a subtest are required. Examiners may administer a subset of the subtests or subtest conditions if all the index scores are not required. Scaled scores are derived from the subtest raw scores and have a mean of 10 and a standard deviation of 3. Subtest and index abbreviations are used throughout the WMS-IV manuals and this book. Rapid Reference 1.3 lists the abbreviations used for the WMS-IV subtests and indexes.

Five index scores can be obtained with the WMS-IV (Auditory Memory, Visual Memory, Visual Working Memory, Immediate Memory, and Delayed

≡ Rapid Reference 1.3

WMS-IV Subtest and Index Abbreviations

Subtest/Index	Abbreviation
Brief Cognitive Status Exam	BCSE
Logical Memory	LM
Verbal Paired Associates	VPA
Designs	DE
Visual Reproduction	VR
Spatial Addition	SA
Symbol Span	SSP
Auditory Memory Index	AMI
Visual Memory Index	VMI
Visual Working Memory Index	VWMI
Immediate Memory Index	IMI
Delayed Memory Index	DMI

Figure 1.2 Organization of Subtests into Index Scores (Adult Battery)

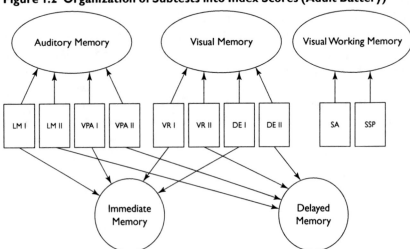

Memory), each comprised of at least two conditions or subtests. Four index scores are available for the Older Adult battery; the Visual Working Memory Index is not available because Spatial Addition is not included in the Older Adult battery. Figures 1.2 and 1.3 depict the organization of the subtests into the index scores for the Adult and Older Adult batteries, respectively. Unlike the WMS-III, General Memory and Recognition Indexes are not derived in the WMS-IV, and Auditory Memory and Visual Memory are not divided into immediate and delayed index scores. The Working Memory Index of the WMS-III has been replaced by the Visual Working Memory Index and is comprised of two new subtests. Standard scores are derived for each of the five indexes, with a mean of 100 and a standard deviation of 15.

Scores from the CVLT-II (Delis, Kramer, Kaplan, & Ober, 2000) may be substituted for the VPA scores required for computing index scores. Both VPA and CVLT-II are list-learning tasks and measure auditory verbal memory. This substitution allows an alternative measure for individuals who have difficulty comprehending the pairing of unrelated words required for VPA. The substitution of CVLT-II reduces testing time across a battery of tests when both CVLT-II and WMS-IV are administered. Figure 1.4 illustrates the composition of the WMS-IV index scores when CVLT-II scores are substituted for VPA I (immediate) and II (delayed) scores.

Don't Forget

....

CVLT-II scores can be substituted for VPA scores in computing index scores, but the CVLT-II itself is not included in the WMS-IV kit.

Figure 1.3 Organization of Subtests into Index Scores (Older Adult Battery)

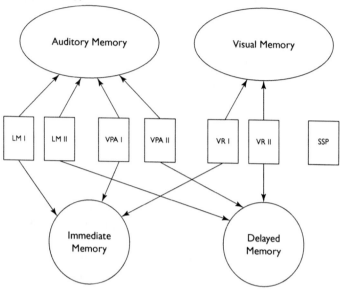

Figure 1.4 WMS-IV Index Structure with Substitution of CVLT-II for VPA, by Battery

	Adult Battery	Older Adult Battery
Auditory	Logical Memory I and II	Logical Memory I and II
	CVLT-II Trials 1–5 and Long Delay Free Recall	CVLT-II Trials 1–5 and Long Delay Free Recall
Visual	Designs I and II	Visual Reproduction I and II
	Visual Reproduction I and II	
Visual Working Memory	Spatial Addition	Symbol Span
	Symbol Span	(no index score available)
Immediate Memory	Logical Memory I	Logical Memory I
	CVLT-II Trials 1–5	CVLT-II Trials 1–5
	Designs I	Visual Reproduction I
	Visual Reproduction I	

(*continued*)

Figure 1.4 (Continued)

Delayed Memory	Logical Memory II	Logical Memory II
	CVLT-II Long Delay Free Recall	CVLT-II Long Delay Free Recall
	Designs II	Visual Reproduction II
	Visual Reproduction II	

Process scores provide additional information about WMS-IV performance and are provided as either scaled scores or cumulative percentages. Raw scores for all delayed recognition conditions and an optional copy condition for Visual Reproduction are converted to cumulative percentages presented in seven broad bands: ≤2, 3–9, 10–16, 17–25, 26–50, 51–75, and ≥75, reflecting the percentage of examinees in the standardization sample with the same or lower scores. Ranges are used in place of a specific cumulative percentage to account for measurement error in these scores. Separate content and spatial scores are provided for the Designs subtests and are converted to scaled scores. In addition, Word Recall, an optional free recall condition added to VPA, produces a scaled score.

Contrast scaled scores provide information about performance on one task adjusted for performance on another task. Similar to the manner in which demographic adjustments are derived for normative scores, one score is adjusted for performance on a separate score. For example, the Immediate Memory Index versus Delayed Memory Index Contrast Scaled Score adjusts the Delayed Memory Index for performance on immediate memory. The new score represents the examinee's performance on delayed memory in comparison to individuals of similar immediate memory ability. Contrast scaled scores are provided at the subtest and index level and are presented as scaled scores with a mean of 10 and a standard deviation of 3. Contrast scores are used to interpret scores in relation to similar ability peers; they do not replace subtest scaled scores and should not be substituted for subtest scores in reports or to compute index scores. Detailed information on the interpretation of contrast scaled scores is provided in Chapter Four.

Advanced Clinical Solutions (ACS) Additional WMS-IV Scores

Some of the scores available in the WMS-III were not used by the majority of users. Many of these scores were removed from the WMS-IV and included in the ACS to support ongoing research and clinicians who utilize the scores. This streamlined the WMS-IV for the general user. Additional process scores for the WMS-IV are provided in the ACS. The process scores in the WMS-IV and ACS describe the specific cognitive skills utilized in memory functioning that are not evident in the subtest or index scores. The process approach to cognitive assessment, which requires quantifiable scores but emphasizes qualitative interpretation of performance (e.g., error analysis), was pioneered by Heinz Werner (1937) and popularized by Edith Kaplan (1988). The ACS scores do not require any additional administration beyond the normal administration of WMS-IV. However, they do require additional scoring. These scores are not required; they enhance the interpretation and application of WMS-IV results. See Figure 1.5 for a list of the additional scores. ACS scores are included in this book as they can be obtained without administration beyond the standard WMS–IV. The ACS scores are presented as subtest scaled scores, cumulative percentages, index standard scores, or contrast scaled scores.

Figure 1.5 Additional WMS-IV Scores in ACS

Additional Index Scores	Auditory Immediate
	Auditory Delayed
	Auditory Recognition
	Visual Immediate
	Visual Delayed
	Visual Recognition
	Designs Spatial
	Designs Content
Additional Subtest Scores	LM I Story A First Recall*
	LM I Story A Second Recall*
	LM I Story A*
	LM I Story B
	LM I Story C†
	LM II Story A*
	LM II Story B
	LM II Story C†
	LM II Cue Given LM II Story A Recognition*
	LM II Story B Recognition
	LM II Story C Recognition†
	VPA I Recall A
	VPA I Recall D
	VPA I Easy Items
	VPA I Hard Items
	VPA I Extra-List Intrusions
	VPA I Intra-List Intrusions
	VPA I Intrusions
	VPA II Easy Items
	VPA II Hard Items
	VPA II Extra-List Intrusions
	VPA II Intra-List Intrusions

(continued)

Figure 1.5 (Continued)

Additional Subtest Scores (continued)	VPA II Intrusions VPA II Recognition Easy Items VPA II Recognition Hard Items VPA II Recognition Hits VPA II Recognition False Positives VPA II Recognition Discriminability VPA II Word Recall Intrusions VPA II Word Recall Repetitions DE Rule Violation[†] VR I Average Completion Time VR I Additional Design Elements VR II Average Completion Time VR II Additional Design Elements
Additional Contrast Scaled Scores	Index-Level Auditory Immediate Index versus Auditory Delayed Index Auditory Recognition Index versus Auditory Delayed Index Visual Immediate Index versus Visual Delayed Index[†] Visual Recognition Index versus Visual Delayed Index[†] Designs Spatial Index versus Designs Content Index[†] Subtest-Level LM I Story A First Recall versus Story A Second Recall[*] LM Story A First Recall versus Story A Delayed Recall[*] LM Story B Immediate Recall versus Delayed Recall LM Story C Immediate Recall versus Delayed Recall[†] VPA I Recall A versus Recall D VPA I Easy Items versus Hard Items VR I Average Completion Time versus Immediate Recall VR II Average Completion Time versus Delayed Recall

[*]Score is available for ages 65–90 only.   [†]Score is available for ages 16–69 only.

THEORETICAL AND RESEARCH FOUNDATION

The evolution of the WMS reflects the growing research on and theories of learning and memory, concepts that are closely intertwined. *Learning* is the process through which new information is acquired, and *memory* is the persistence of learning so that it can be recalled at a later time (Squire, 1987). Learning and memory are frequently discussed in terms of encoding, storage or consolidation, and retrieval. *Encoding* is the transformation of external information into mental representations or memories. It represents the concept of *how* information is taken in to the memory system. *Consolidation* is the process through which information in immediate memory is solidified into long-term memory stores, and bringing this information from storage into conscious awareness is *retrieval*.

Many theories of memory divide the construct into short-term memory and long-term memory (e.g., Atkinson & Shiffrin, 1968). *Short-term memory* refers to brief, temporary storage of information, lasting from a few seconds to a few minutes. Permanent or long-lasting memories, from hours to years, are considered *long-term memory*. The WMS-IV measures both short- and long-term memory with the immediate and delayed conditions of LM, VPA, DE, and VR, respectively. More recent theories incorporate *working memory* into the concept of short-term memory. Working memory is a limited capacity system in which information is temporarily stored and manipulated. In the model proposed by Baddeley and Hitch (1974) and revised by Baddeley (2000, 2003), the working memory system is comprised of the *central executive*, a supervisory system that regulates two information activation/storage systems, the *phonological loop* and the *visuospatial sketchpad*. The phonological loop processes and temporarily stores auditory information while the visuospatial sketchpad does the same with visual information. Figure 1.6 ties the memory processes described to the measures included in the WMS-IV. In addition, the *episodic buffer*, regulated by the central executive, shuttles information into long-term memory and holds interrelated information in working memory. The central executive regulates the working memory system through controlling the flow

Figure 1.6 Memory Processes Measured in the WMS-IV

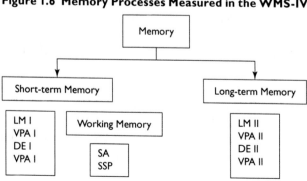

of information and the attention system, and engaging long-term memory as needed. It facilitates learning and other complex cognitive tasks by coordinating cognitive processes.

Long-term memory is often categorized as *implicit* (procedural) or *explicit* (declarative) memory. *Implicit* or procedural memory involves learning from experiences without the conscious awareness of learning, such as riding a bike or driving a car. *Explicit* or declarative memory is the conscious storage and retrieval of information, such as personal knowledge. Explicit memory is further divided into *semantic* and *episodic* memory. *Semantic memory* is the memory for facts and concepts, and *episodic memory* involves recollection of personal events and the contexts in which they occur. The WMS-IV is primarily a measure of declarative episodic memory as the "information presented is novel and contextually bound by the testing situation and requires the examinee to learn and retrieve information" (Wechsler, 2009, p. 2).

Brain Basis for Memory

A thorough examination of the literature on memory and neuroanatomy is beyond the scope of this book. This section provides a broad overview of theories on the brain and memory. For more comprehensive reviews, the reader is referred to other sources, such as Bauer (2008), Eichenbaum (2008), or Squire and Schacter (2002).

Multiple processes are involved in aspects of memory and must be intact for normal encoding, consolidation, and retrieval of information to be accomplished. Various injuries or disorders of the brain can affect different aspects of memory processes. In addition, problems with brain systems not directly associated with memory may also impact memory functioning. For example, attentional processes can impact normal memory functioning and should be considered when interpreting results. The brain systems that underlie episodic memory do not exclusively support episodic memory; they also activate during semantic and working memory tasks. The interdependence of abilities across systems and regions makes the specification of brain–memory relationships difficult.

A large volume of research has accumulated on the neuroanatomy of memory, implicating multiple regions and processes, particularly the structures within the medial temporal cortex. Memory circuitry in the brain involves the interaction of a number of brain regions; however, lesions in a specific region within the circuit may or may not produce complete amnesia. Dual systems hypotheses indicate that parallel memory systems, one involving the hippocampus and the other the amygdala, are critical in understanding memory impairment (Bauer, 2008). Lesions involving both the hippocampus and the amygdala, or those involving both the perirhinal and parahippocampal gyri can produce a severe amnestic syndrome. Additional amnestic syndromes may occur in the presence of lesions including both antero- and dorsomedial thalamic nuclei or in lesions involving structures within the basal forebrain (Bauer, 2008). The observed memory impairments will vary, depending on which structures are damaged.

Encoding of novel information involves the medial temporal lobe, particularly the hippocampus, and midline diencephalon. Damage to the medial temporal lobe region, as exemplified by the case of H. M. (Scoville & Milner, 1957), results in the inability to form long-term memories or anterograde amnesia, although procedural memory and short-term memory remain intact. Neurologic conditions that produce amnesia affect the hippocampus, amygdala, and nearby areas (e.g., fornix, mamillary bodies of the hypothalamus, and/or medial thalamic nuclei) (Bauer, 2008; Cummings & Mega, 2003).

Information appears to be stored in the medial temporal lobe temporarily before being consolidated into long-term memory (Shimamura, 2002; Squire, Cohen, & Nadel, 1984). Research suggests longer term storage occurs in the posterior neocortex, although the hippocampus plays a role in the long-term storage of episodic memories (Nadel & Moscovitch, 1997; Shimamura & Wickens, 2009). The hippocampus interacts with cortical structures via circuits involving mamillary bodies, thalamic nuclei, and the posterior cingulate and also through projections from the perirhinal and parahippocampal cortex (Bauer, 2008). Interactions are observed during consolidation and retrieval of memory, reflecting involvement of the hippocampus and the neocortex (Kryukov, 2008; Takashima et al., 2009; Wang & Morris, 2010). The inferior parietal cortex and anterior prefrontal cortex are implicated in the retrieval process (Buckner, 2003).

The frontal lobes also influence memory, with impairments producing deficits in episodic memory due to poor screening of irrelevant information, poor encoding of information, failure to employ an appropriate strategy during learning, poor initiation of recall, and/or low productivity (Nyberg, 2008). Individuals with frontotemporal dementias frequently demonstrate retrieval deficits along with executive dysfunction (Cummings & Mega, 2003). When deeper processing of information is achieved during encoding or retrieval, the dorsolateral prefrontal cortex is activated. Imaging studies show the importance of the dorsolateral and ventrolateral prefrontal cortex during encoding and retrieval (Buckner &

Koutstaal, 1998; Ranganath & Blumenfeld, 2008). Damage to the dorsolateral prefrontal or medial frontal cortex can result in memory impairment. Finally, patients with damage to the basal ganglia also show memory impairments (Packard & Knowlton, 2002). The utilization of working memory involves the complex interaction of multiple neurological systems. In general, the posterior brain regions seem to contribute storage functions to working memory, while rehearsal and executive functions are managed by prefrontal regions (Postle, Druzgal, & D'Esposito, 2003). Further, working memory appears to be processed in different regions depending on the type of memory involved. Spatial working memory, for example, activates the right prefrontal and parietal networks as well as the right dorsal stream of vision. Visual object working memory activates the left inferotemporal region and the left ventral stream of vision (Buchsbaum & D'Esposito, 2008).

STANDARDIZATION AND PSYCHOMETRIC PROPERTIES

The standardization sample for the WMS-IV was comprised of 1,400 individuals selected to form a representative sample of the U.S. population based on the 2005 U.S. Census data. It was stratified based on age, sex, race/ethnicity, education level, and geographic region. Sex was evenly sampled for ages 16–69 and representative of the population for ages 70–90. Fourteen normative age bands were created, each with a sample of 100 participants. Nine age bands were given the Adult battery and five were administered the Older Adult battery. Two groups were collected for individuals ages 65–69, one for each battery. The CVLT-II was completed by 380 individuals from the normative sample to allow for calculation of VPA I and II equivalent scaled scores.

Average split-half reliability coefficients for the index scores range from 0.93 for the VWMI to 0.96 for the VMI in the Adult battery and from 0.92 for DMI to 0.97 for VMI in the Older Adult battery. In a sample of 555 individuals diagnosed with a variety of clinical disorders, the average split-half reliability coefficients range from 0.93 for VWMI to 0.98 for VMI. Average subtest reliability coefficients for the normative samples range from 0.82 for LM I to 0.97 for VR II in the Adult battery and from 0.74 for VPA II to 0.96 for VR II in the Older Adult battery. In the clinical sample, the average split-half reliability coefficients range from 0.86 for LM I to 0.97 for VR II. Rapid Reference 1.4 provides the split-half reliability for all index and subtest scores in the normative sample. Sattler (2008) suggests that reliabilities should be above 0.80 for individual assessments. It is suggested that scores with reliabilities below this level be interpreted with caution, with greater care for those with reliabilities below 0.75.

≣ Rapid Reference 1.4

Reliability and Stability Coefficients for Subtest and Index Scores

Average WMS-IV Index and Subtest Internal Consistency and Test–Retest Reliability Coefficients by Battery

	Adult Battery		Older Adult Battery	
	Average Reliability r_{xx}	Average Test–Retest r_{12}	Average Reliability r_{xx}	Average Test–Retest r_{12}
Index Scores				
Auditory Memory Index	0.95	0.81	0.95	0.82
Visual Memory Index	0.96	0.80	0.97	0.79
Visual Working Memory Index	0.93	0.82		
Immediate Memory Index	0.95	0.81	0.95	0.84
Delayed Memory Index	0.94	0.79	0.92	0.80
Subtest Scores				
Logical Memory I	0.82	0.72	0.86	0.77
Logical Memory II	0.85	0.67	0.87	0.71
Verbal Paired Associates I	0.94	0.76	0.93	0.76
Verbal Paired Associates II	0.85	0.76	0.74	0.77
Designs I	0.85	0.73		
Designs II	0.85	0.72		
Visual Reproduction I	0.93	0.62	0.93	0.79
Visual Reproduction II	0.97	0.59	0.96	0.64

(continued)

	Adult Battery		Older Adult Battery	
	Average Reliability r_{xx}	Average Test-Retest r_{12}	Average Reliability r_{xx}	Average Test-Retest r_{12}
Spatial Addition	0.91	0.74		
Symbol Span	0.88	0.72	0.84	0.69

Note. Average reliability coefficients were calculated with Fisher's z transformation.

Standardization data from the Wechsler Memory Scale–Fourth Edition (WMS-IV). Copyright ©2009 NCS Pearson, Inc. Used with permission. All rights reserved.

The test–retest sample consisted of 244 individuals, 173 completed the Adult battery and 71 completed the Older Adult battery. Testings were an average of 23 days apart (range: 14–84). Memory and learning measures are particularly susceptible to practice effects that lower test–retest correlations (Strauss, Sherman, & Spreen, 2006) due to repeated exposure of the stimuli to be recalled. This is observed in the WMS-IV data. Test–retest reliabilities for all index and subtest scores are listed in Rapid Reference 1.4. Test–retest coefficients for the Adult battery ranged from 0.79 to 0.82 for the index standard scores and from 0.59 to 0.76 for the subtest scaled scores. For the Older Adult battery, test–retest coefficients ranged from 0.79 to 0.84 for the index standard scores and from 0.64 to 0.77 for the subtest scaled scores. The effect sizes ranged from 0.29 to 0.95 across the index scores and from 0.20 to 0.96 across the subtest scores, indicating small to large changes in performance across testing. The smallest changes were observed on the VWMI, while changes approaching 1 standard deviation were observed between testings on the AMI, IMI, and DMI. Given the high degree of change in these scores, it is suggested that WMS-IV memory subtests not be given a second time within a short time interval (e.g., 1–3 months). If a second administration is given within a short time frame, practice effects should be considered when interpreting differences between scores.

CAUTION

Memory and learning measures are particularly susceptible to practice effects, and changes approaching 1 standard deviation on some index scores may be observed if the WMS-IV is readministered after a short time interval (i.e., 1–3 months).

COMPREHENSIVE REFERENCES ON TEST

The most detailed and comprehensive information on the WMS-IV can be found in the *WMS-IV Administration and Scoring Manual* and *WMS-IV Technical and Interpretive Manual.* The *WMS-IV Administration and Scoring Manual* provides an overview of the test, descriptions of each subtest and score, and detailed information on subtest administration and scoring, calculating the index scores, and completing discrepancy analyses. Information on the theoretical underpinnings, development and standardization, reliability, validity, and interpretation is provided in the *WMS-IV Technical and Interpretive Manual.* Detailed information on the ACS Additional Scores can be found in the *ACS Administration and Scoring Manual* and the *ACS Clinical and Interpretive Manual.* In addition, the ACS manuals provide an overview of the use of demographic adjustments to WMS-IV norms, and information on premorbid memory prediction, effort assessment, and serial assessment with WMS-IV.

Tulsky et al. (2003) provide a thorough review of the Wechsler Memory Scales, the application and clinical use of the WMS–III, and related research in *Clinical Interpretation of the WAIS-III and WMS-III.* A chapter by Holdnack and Drozdick in *WAIS-IV Clinical Use and Interpretation: Scientist–Practitioner Perspectives* (Weiss, Saklofske, Coalson, & Raiford, 2010) is devoted to the use of the WMS-IV with WAIS-IV. Groth-Marnat (2009) devotes a chapter in *Handbook of Psychological Assessment–Fifth Edition* to the Wechsler Memory Scales, with a detailed overview of the WMS-IV and its clinical use. It is expected that more research on the WMS-IV will become available as the revision is more widely used. Rapid Reference 1.5 provides basic reference and publication information on the WMS-IV.

Rapid Reference 1.5

Publication Data for WMS-IV

Author: David Wechsler

Publication Date: 2009

What Test Measures: Auditory and Visual Memory, Visual Working Memory, Immediate and Delayed Memory, Cognitive Status

Age Range: 16–90

Administration Time:

Adult Battery: 90 minutes for complete battery

Older Adult Battery: 45 minutes for complete battery

(*continued*)

Qualification of Examiners: Graduate- or professional-level training in
  psychological assessment

Publisher: Pearson

19500 Bulverde Road

San Antonio, TX 78259

Order Phone Number: 1-800-211-8378

www.PsychCorp.com

Price: Complete Kit (as of June 2010): $699.00

🐾 TEST YOURSELF 🐾

1. **One of the biggest changes from the WMS-III to the WMS-IV is the
   introduction of different batteries for examinees based on age. The
   Older Adult battery is shorter than the Adult battery to decrease
   administration time and to lower the floor in older adults. Which index
   is not included in the Older Adult battery?**

   (a) Visual Memory Index

   (b) Visual Working Memory Index

   (c) Immediate Memory Index

   (d) Delayed Memory Index

2. **The General Memory Index (GMI) of the WMS-III was a measure of
   global delayed memory. This was replaced with the Delayed Memory
   Index (DMI) in the WMS-IV. What is the main difference between the
   WMS-IV DMI and the GMI of the WMS-III?**

   (a) Recognition tests were included in the GMI but were not included in the
        DMI.

   (b) The DMI is comprised of auditory memory only, while the GMI included
        both auditory and visual memory.

   (c) The GMI was comprised of visual memory only, while the DMI includes
        both auditory and visual memory.

   (d) The DMI includes recognition memory, but the GMI included only
        delayed recall memory.

3. **A new capability in the WMS-IV involves the substitution of scores from the CVLT-II for two subtest scores. For which subtest scores can scores from the CVLT-II be substituted?**

   (a) Logical Memory I and II

   (b) Visual Reproduction I and II

   (c) Verbal Paired Associates I and II

   (d) Symbol Span and Spatial Addition

4. **Auditory Immediate Index, Auditory Delayed Index, and Auditory Recognition Index are all part of the:**

   (a) Advanced Clinical Solutions for the WAIS-IV and WMS-IV

   (b) Auditory Memory Index of the WMS-IV

   (c) General Memory Index of the WMS-III

   (d) Delayed Memory Index of the WMS-IV

5. **Contrast scaled scores adjust one score for performance on another score. When should contrast scaled scores be used?**

   (a) To substitute for an invalid subtest scaled score

   (b) To compute index scaled scores for individuals at the extremes of the distribution

   (c) To contrast scores obtained on one subtest with those obtained on another unrelated subtest

   (d) To assist in interpretation of performance in relation to similar ability peers

6. **The ACS additional scores can be obtained with a standard WMS-IV administration.**

   True/False

7. **The WMS-IV is a measure of:**

   (a) Global memory ability

   (b) Declarative episodic memory and visual working memory

   (c) Implicit memory and working memory

   (d) Visual working memory and auditory working memory

8. **Systems utilized in episodic memory encoding, storage, and retrieval are exclusive to those functions.**

   True/False

Answers: 1. b, 2. a, 3. c, 4. a, 5. d, 6. True, 7. b, 8. False

Chapter Two

HOW TO ADMINISTER THE WMS-IV

Due to the long history and use of the Wechsler Memory Scales, you may be familiar with many aspects of WMS administration. However, the Wechsler Memory Scale–Fourth Edition (WMS-IV) is a significant revision and introduces new procedures that will not be familiar. Proper administration of the WMS-IV requires adherence to the guidelines and instructions provided in the *WMS-IV Administration and Scoring Manual*. The standard instructions were developed to ensure consistent administration across examiners, decrease measurement error due to use by multiple examiners, and increase reliability of results. Failure to follow the standardized presentation, administration, recording, and scoring instructions may result in the inability to apply normative data. Detailed instructions on developing rapport, setting up the testing environment, correctly using the kit materials, administering each subtest, and recording responses are provided in the *WMS-IV Administration and Scoring Manual*. In addition, general instructions used across subtests, such as start and stop rules, prompts and timing, are provided. Before using the WMS-IV, familiarize yourself with the administration guidelines and instructions. You may find it helpful to administer a few practice cases to become accustomed to the materials and instructions. The more familiar you are with the WMS-IV prior to administration, the greater attention you can place on the examinee during the test session.

Clinical questions or behaviors observed during testing may suggest the need to "test the limits" with an examinee. For example, an examinee may not recall any items on the delayed condition of Visual Reproduction (VR). To test the extent of impairment, you may want to provide cues to assist in recall, such as "This design had flags." This further testing allows a more thorough evaluation of an examinee's strengths and weaknesses through testing of hypotheses related to the examinee's performance. While the information gained from deviating from standard administration may be diagnostically and therapeutically useful, it is imperative that any modifications occur after the standard administration is completed. In the previous example on VR delayed recall, the cuing should occur only after the standard administration of delayed recall, and scores should not include those items recalled after cuing. Scores obtained under unstandardized administration may be invalid. It should be noted that some modifications may impact performance on later conditions within the same subtests. Continuing with the VR delayed recall example, cuing immediately after delayed recall could enhance performance on the recognition condition, even if the recognition task is administered in the standard manner.

APPROPRIATE TESTING CONDITIONS

Testing Environment

The ideal testing environment for the WMS-IV is a quiet, well-lit room with minimal distractions. This environment can be set up in a variety of locations, including clinics, offices, schools, and hospitals. The examinee should sit with his or her back to any large visual distractions, such as windows or computer monitors. In addition, if you are administering the Brief Cognitive Status Exam (BCSE), any clocks in the room should be out of direct sight of the examinee. Every attempt to minimize interruptions during testing should be made. For example, when testing in a school, attempt to schedule the test session around class transition times to avoid bells or loud hallway noise. Ensure adequate time is allowed for testing or divide testing into multiple sessions. If multiple sessions are planned, administer all conditions of a subtest in the same session. Although you may not have access to an ideal testing environment to administer the WMS-IV in all cases, every effort should be made to ensure the examinee's performance is not negatively affected by the testing environment.

Prior to testing, put some effort into setting up the room. The WMS-IV should be administered at a table or desk wide enough to support the width of the stimulus book. The height of the table and chairs should be appropriate for the individual being tested so that his or her feet rest comfortably on the floor. If you use a desk for testing, ensure adequate legroom under the desk for comfortable sitting space for the examinee. You may also want to ensure the examinee sits in a chair without wheels to reduce excessive movement during testing, particularly if hyperactivity or motor tics are a concern. The surface of the table should be smooth to easily accommodate written responses. If the table is rough or uneven, place cardboard underneath the response booklet when administering the BCSE and VR.

During testing, the examinee should sit directly across from you within easy reach of presented test materials. Sitting across from the examinee allows you to fully observe the examinee throughout testing and maintain control over the test materials. The stimulus books are presented flat on the table between you and the examinee to allow you a clear view of the instructions and the examinee's responses. All correct responses are included on the record form, not the stimulus books, to accommodate the flat presentation. To present the stimulus book correctly, place the stimulus book on the table with the cover facing you and turn the pages toward the examinee. Several subtests require pointing for responses so place the stimulus book within a comfortable distance from the examinee to allow pointing. Materials not in use should be placed out of sight and reach of the examinee but within easy reach for you, for example, on a chair or small table to the side of your chair. Keeping materials out of sight of the examinee will help reduce anxiety about future subtests or the length of testing, and minimize distractions during testing. This is particularly important on the WMS-IV, as poor attention on the immediate condition can impact performance on multiple delayed conditions of a subtest. Keep an eye out for signs of discomfort in the examinee, including increased shifting in the chair, and take a break or adjust the room accordingly.

Throughout testing, the record form should be placed on a clipboard to keep it out of sight of the examinee and to provide a hard surface on which to record responses. The stories and word lists for the verbal memory subtests and correct responses for most of the subtests are presented in the record forms. You will need to read these stimuli from the record form, so place the record form on the clipboard to easily read the verbal stimuli. Ensure you are using the correct record form for the examinee's age. If you are administering the complete WMS-IV, administer subtests in the order they are presented in the record form. A stopwatch is required during the visual working memory subtests and may be placed in your lap or on the table, whichever is most comfortable for you. You may also record completion times for VR items. Try to avoid obvious attempts to conceal materials as this may make the examinee uncomfortable and damage rapport. You will also need access to a clock or watch if you administer the BCSE.

You and the examinee should be the only individuals in the room during testing. However, in some cases this is not feasible or desirable such as when an aide or caregiver needs to remain with the examinee. In such cases, speak to the aide prior to the test session and establish rules regarding his or her assistance during the session. It should be made clear that he or she cannot assist the individual in responding to items as the test needs to be administered under the same rules to everyone in order to obtain a true picture of the examinee's abilities. For caregivers of individuals with communication problems, it may help to clarify that you will ask them for assistance when it is needed. Establishing the rules before the testing session will help the assessment go more smoothly and avoid conflict during the session, which may influence the examinee's performance.

Testing Materials

The majority of items required for administering the WMS-IV are included in the WMS-IV test kit. In addition to the kit materials, you will need to supply a stopwatch for timing, a watch to administer the BCSE time estimation item and to measure time between completing an immediate condition and beginning a delayed condition, two pencils (one with an eraser and one without) for administering the BCSE and VR items in the response booklet, a pencil or pen for recording responses in the record form, and a clipboard. Although space is provided on the record forms for observations, you may want to have additional paper to take notes on during the test session. The stimulus books contain all the administration directions required for administering the WMS-IV and are displayed throughout the test session. The *WMS-IV Administration and Scoring Manual* contains detailed scoring information required for obtaining scores upon completion of the test session but is not required during the test session. Rapid Reference 2.1 lists the materials contained in the WMS-IV test kit.

Rapid Reference 2.1

WMS-IV Test Kit Materials

WMS-IV Administration and Scoring Manual
WMS-IV Technical and Interpretive Manual
Adult Battery Record Forms
Older Adult Battery Record Forms
Response Booklets
Stimulus Books 1 and 2
Memory Grid
Designs and Spatial Addition Cards in Card Box
Scoring Template
Training CD

CAUTION

....

Additional Materials Required for Administering the WMS-IV

- Stopwatch
- Watch or clock
- Pencils with erasers
- Pencils without erasers
- Pencil or pen for examiner
- Clipboard
- Blank paper for taking notes

The memory grid is a new item in the WMS-IV kit and is used for the Designs (DE) and Spatial Addition (SA) subtests. It is not required for administration of the Older Adult battery. It may take several practice attempts to master administration of items using the grid and recording of responses. Follow the guidelines in the *WMS-IV Administration and Scoring Manual*, which are demonstrated in the training CD, to properly use the memory grid. Rapid Reference 2.2 lists general guidelines for using the memory grid.

≡ *Rapid Reference 2.2*

....

Guidelines for Use of the Memory Grid

- All words on the grid should appear upside up or in correct orientation to you throughout use of the grid.
- Cards should be presented in a stack with the design/circle side up.
- Cards do not need to be pushed completely into the grid in order to stay in place when the grid is lifted.
- Assist examinees in placing cards in the grid if necessary, but don't suggest which card or in which location to place the card.
- To record a response, invert the grid by lifting the side closest to you so that you can see the card identifiers through the holes in the grid. Record the card identifiers in the miniature grid on the record form.
- Remove cards by pushing your finger through the holes in the grid.

ORDER OF TEST ADMINISTRATION

When administering one of the standard WMS-IV batteries, the subtests should be presented in the order listed in the record form for the chosen battery. The Adult and Older Adult batteries have different administration orders. The stimulus books present the subtests in the administration order for the Adult battery. When you are administering the Older Adult battery, be sure to follow the order on the record form. If California Verbal Learning Test–Second Edition (CVLT-II) scores are being substituted for Verbal Paired Associates (VPA) scores, skip over VPA during administration. Administration of the CVLT-II should be completed either before or after the completion of the WMS-IV; it should not be administered in place of VPA I and II during administration of the WMS-IV.

It is important to note that not all conditions of a subtest need to be administered during a standard administration. Only the immediate and delayed recall conditions are used to calculate index scores. For example, on VPA, if you only want to obtain the index scores, the recognition and word recall conditions do not need to be administered. All the administration times listed in the *WMS-IV Administration and Scoring Manual* are based on the administration of all of the available conditions in a subtest.

The WMS-IV is a thorough assessment of memory ability, requiring sustained effort by the examinee. It should be administered near the beginning of a series of instruments, after a less effortful test if possible. Frequently, the WMS-IV is given with a measure of general intellectual ability, such as the Wechsler Adult Intelligence Scale–Fourth Edition (WAIS-IV), Kaufman Adolescent and Adult Intelligence Test (KAIT; Kaufman & Kaufman, 1993), Woodcock–Johnson Tests of Cognitive Ability–Third Edition (WJ-III; Woodcock, McGrew, & Mather, 2000), Wechsler Abbreviated Scale of Intelligence (WASI, Pearson, 2000), or other measure of intelligence. The administration of both intelligence and memory measures allows the examination of memory within the context of general ability level. Joint norms were collected during the conorming of the WAIS-IV and WMS-IV, allowing direct comparisons of performance between the two measures through the creation of comparative statistics and contrast scores. Interpretation of performance across WAIS-IV and WMS-IV is discussed in Chapter Six. It is recommended that WMS-IV be given prior to WAIS-IV as research on earlier versions demonstrated small order effects on performance on the WMS-III when WAIS-III was given first, but not vice versa (Zhu & Tulsky, 2000).

ADMINISTERING A PARTIAL WMS-IV BATTERY

Unlike previous editions of the WMS, the only optional subtest included in the WMS-IV is the BCSE. Therefore, to obtain all the available index scores, all subtests in the appropriate battery need to be administered. In many clinical situations, a complete WMS-IV is not feasible or necessary to answer the clinical questions for a particular client. Many examiners choose to administer subsets of the WMS-IV based on the clinical needs of the examinee. For example, Logical Memory (LM) and VR are frequently administered outside of the administration of a full WMS-IV. Moreover, subtests from the WMS-IV are frequently used within a larger assessment battery designed by the examiner. This selection of subtests allows examiners to focus limited testing time on measuring abilities related to the referral question.

When choosing to give a portion of the WMS-IV, it is important to select subtests that will ensure you obtain the information you need to answer the referral question. Developing a partial battery of subtests often involves changing the administration order of the subtests. There are several issues that need to be considered when re-ordering subtests. Do not administer SA between the immediate and delayed conditions of DE, as the spatial component of SA may interfere with the delayed recall of the spatial placement of the cards in DE. SA may be administered prior to DE I or following DE II. Symbol Span (SSP) should not be administered between either of the visual memory subtests, as the symbols could interfere with the recall of the content of these subtests. Also, if you are not administering VR I as the first memory subtest, you will need to add a prompt to the subtest you administer first. At the end of the immediate recall condition, say, "Later I will ask you to (tell me the stories, remember the designs and where they are on the page, say the words) again, so try to remember them." You need to give this prompt only once since it creates the cognitive set for the following memory subtests. Finally, it is generally a good idea to switch between visual and verbal memory as you administer subtests. This helps testing remain interesting for the examinee and does not overly tax one memory system.

CAUTION

Warnings on Changing Administration Order

Don't give Symbol Span before or between Visual Reproduction I and II.

Don't give Symbol Span between Designs I and II.

Don't give Spatial Addition between Designs I and II.

Add delayed recall prompt to first subtest administered if Visual Reproduction is not administered first.

A partial battery that samples each of the memory domains and can be used across both batteries includes VR, SSP, and either LM or VPA. A 20-minute delay is required between the immediate and delayed conditions; therefore, some time will need to be filled with other tasks (e.g., BCSE, Trail Making Test from Delis–Kaplan Executive Function System [DKEFS; Delis, Kaplan, & Kramer, 2001]) since SSP cannot be given between VR I and VR II and administration of LM I or VPA II will not fill the entire delay period.

Following publication of the WMS-IV, Pearson released the WMS-IV Flexible Approach (Pearson, 2010). The WMS-IV Flexible Approach manual is included in the standard kit and contains normative data on alternate indexes for various subtest configurations of the WMS-IV (e.g., LM and VR). The alternate indexes do not replace the standard WMS-IV indexes due to lower reliability and less comprehensive content coverage but do offer normative information for clinicians needing briefer assessments of memory functioning.

DEVELOPING RAPPORT WITH EXAMINEES

Establishing Rapport

One of the key skills required for administering standardized tests is the ability to establish rapport with examinees. In many evaluations, the first contact with the examinee occurs just prior to the test session. Establishing and maintaining rapport with the examinee is critical in these situations to elicit optimal performance on the WMS-IV.

Each examinee should be approached differently, depending on the purpose of the testing, the setting in which the testing is done, the examinee's familiarity with the examiner and testing situations, the examinee's approach to and motivation for testing, and other related factors. Use your experience and knowledge of the examinee to determine the most effective way to establish rapport. Begin the test session by putting the examinee at ease, perhaps with some informal conversation about the examinee's activities or interests. Spend some time explaining the purpose and content of the evaluation and address any questions and concerns raised. Be prepared to answer questions about the potential use of results, particularly if the evaluation is a "third-party" evaluation (e.g., court-ordered assessment). It may be helpful to have a parent, friend, or care provider accompany the examinee during this initial meeting period to alleviate concern and provide support for the examinee. This is particularly helpful when the examinee has communication difficulties or is easily overwhelmed or confused. The time needed for building rapport depends on the examinee's needs.

As previously mentioned, the WMS-IV requires sustained effort by the examinee. Given the high stakes frequently associated with memory assessment, it is appropriate to address concerns about performance with the examinee and prepare him or her for the length of testing. There is not a standard introduction to the WMS-IV, but all examinees can be provided with a basic overview of testing. A general introduction describing the WMS-IV as a comprehensive assessment of learning and memory is appropriate. In addition, an examinee can be informed that his or her performance will be compared to similar age peers. This may be particularly reassuring to older adults for whom memory assessment may be especially anxiety provoking. Detailed information on the content is not recommended; however, preparing the examinee for 45–90 minutes of sustained effort might prove helpful in establishing and maintaining rapport. Assuring examinees that not all items are completed by all examinees and that some items may be difficult will help normalize the testing experience and reduce performance anxiety. Encourage individuals to try their best and emphasize effort over getting everything right. Finally, it is important to address the outcomes of testing, including when and if results will be provided and with whom. It may be helpful to address specific concerns the examinee may have regarding the use of results (e.g., loss of independence, financial control).

Maintaining Rapport

Maintaining rapport requires your full attention during test administration. Prior to test administration, you must master the mechanics of the WMS-IV, such as giving directions, handling materials, and timing and recording responses. Mastering these details will enable you to focus your efforts on the examinee rather than on learning the materials. This focus will help you observe the examinee's verbal and nonverbal cues for signs of discomfort, unease, or frustration. If you notice signs of frustration, you may remind the examinee that the test was designed to include very difficult items and very few people obtain perfect scores. Praise the examinee's effort instead of performance (e.g., "You're working hard" instead of "Correct"); never inform the examinee if a response was correct unless explicitly stated in the instructions. If an examinee becomes discouraged, provide encouragement by saying, "Just try your best," or provide a break. Occasionally, an examinee may ask for help beyond that allowed in the standard administration or ask you to complete the item. In such extreme cases, you will need to redirect him or her by saying something such as, "I want to see how well you can do it yourself." If this becomes a frequent request, a break may be warranted. Paying close attention to the examinee will help maintain rapport through appropriately timed statements of support and reassurance.

If the examinee becomes fatigued, bored, or overly anxious, you may engage in brief conversations between subtests; however, be careful not to let small talk slow down the pace of administration or interfere with standard instructions. If a brief rest period is needed, make sure to take it at the completion, not in the middle, of a subtest. In addition, ensure that a break does not extend the delay time beyond 30 minutes between immediate and delayed conditions of a subtest. The best time for a break during administration of the Adult battery is between LM II and VPA I.

Forensic evaluations and other "third-party" evaluations present a unique challenge to building rapport. It is important to assure the examinee that the goal of testing is to provide an accurate assessment of his or her strengths and weaknesses and good cooperation and effort are the most likely way for the results to be valid. Most examinees are willing to participate in testing and give good effort; however, some may display suboptimal effort or refuse to complete testing. For those who refuse to complete testing, stopping the test session is the best approach. The client can be encouraged to reschedule the test session if cooperation is more likely at a later time.

Suboptimal effort is less obvious and can occur for a variety of reasons such as illness, fatigue, poor understanding of the purpose of testing, and, in some instances, personal gain. It is appropriate to administer additional measures of effort if suboptimal effort is suspected (e.g., Advanced Clinical Solutions [ACS], Test of Memory and Malingering; Tombaugh, 1997). There is some debate in the field as to whether examinees should be warned that effort measures will be administered during testing (Slick, Tan, Strauss, & Hultsch, 2004). For a comprehensive review of issues in assessing and reporting suboptimal effort, see Bush et al. (2005).

TESTING INDIVIDUALS WITH SPECIAL NEEDS

Clinicians frequently assess individuals with special needs, such as hearing or visual impairment, physical and cognitive disabilities, and language or communication difficulties. In addition, the prevalence of auditory, visual, and motor deficits increases with age. Prior to testing any individual, you should familiarize yourself with his or her particular needs and plan accommodations accordingly. In addition, educational and cultural influences, such as fluency in English, may need to be accommodated for during testing and should be assessed prior to testing. It is important to select instruments that are designed to address the needs of the particular client. In some situations, such as with severely disabled individuals or non-English-speaking clients, the WMS-IV may not be an appropriate measure to use.

In most situations, the WMS-IV can be administered in the standard manner with few or no modifications. Often, the need for a standard administration outweighs the need to provide individual accommodations. Depending on the nature of the client's impairment, obtained scores may underestimate the examinee's true ability when administered under standard conditions. For example, an older individual with language production difficulties following a stroke may have difficulty on tasks requiring verbal responses. If an examinee's performance is affected by factors other than memory ability, it is imperative to note this during interpretation of results. Attributing low performance to memory impairment when other known deficits affected performance could result in misdiagnosis and inappropriate treatment.

Occasionally, modifications are necessary to ensure meaningful data. Small changes to standard procedures may not impact the validity of results while allowing the client to accurately exhibit his or her abilities. However, your clinical experience and judgment is needed to determine if a modification could result in the inability to apply normative data. For example, administering a partial battery in order to decrease testing time and focus the assessment is unlikely to affect subtest level scores but should be considered when interpreting performance, as this is not how the normative data was collected. However, allowing an examinee an alternate response style, such as writing responses instead of responding verbally, may better capture the examinee's performance but changes the test significantly and may influence performance enough for normed scores to be invalid. All permutations of accommodations have not been tested to determine their effect on normative data so your judgment is crucial in this determination. Rapid Reference 2.3 provides some suggestions on modifying the WMS-IV to accommodate individuals with special needs. It is important to note any accommodations from the standard administration in your final report and on the record form. For more information on modifying instruments for examinees with special needs, see Mitrushina et al. (2005), Sattler (2008), Simeonsson and Rosenthal (2001), and/or Strauss et al. (2006).

≡ Rapid Reference 2.3

Modifications to the WMS-IV to Accommodate an Examinee's Special Needs

Hearing Difficulties

Within standard administration: Ensure that the testing environment is quiet and free from outside noise. Sit in close proximity to the examinee and sit on the side with better hearing, if applicable. Although speaking in a louder tone may help, it can also distort speech, so assess whether speaking more loudly helps before doing so throughout the assessment. You may repeat directions but do not repeat items. Have the examinee repeat instructions back to you to ensure clear communication. On VPA, if the examinee consistently misarticulates an item (e.g., says "quite" in place of "quiet" every time), it is counted as correct. When facing the examinee, ensure that the examinee can clearly see your face as this may help decode speech.

Beyond standard administration: Provide written instructions to help communicate instructions. Provide written stimuli for verbal memory tests.

Visual Difficulties

Within standard administration: Adjust lighting or sitting positions to accommodate visual difficulties. Administer only the auditory subtests.

Beyond standard administration: Allow use of magnifying aide. Enlarge stimuli.

Motor Difficulties

Within standard administration: Assist the examinee with placement of the cards on DE and SA. *Note:* Do not assist with where to place the cards, only actually placing the cards. Provide a larger pencil for individuals with grip problems. Instead of pointing, the examinee may respond with the response number. In extreme cases, you may want to avoid VR. Take breaks as needed but keep delay time in mind.

Beyond standard administration: Use larger response sheets.

Communication Difficulties

Within standard administration: Allow pointing to responses instead of verbal responses when appropriate.

Beyond standard administration: Allow written responses to verbal subtests. Rephrase instructions to increase comprehension. Redirect if responses do not make sense.

Non-English Speakers

Beyond standard administration: Use an interpreter during testing. Administer the test in the language spoken by the examinee. Use a translated version of the test.

The use of the WMS-IV with non-English speakers presents an interesting dilemma. The ideal solution is to utilize an adapted version with targeted norms; however, instruments in an examinee's native language are frequently not available. Moreover, if tests are available in the main language, the examinee may speak a dialect that is not included in the translation, or available norms may not be appropriate for the individual being tested. Several accommodations, including the use of an interpreter, using a translated or adapted version, or administering the test bilingually or in the examinee's language, may be utilized with the WMS-IV, but each of these approaches threatens the validity of using the WMS-IV standard normative data. The WMS-IV normative data were collected in examinees fluent in English. Translations or bilingual administration of the WMS-IV deviate from the standard administration and should be considered in score interpretation. Auditory memory subtests are likely the most susceptible to problems, as word difficulty and frequency of use vary across languages and straight translations do not account for these differences. For a comprehensive review of issues related to adapting tests for use in cross-cultural evaluations or testing bilingual or non-English speakers, see Hambleton, Merenda, and Spielberger (2005); Judd et al. (2009); and/or Sattler (2008).

Testing Older Adults

Assessment of memory functioning is crucial when assessing older adults. Not only is memory loss a major concern among older adults, but chronic medical conditions that may affect performance are also more prevalent in older adults. Moreover, it is important to identify pathological memory loss early to maximize the effects of intervention. Therefore, identifying pathological memory loss is a frequent referral question among older adults.

For most older adults, test administration will not differ greatly from that with younger adults. However, certain medical conditions and impairments increase in prevalence as individuals age. It is imperative when testing older adults that you consider common physical problems that could compromise performance, such as hearing and visual impairment. Hearing impairment is particularly common and may be indicated by the examinee speaking in a loud tone, complaining about outside noise, frequently requesting you to repeat statements, mishearing you or failing to respond to questions, or exhibiting a tendency to focus intently on you when you are speaking. Visual impairments are also a common problem in older adults and may be indicated by leaning in to look at the stimulus books, squinting, asking for information about the stimulus, or adjusting body position to see the stimulus. Remind examinees to bring and wear corrective lenses during testing. If possible, make accommodations to assist the examinee in compensating for impairment to ensure that scores reflect the examinee's ability instead of his or her impairment.

In general, knowledge of an examinee's health and medication status will assist you in planning test sessions. For example, many medications produce drowsiness, particularly when they are first taken. For individuals on certain medications, it may be beneficial to plan testing time around medication to ensure that the examinee is alert and able to give his or her best effort. Care providers can supply information about the best time of day for individuals with significant health problems or cognitive impairment. Additionally, for medically frail individuals, it may be prudent to plan breaks throughout testing, particularly if the WMS-IV is being administered within a larger battery. The assessment of older adults, particularly medically frail older adults, is complex and beyond the scope of this book. For more information on the assessment of older adults, see Attix and Welsh-Bohmer (2006); Carstensen, Edelstein, and Dornbrand (1997); Lezak, Howieson, and Loring (2004), and/or Lichtenberg (2010).

≡ Rapid Reference 2.4

Battery Recommendations for Ages 65–69

Administer Adult Battery	Administer Older Adult Battery
Individuals with problems with spatial memory	Individuals for whom fatigue is a concern
Individuals who need a comprehensive assessment of visual memory	Medically frail individuals
Individuals who need working memory assessment	Individuals with lower education
Highly educated individuals	Individuals with lower memory ability or who are cognitively impaired
Individuals with high memory ability	Individuals who may need retesting and may "age out" of the Adult battery norms

For individuals ages 65–69, you may choose to administer either the Adult or Older Adult battery. For highly educated or high-ability older adults, those for whom spatial memory is a question, or those for whom a full battery is warranted, the Adult battery may be more appropriate. For those with established medical and clinical diagnoses or for whom fatigue is a concern, the Older Adult battery may be more appropriate. In addition to being shorter, the Older Adult battery has a lower floor in this age range, making it more appropriate for individuals with below-average memory ability. Also, if you plan to retest the examinee over several years, the Older Adult battery may be preferable as the examinee may "age out" of the norms for the Adult battery between testings. Thus, the same battery could be compared across testings. Rapid Reference 2.4 lists the suggested battery for various groups of individuals aged 65–69.

Recording Responses

Documenting the examinee's exact responses is crucial to ensure accurate scoring, particularly on those subtests where scoring occurs at a later time. It is generally recommended that you always record the examinee's responses, even when scoring is easily completed, such as on SA. This will allow you to examine error patterns and memory processes in greater detail. In addition, if you plan to obtain the ACS Additional Scores, accurate recording of responses is essential.

Space to record responses is provided on the record forms for each subtest. For LM, room is provided at the bottom of the page to record the entire response given by the examinee. Although scoring can occur during the examinee's response, you may find it helpful to write the response verbatim and score it later, as you may miss part of the response while scoring. This may be particularly helpful when you are first learning the test and are not familiar with specific scoring criteria. Always double-check scoring after the completion of the testing session to ensure accuracy.

Over the years, a series of abbreviations has been utilized across many standardized instruments that may be helpful in quickly capturing responses. Rapid Reference 2.5 provides a list of some of the common abbreviations used in standardized testing. The use of abbreviations increases your speed of recording, improves accuracy, and allows you to keep up with the examinee throughout a lengthy response. This enables greater attention to the examinee while recording, enhancing and maintaining rapport.

≡ Rapid Reference 2.5

Common Abbreviations Used in Standardized Testing

Abbreviation	Meaning
P	Prompt given
R	Repeated item

(continued)

Abbreviation	Meaning
SC	Self-corrected
DK	Don't Know
DR	Don't Remember
√	Correct Response
NR	No response
DC	Discontinue

Start Points, Reversal Rules, and Discontinue Rules

The basic administration rules of the WMS-IV are relatively easy to learn, as most subtests of the WMS-IV are administered in their entirety. However, SA uses start points and a reversal rule, and both SA and SSP use a discontinue rule. Thus, for these subtests, not all items are administered to every examinee. The start point, reversal and discontinue rules ensure an examinee takes only those items appropriate for his or her ability level. On SA, individuals ages 16–54 begin on Item 6. If an examinee obtains a score of 0 on either Item 6 or 7, administer the items in reverse order (e.g., Item 5 then Item 4) until a score of 1 is obtained on two consecutive items. Detailed directions on the application of the reversal rule can be found in the *WMS-IV Administration and Scoring Manual*.

Discontinue rules describe the requirements for stopping administration of items on a subtest. It should be noted that to discontinue SSP, an examinee needs to obtain four consecutive imperfect scores. An imperfect score is less than the maximum value for an item (i.e., less than 1 on items 1–2 or less than 2 on items 3–26). Typically an examinee needs to score 0 points, as in the discontinue rule on SA, so ensure you discontinue appropriately on SSP.

Querying, Prompting, and Repeating

Administration of the WMS-IV involves ensuring the examinee is given the best opportunity to exhibit his or her ability. To this effort, rules for prompting examinees and repeating instructions are clearly described in the *WMS-IV Administration and Scoring Manual*. To maintain standard administration, ensure that you are familiar with these rules to avoid the need to review the manual during administration. Subtest specific prompts are included in the stimulus books. Prompting allows you to redirect an examinee that has become distracted or forgotten the task.

≋ *Rapid Reference 2.6*

WMS-IV General Prompts

Behavior	Prompt
Examinee fails to respond to an item.	Just try it once more.
Examinee hesitates during a response.	Try it just a little longer.
	I think you can do it.
Examinee asks for help.	I want to see how well you can
Examinee asks you to do the task.	do it yourself.
Examinee provides an ambiguous or incomplete response.	Explain what you mean.
	Tell me more about that.
Examinee fails to respond to a prompt.	Let's go on.

Prompts may also provide encouragement or support when an examinee is a little hesitant to respond. The prompts listed in Rapid Reference 2.6 are incorporated into the standard instructions and may be used across subtests.

Repetition is particularly regulated during administration of the WMS-IV. In general, instructions can be repeated as needed to clarify the instructions to the examinee. However, memory stimuli should never be repeated or reexposed to the examinee. Presenting the stimuli more than once will invalidate the subtest results as repetition enhances recall.

DON'T FORGET

General Administration Tips for All Subtests

Prior to using the WMS-IV, familiarize yourself with the test administration and materials.

Prior to testing, remind the examinee to bring any visual or hearing aids to testing. Ask about any visual or hearing difficulties that may affect performance (e.g., double vision, nearsightedness, farsightedness, hearing loss).

Plan your test session ahead of time. This includes determining which subtests are to be administered and in what order, planning any modifications or accommodations, and considering the need for and frequency of breaks.

(continued)

Plan breaks between subtests, not during a subtest. Also, ensure breaks do not extend the elapsed time between immediate and delayed conditions beyond the 20–30 minutes allowed. The best break in the Adult battery is between LM II and VPA I.

During administration, maintain attention to the examinee's behavior and needs. Provide direction and feedback as needed to obtain the examinee's best effort throughout testing.

Provide encouragement by praising effort, not accuracy. Do not provide feedback on any items or responses unless directed to do so in the instructions.

Record all responses during testing and note any unusual behaviors or responses. You can evaluate all the responses later as needed.

SUBTEST-BY-SUBTEST RULES OF ADMINISTRATION

The WMS-IV stimulus books contain all of the administration directions for the WMS-IV subtests. They are presented in the order of administration of the Adult battery. If you are administering the Older Adult battery you will need to use the tabs to find the subtests in the administration order presented in the record form.

Subtests are presented by laying the stimulus book flat on the table. Ensure that the table is wide enough to allow the stimulus book to lie flat, and turn the pages toward the examinee. The flat presentation allows you to see the examinee's pointing responses and presents stimuli on the same plane as the examinee must recall the stimuli. The first page of each subtest presents the general directions for the subtest, including key directions for recording responses. In addition, a sidebar provides a brief overview of key points, including materials, start points, reversal and discontinue rules, timing, and scoring. All directions appear on the examiner pages, facing you. If the examinee is being shown a stimulus, it will appear on the examinee side of the stimulus book. Correct responses are not included in the stimulus books as they might be seen by the examinee. The record forms contain the correct responses as well as the stimuli for the verbal memory subtests. Note any unusual behavior that occurs during testing either in the margins of the record form or on a separate piece of paper. This will help when you interpret test results. The *WMS-IV Administration and Scoring Manual* provides examples of recording and detailed scoring information for each subtest.

The administration of each subtest is briefly described within this section, but it does not replace a thorough review of the stimulus books and *WMS-IV Administration and Scoring Manual*. Each subtest section includes behaviors to watch for during administration of that subtest and a "testing the limits" section to help go beyond standard administration. Appendix A of this book provides a checklist of WMS-IV administrative procedures for each subtest and overall. This checklist may be particularly helpful for individuals learning the instrument or teaching administration of the WMS-IV to graduate students or other examiners.

Brief Cognitive Status Exam (BCSE)

The BCSE is the only optional subtest included in the WMS-IV. It is administered from stimulus book 1 and the record form and requires the response booklet. Every item is administered to each examinee. The subtest is organized into seven sections, each of which has unique administration directions. The subtest begins with a series of orientation items that require the examinee to supply the date and current president. For the time estimation item, the examinee is asked to guess the time of day without using a clock or watch. Then the examinee is asked to name four visual stimuli before completing two mental control items that require the examinee to recite a common sequence in reverse order. The examinee then draws an analog clock, placing hands in the clock to designate a specified time. After completing the mental control and clock-drawing items, the examinee is asked to recall the visual stimuli shown earlier. The examinee was not told to remember the visual stimuli so this is considered incidental recall. An inhibition item is given next and includes a practice and a test item. During the practice item, the examinee names the shapes presented in an array containing rows of rectangles and triangles. On the test item, using the same array of rectangles and triangles, the examinee must inhibit the correct name of each shape and say the name of the other shape (i.e., say "triangle" when seeing a rectangle and vice versa). Finally, for verbal production, the examinee names as many colors as possible in 30 seconds.

The majority of the items on the BCSE are easy to administer, although tracking responses on inhibition and recording responses on verbal production can be a little difficult. Both can be mastered fairly easily with a little practice. Read each item as presented in the stimulus book. If an examinee's response is unclear, you may ask for clarification or repeat a question if necessary. Record responses to scored items verbatim for further evaluation following administration. In addition, mark skipped responses, self-corrections, and responses made out of sequence. It may also be helpful to record the responses during naming, even though they are not scored, to help you score and evaluate them later during incidental recall, particularly if they are misnamed initially. On clock drawing, be sure to indicate the order in which the examinee draws numbers in the clock, as this is used in scoring and cannot be recovered from the drawing. A box on the record form reminds you to capture this information during administration.

Even though the BCSE is optional, it is recommended that it be given in most clinical situations. It is a relatively easy set of tasks for most examinees, providing a measure of success at the beginning of the examination. It also provides a quick overview of the examinee's cognitive functioning, which may lead you to modify later subtest administration. For example, if an examinee misnames one of the visual stimuli but recalls the erroneous name on recall, it could indicate perceptual problems that may require modification of later administration or suggest an interpretation for later scores.

Possible Behavioral Observations During the BCSE

- Confusion over a specific item type, for example, difficulty drawing a clock but easily recalling items
- Disorientation as indicated by responses to the orientation items
- Attempts to use memory aids or visual cues, for example, attempting to use a watch during the time estimation item or to view a calendar during the orientation items
- Poor working memory as demonstrated by difficulty with reverse sequences
- Misnaming visual stimuli
- Poor motor skills or organization on clock drawing
- Difficulty inhibiting the correct shape name on inhibition
- Content and speed of responses on verbal production: Are the colors arranged in any manner? Is there a steady production of words or long pauses between responses?
- Multiple repeated responses on the verbal fluency item
- Expressions of frustration or confusion
- Hesitations, restarts, or frequent self-corrections that indicate the examinee has difficulty beginning, inhibiting, or monitoring responses. For example, on Mental Control, the examinee might say, "December (long pause), November, December, no wait, November (pause), October."

Testing the Limits

- To assess whether memory aids can improve performance on orientation items, allow the examinee to use a calendar.
- To assess retrieval problems, have the examinee select the response from multiple choices for orientation and recall items.
- Test knowledge of the forward sequences for the mental control items to ensure the examinee is familiar with the sequences.

- Have examinee copy an analog clock to determine the role of motor problems.
- Rephrase the time for the clock drawing. For example, say, "Make the hands tell the time nine-ten."
- Present the inhibition item line by line instead of in the full array.
- Try other semantic categories for verbal production.

Visual Reproduction I (VR I)

VR I is administered from stimulus book 1 and requires the response booklet. Ensure the correct page of the response booklet is placed in front of the examinee for each item. Although completion time may be recorded, it is only used to compute VR I additional scores. Scoring is done after administration is completed. Due to the small amount of recording required on this subtest, it offers a good chance to observe the examinee's response style.

In this subtest, the examinee is presented with five designs in succession and asked to draw each design immediately after its presentation. The last two items contain two designs. Present each item for 10 seconds, remove it from view, and ask the examinee to draw the item. If the examinee is reluctant to draw or states that he or she is not an artist, provide encouragement by saying, "Don't worry about your artistic ability; just draw it as best you can." Alternately, if the examinee is reluctant to draw because of poor memory or says he or she can't remember anything, say something such as, "Well, just draw it as well as you remember." There is not a time limit for drawing the items, so provide the examinee time to recall the design. In most situations, it is clear when the examinee has finished and is ready to proceed. Occasionally, an examinee will stop drawing, and it is unclear if he or she is finished. In this situation, it is okay to ask the examinee if he or she is finished. However, do not prompt him or her to draw more or provide specific information on the designs. Once all five items are complete, tell the examinee to remember the designs, as you will ask about them again later. This is the only subtest where this prompt is given. You will need to record the time you complete VR I so you can administer VR II within 20–30 minutes.

Possible Behavioral Observations During VR I

- Poor motor abilities that may impact performance
- Tremor or other motor difficulty
- Recalling elements of a previous design in a later recall, for example, drawing flags on items 3–5 or dots on item 4 or 5

- Failure to recall any component of an entire item, resulting in a score of 0
- Lack of details in the drawing or including additional elements
- Recalling details but losing overall structure
- Recalling only left or right designs on items 4 and 5
- Expressions of frustration or confusion
- Drawing excessively fast, demonstrating a lack of effort or impulsivity, which affects the quality of the response
- Statements regarding memory processes, particularly verbalization of designs, for example, "I remember this as an X with flags."
- Hesitations, restarts, or frequent self-corrections that indicate the examinee has difficulty beginning, inhibiting, or monitoring responses
- Poor motivation or stating he or she cannot recall anything

Testing the Limits

Note: All modifications on VR I will affect performance on VR II.

- Allow longer exposure time.
- Have the examinee copy the items before recalling them.
- Provide larger stimuli or stimuli with thicker or heavier lines.
- Provide larger size response booklet.
- Administer recognition items after immediate recall.

Logical Memory I (LM I)

LM I is administered from stimulus book 1 and the record form. It is a good idea to write the examinee's entire response to score later, instead of attempting to record and score at the same time, as this may result in missing portions of the examinee's response. Alternately, you may record the examinee's responses using a tape recorder or some other method. If you choose to record, inform the examinee by saying something such as, "I am going to record your response so that I can write it down accurately later."

In this subtest, the examinee is read two stories out loud. Ensure that you are administering the correct stories for the chosen battery, as one of the stories differs between the Adult and Older Adult batteries. Story A describes the friendship between two people who meet weekly for lunch, Story B describes a woman who reports a robbery to the police, and Story C describes a man changing his evening plans following a weather bulletin. All of the stories contain many details, although Story A is shorter and contains fewer details. Stories A and B are included in the Older Adult battery and Stories B and C are included in the Adult battery.

In the Older Adult battery, Story A is administered twice with recall required after each administration and Story B is administered once. Each story is administered only once in the Adult battery. Read each story in a conversational manner, with natural pauses between sentences. Speak at a regular pace without significant inflection or dramatic emphasis. You may want to practice reading the stories aloud a few times before administering them to an examinee. Occasionally, an examinee may interrupt you during a story; gently redirect him or her to wait until the story is complete or provide a nonverbal cue that he or she is to wait until you have finished the story.

Following each presentation of a story, instruct the examinee to begin at the beginning of the story and repeat what he or she remembers about the story. There is no time limit on recall so provide the examinee ample time to recall the story. Although you can encourage an examinee to recall as much information as possible, do not prompt for specific information. You will need to record the time you complete LM I so you can administer LM II within 20–30 minutes.

CAUTION

Differences Between Adult and Older Adult Batteries on Logical Memory I

Adult Battery	Older Adult Battery
Administer Stories B and C	Administer Stories A and B
Administer Story B one time	Administer Story A two times
Administer Story C one time	Administer Story B one time

Possible Behavioral Observations During LM I

- Asks for repetition of story
- Organizing the story recall: Did the examinee organize the response or recite a list of details?
- Interrupting during the story to ask questions, for example, asking, "Did the girl go to the nearest police station?"
- Personalization in the story recall, for example, "I like meeting my friends for lunch, too."

- Paucity or embellishment of content during recall
- Combining the elements of the stories, for example, recalling the name of a character from the first story during recall of the second story
- Perseverative responding or repeating details of the story
- Statements regarding memory processes, for example, "I remembered her name because I have a friend with that name."
- Expressions of frustration or confusion
- Hesitations, restarts, or frequent self-corrections that indicate the examinee has difficulty beginning, inhibiting, or monitoring responses
- Poor motivation or stating he or she cannot recall anything

Testing the Limits

Note: All modifications on LM I will affect performance on LM II.

- Provide written stories for the examinee to read.
- Repeat stories more than allowed.
- Present stories sentence by sentence and allow recall after each sentence.
- Prompt for specific information during recall.
- Administer recognition following immediate recall.

Spatial Addition (SA)

SA is administered from stimulus book 1 and the record form and requires the Spatial Addition cards and memory grid. It is administered only as part of the Adult battery. Scoring is completed during administration in order to apply the reversal and discontinue rules correctly. This is the first use of the memory grid and cards in a standard administration. Rapid Reference 2.2 lists general guidelines on use of the memory grid. It takes some practice to smoothly handle the various components and record quickly and efficiently. Review the administration provided on the training video to ensure correct placement of materials and recording. In addition, an alternate scoring template is included on the training CD that provides views of the correct grids from the top of the grid so you can score the responses without flipping over the grid.

It is common on this subtest for an examinee to express frustration or difficulty with the task. Tasks requiring pure visual memory with little chance to verbalize are not common and require more concentration than those visual memory tasks that can be verbalized. You may reassure the examinee using the general prompts discussed earlier.

In this subtest, the examinee is shown a grid for 5 seconds and then shown a second grid for 5 seconds. Each grid contains red and/or blue circles. The examinee is told to pay attention to the location of the blue circles across the grids and to ignore any red circles. The examinee must mentally combine the blue circles across the two grids. For each cell in the grid where a blue circle appears in only one of the grids, the examinee should place a blue circle card. For each cell where a blue circle appears on both grids, a white circle should be placed. For all cells where either no circle appeared or a red circle appeared, no card should be placed. Several demonstration and sample items are presented, and early items help solidify correct responding. Use the demonstration item to teach the task to the examinee. Be sure to provide all the corrective feedback provided in the demonstration and sample items to ensure that the examinee understands the task before beginning test items. If the examinee has difficulty or is reluctant to place cards in the grid, you may assist but do not suggest where cards should be placed.

Some examinees may attempt to use physical cues, such as putting fingers in the empty memory grid during administration or attempting to place cards in the grid while the stimulus is still showing. If this happens, say, "Do not touch the grid until I tell you to do so." There is not a time limit on these items, so provide the examinee time to respond. Occasionally, an examinee will stop actively putting cards in the grid but it is unclear if he or she is finished. In this situation, it is okay to ask if he or she is done. However, do not suggest that cards are missing or provide feedback on the response. Although not required, recording responses in the grid on the record form allows later review of error patterns.

Possible Behavioral Observations During SA

- Interrupting during the instructions to ask questions or clarify the instructions, for example, asking, "So you want me to ignore all the red circles?"
- Consistent misunderstanding of a particular rule, for example, failing to ignore the red circles
- Organizing the cards in a manner to assist in correct responding, for example, placing all the red cards at the bottom of the stack or trying to put them to the side
- Watching you for signs that a card still needs to be placed
- Difficulty inserting the cards into the grid
- Perseverative responding, for example, always placing blue circles in the corners across items

- Consistently placing fewer or more than the required number of cards in the response
- Random responding
- Verbalizing the task, for example, labeling the cells by creating row and column names (e.g., A-1, A-2)
- Expressions of frustration, confusion, or discouragement
- Hesitations, restarts, or frequent self-corrections that indicate the examinee has difficulty beginning, inhibiting, or monitoring responses
- Poor motivation or stating he or she cannot perform the task or inconsistent effort across items

Testing the Limits

- Allow the examinee to use physical cues during administration.
- Teach the examinee a method to approach the task; for example, "It is easier to remember which cells the cards were in if you number the cells."
- Readminister missed items.
- Show the two grids at the same time.
- Display the two grids during the response.
- Remove red circles from response cards.

Visual Reproduction II (VR II)

VR II is administered from stimulus book 2 and requires the response booklet. It is administered 20–30 minutes after VR I. Ensure that the correct page of the response booklet is placed in front of the examinee for each item. When setting up the response booklet for the delayed recall condition, do not display the previously drawn items, as this will provide a cue for the examinee. Although completion time may be recorded, just as with VR I, it is used only to compute additional scores. If desired, the recognition task may be given after delayed recall. For cases where motor speed and ability are a concern, the copy task can be used to determine to what degree motor performance is impacting the score. Recognition should always be given before the copy condition. Scoring occurs after administration is completed.

In this subtest, the examinee recalls the five designs presented during VR I. He or she may recall the designs in any order; no redirection is used when the designs are recalled in a different order than they were presented. Do not provide any prompts to assist in the recall of a particular design. If the examinee is reluctant to draw or states that he or she is not an artist, encourage him or her by saying, "Don't worry about your artistic ability; just draw it as best you can." Alternately, if the examinee is reluctant to draw because of poor memory or states that he or she can't remember anything, say something such as, "Well, just draw it as well as you remember." There is not a time limit on these items, so provide the examinee time to recall the design. Occasionally, examinees will stop drawing and it is unclear if they are finished. In this situation, it is okay to ask if they are finished. During the recognition task, the examinee is shown six designs and asked to select the designs previously shown. In the copy condition, the original stimuli are displayed and the examinee is asked to replicate the design while it is displayed.

Possible Behavioral Observations During VR II

- Poor fine motor abilities that may be impacting performance
- Tremor or other motor problems
- Perseveration of a particular design or elements of a particular design
- Rotation of a design
- Mismatching designs for items 4 and 5
- Self-talk during drawing, for example, "Draw an X and then add flags."
- Speed of responding: Does it take longer to recall the fourth or fifth design?
- Drawing excessively fast, demonstrating a lack of effort or impulsivity, which affects the quality of the response
- Paucity or embellishment of content
- Drawing other designs seen during testing, such as a clock
- Expressions of frustration or confusion
- Hesitations, restarts, or frequent self-corrections that indicate the examinee has difficulty beginning, inhibiting, or monitoring responses
- Poor motivation or stating he or she cannot recall anything

Testing the Limits

- Provide cues for each item in recall (e.g., "One had flags.").
- Match the recognition items to the actual stimuli.
- Provide larger response booklet.

Logical Memory II (LM II)

LM II is administered from stimulus book 2 and the record form. It is administered 20–30 minutes after LM I. As with LM I, it is a good idea to write the examinee's entire response or record it to score later, instead of attempting to record and score at the same time.

In this subtest, the examinee is asked to recall the two stories previously read out loud. The examinee does not need to recall them in the same order as they were presented. Do not stop the examinee during recall of one story to ask for recall of the other story. Ensure that you are administering the correct stories for the chosen battery as the directions for the Adult and Older Adult batteries are presented separately and cues and recognition items differ as well. Instruct the examinee to begin at the beginning of the story and repeat what he or she remembers about the story. If the examinee does not recall any details of a story, use the prompts in the stimulus book to encourage some response. There is no time limit on this subtest, so provide the examinee time to recall each story. Do not prompt the examinee for specific information. Occasionally, an examinee may recall details of a story after completing the response for that story, such as during the recall of the second story. If it is clear that the examinee is amending his or her earlier response, consider it as a self-correct and award credit for the recall. For example, during recall of Story C, the examinee says, "Wait, I just remembered that the lady who was robbed in the other story had four kids who were hungry." If, however, the examinee incorporates the details into the recall of the second story, do not award credit. For example, "John decided to stay home because the television showed the story of a lady with four kids who was robbed."

Following delayed recall, a recognition task may be administered. Read the questions from the record form for each story. Do not provide any cues or inflection as to the correct response. Read each question in a conversational tone. If a question elicits a memory by the examinee (e.g., responding to a question about the gender of the story character elicits spontaneous recall of the character's name), do not give credit for the story detail in delayed recall. In other words, do not award credit on delayed recall for details recalled during the recognition task, even if they occur prior to a question directly related to the recalled detail.

Possible Behavioral Observations During LM II

- Organization of story recall: Did the examinee organize the response or recite a list of details?
- Pace of recall: Are there long pauses or rapid telling of information?
- Personalization in the story recall: For example, "I like meeting my friends for lunch, too."

- Combining the elements of the stories: For example, recalling the name of a character from the first story during recall of the second story
- Paucity or embellishment of content
- Perseverative responding or repeating story details
- Spontaneous recall of information during recognition
- Verbalizations that provide insight on mnemonics used to remember the story: For example, "I remember her name was Ruth because my cousin is Ruth and I pictured her doing everything while you were reading the story."
- Expressions of frustration or confusion
- Hesitations, restarts, or frequent self-corrections that indicate the examinee has difficulty beginning, inhibiting, or monitoring responses
- Poor motivation or stating that he or she cannot recall anything

Testing the Limits

- Cue for more detail during recall.
- Allow written responses.
- Provide written versions of recognition items.

Verbal Paired Associates I (VPA I)

VPA I is administered from stimulus book 2 and the record form. In this subtest, the examinee is read either 10 or 14 word pairs, depending on which battery is administered, and asked to recall the second word in the pair when given the first word. The word pairs are presented four times in varying orders, with the examinee recalling the second words in the pairs following each presentation of the entire list.

Four of the word pairs are semantically related, while the rest of the pairs are unrelated. Ensure that you are administering the correct word pair list for the battery you are administering, as they differ between the two batteries. The Older Adult battery has four fewer pairs than the Adult battery. Read each word of each word pair about 1 second apart, with 2 seconds between presentation of each word pair. Present the words in a similar tone, without inflection or emphasis. You may want to practice reading the word pairs a few times aloud before administering them to an examinee. Occasionally, an examinee may begin to recite word pairs before you have finished presenting the list. If this occurs, stop reading and redirect him or her to wait until you are finished reading the entire list. Following each administration of the word pair list, ask the examinee to recall the second word of each pair by saying, "Which word goes with (insert first word of pair)?"

Allow 5 seconds for the examinee to respond to each item before proceeding to the next pair. Record the examinee's response on the record form verbatim or with a checkmark indicating a correct response. Feedback is provided on every response. You will need to record the time you complete VPA I so you can administer VPA II within 20–30 minutes.

CAUTION

....

Differences Between Adult and Older Adult Batteries on VPA

Adult Battery	Older Adult Battery
Administer 14 items	Administer 10 items

Possible Behavioral Observations During VPA I

- Interrupting the presentation of the word list to begin response
- Recitation of items during presentation of the list, quietly rehearsing or lip movement that suggests internal repetition
- Poor understanding of the task as indicated by frequent statements of "those don't go together"
- Responding with words related to the cue word instead of the target word.
- Types of intrusion errors: Are they mispaired words, semantically related words, novel words?
- Repeating the same response across cue words
- Expressions of frustration or confusion
- Hesitations, restarts, or frequent self-corrections that indicate the examinee has difficulty beginning, inhibiting, or monitoring responses
- Poor motivation or stating that he or she cannot recall anything

Testing the Limits
Note: Changes to VPA I will affect VPA II.

- Provide additional coaching or training.
- Teach the word pairs in the same manner they will be recalled, "X goes with Y."
- Administer recognition items following immediate recall.

Designs I (DE I)

DE I is administered from stimulus book 2 and the record form and requires the Designs cards and memory grid. It is administered only as part of the Adult battery. Some practice is needed to smoothly utilize the memory grid during administration. Rapid Reference 2.2 lists general guidelines on use of the memory grid. Review the administration provided on the training video to ensure correct placement of materials and recording. It is common on this subtest for an examinee to express frustration or difficulty with the task. Tasks requiring pure visual memory with little chance to verbalize stimuli are not common and require more concentration and effort than those visual memory tasks that can be verbalized. You may reassure the examinee using the general prompts discussed earlier and provided in Rapid Reference 2.6.

In this subtest, the examinee is shown a grid with four designs in the cells of the grid for 10 seconds. A blank grid and eight cards are then given to the examinee, and the examinee must select the correct cards and place them in cells on the grid to produce a grid that matches the one previously shown. On the back of each card is a card identifier. Ensure that the correct cards are presented for each design. The grid is then emptied and a new grid with more designs is shown for 10 seconds before the examinee is asked to recreate the grid. A total of four grids are displayed and recalled. If the examinee appears not to be attending to the grid during presentation, redirect him or her to the page. Responses are recorded after each response, but scoring is a little tricky and should be completed after administration.

Several prompts are provided, based on examinee responses. If the examinee fails to respond, encourage him or her to guess by saying something like, "Just do the best you can; put in the cards you think were there." If the examinee does not understand what to do, use the prompt in the stimulus book to help him or her understand the task. When an examinee places more cards in the grid than allowed for a specific item, ask him or her to remove a card or indicate to you which card to remove. If the examinee places fewer cards in the grid than required, no prompt is given. However, if the examinee asks how many cards should be placed in the grid, you may say how many cards are required. A demonstration item is provided to familiarize the examinee with the memory grid and cards. Be on the lookout for unusual response patterns, such as trying to put the cards in the grid oriented toward your perspective. If this occurs, say, "Place the cards in the exact way you saw them on the page, not from my direction." Do not provide any additional prompts to assist the examinee's recall. Occasionally, an examinee will stop and it is unclear if he or she is finished. In this situation, it is okay to ask if he or she is finished. If an examinee has difficulty picking up the cards and placing them in the grid, you may lay the cards out in front of the examinee and have him or her select a card and then point to a location in the grid. You may then place the card in the grid for the examinee. Use caution and avoid helping the examinee identify a correct card or location when providing motor support.

Possible Behavioral Observations During DE I

- Poor fine motor abilities that may be impacting performance
- Tremor or other motor problems
- Approach to responding: Does the examinee sort the cards first and then put them in the grid or place the card in the grid as soon as he or she identifies it?
- Similar spatial responses to each item, for example, always placing cards in the four corners of the grid
- Requests for help or attempts to use card identifiers to place cards
- Self-talk during responding
- Placing too few cards in the grid
- Frequently putting too many cards in the grid
- Expressions of frustration or confusion
- Hesitations, restarts, or frequent self-corrections that indicate the examinee has difficulty beginning, inhibiting, or monitoring responses
- Poor motivation or stating that he or she cannot recall anything

Testing the Limits

Note: Changes to DE I will affect DE II.

- Have examinee match correct cards to the grid.
- Have the examinee copy the grid before recall.
- Provide only the correct cards during recall.
- Administer recognition items following immediate recall.

Symbol Span (SSP)

SSP is administered from stimulus book 2 and the record form. Scoring is completed during administration in order to discontinue item administration correctly. Scoring is fairly straightforward; however, note that scores of 1 on items 3–26 are counted toward the discontinue rule. Record response sequences for each item. Although a checkmark can be used to indicate a correct response, it will be easier to record incorrect sequences if you record all responses during testing.

In this subtest, the examinee is shown an array of abstract designs for 5 seconds. Then a new array is displayed that includes both the designs from the previous array and new designs. The examinee must select the correct designs in the order they were presented in the original array. He or she may point to the designs or read the letter associated with each design. Partial credit is awarded for correct recall of the designs in an incorrect order. A sample item is presented to familiarize the examinee with the task. Use the sample item to teach the task to the examinee. Be sure to provide all the corrective feedback from the sample item to ensure that the examinee understands the task before beginning test items. There is not a time limit on these items, so provide the examinee time to respond. Occasionally, examinees will stop actively responding but it is unclear if they are finished. In this situation, it is okay to ask if they are finished; however, do not provide feedback on their responses.

CAUTION

Symbol Span Discontinue

Discontinue item administration following four imperfect scores. Imperfect scores include a score of 0 on items 1 and 2 or a score of 0 or 1 on items 3–26.

Possible Behavioral Observations During SSP

- Consistently selecting the correct responses in the incorrect order
- Selecting the same response for every item (e.g., A, B, C, D)
- Consistently selecting fewer or more designs than required in the response
- Watching you for signs that a specific design is correct or that he or she still needs to select a design
- Difficulty differentiating designs
- Selecting the same design multiple times within an item
- Expressions of frustration, confusion, or discouragement
- Hesitations, restarts, or frequent self-corrections that indicate the examinee has difficulty beginning, inhibiting, or monitoring responses
- Poor motivation or stating that he or she cannot perform the task

Testing the Limits

- Provide a longer exposure time.
- Display the recall stimulus during selection of correct response.
- Create a new reordered sheet with only the correct designs.

Verbal Paired Associates II (VPA II)

VPA II is administered from stimulus book 2 and the record form. It is administered 20–30 minutes after VPA I. In this subtest, the examinee is asked to recall the second word from the list of word pairs read to them previously, after hearing the first word in the pair. Ask the examinee to recall the second word of each pair by saying, "Which word goes with (insert first word of pair)?" Allow 10 seconds for the examinee to respond before presenting the next item. Record the examinee's response on the record form verbatim or with a checkmark indicating a correct response. No corrective feedback is given during delayed recall. Ensure that you are administering the correct word pair list for the chosen battery, as the items on the Adult and Older Adult batteries differ.

Following delayed recall, a recognition task may be administered. The examinee is read a series of word pairs and asked to indicate if the pair was from the word pairs list. Incorrect responses include pairs with one word from the list combined with a novel word, two correct words from the list that are incorrectly paired, or two novel words. Do not provide any cues as to the correct response by inflection. Administer every recognition item. An optional word recall condition is also included in VPA II. For this task, the examinee is asked to recall the words from the word pair list without the constraint of correct pairing.

Possible Behavioral Observations During VPA II

- Responding with words related to the cue word instead of the target word
- Types of intrusion errors: Are they mispaired, semantically related, novel?
- Repeating the same response across cue words
- Hesitations, restarts, or frequent self-corrections that indicate the examinee has difficulty beginning, inhibiting, or monitoring responses
- Poor understanding of the task as indicated by frequent statements of "those don't go together"
- Poor motivation or stating that he or she cannot recall anything

Testing the Limits

- Provide a list of correct words and have the examinee pair them.
- Repeat delayed recall after recognition.

Designs II (DE II)

DE II is administered 20–30 minutes after DE I. It is administered from stimulus book 2 and the record form and requires the Designs cards and memory grid. It is administered only as part of the Adult battery. In this subtest, the examinee is asked to recreate the four grids he or she was shown during DE I. On the back of each card is a card identifier. Ensure that the correct cards are presented for each design. Following the examinee's response, the grid is emptied and the next item is administered. Responses are recorded after each grid response, but scoring is a little tricky and should be completed after administration.

When an examinee places more cards in the grid than allowed for a specific item, say, "Remember, do not put more than (insert number) cards in the grid." If the examinee places fewer cards in the grid than required, no prompt is given. If an examinee needs help placing the cards in the grid, you may help but do not provide any direction on which cards to place in the grid or where to place them in the grid. Do not provide any additional prompts to assist the examinee's recall. Occasionally, an examinee will stop and it is unclear if he or she is finished. In this situation, it is okay to ask if he or she is finished.

A recognition task may be administered following the delayed recall condition. Examinees are shown a grid with multiple designs and asked to select the two designs that are both the same design and in the same location on the grid as in the original grids. All recognition items are administered.

Possible Behavioral Observations During DE II

- Poor fine motor abilities that may be impacting performance
- Tremor or other motor problems
- Similar spatial responses to each item
- Requests for help
- Self-talk during responding
- Placing too few or too many cards in the grid
- Expressions of frustration or confusion
- Hesitations, restarts, or frequent self-corrections that indicate the examinee has difficulty beginning, inhibiting, or monitoring responses
- Poor motivation or stating that he or she cannot recall anything

Testing the Limits

- Have the examinee complete the grid while the stimulus is displayed.
- Provide only the correct cards during recall.

DON'T FORGET

....

Common Examiner Mistakes

BCSE

- Failing to record the order in which the examinee draws the numbers in the clock drawing
- Including self-corrections as errors on Mental Control items
- Not including self-corrections as errors on the Inhibition item

Logical Memory

- Administering the wrong stories or recognition questions for the chosen battery
- Reading the story at an inappropriate pace (too quickly or too slowly) or noise level (too loudly or too softly)
- Emphasizing details in the story during presentation
- Administering the delayed condition before 20 minutes or after 30 minutes have elapsed
- Failing to provide the story cue on delayed recall if the examinee does not recall any details

Verbal Paired Associates

- Administering the wrong word pair list or recognition items for the chosen battery
- Failing to present the items at the correct pace, i.e., each word in a word pair 1 second apart with 2 seconds between word pairs
- Failing to provide corrective feedback during the learning trials
- Providing feedback during the delayed recall trial
- Providing more than 5 seconds for an examinee to respond to a recall item
- Failing to award credit for consistent misarticulations
- Administering the delayed condition before 20 minutes or after 30 minutes have elapsed

Designs

- Giving the wrong card set for the item
- Missing a rule violation on an item and allowing too many responses
- Prompting an examinee to add cards to the grid without the examinee's asking how many cards are needed
- Recording responses from the wrong orientation

- Removing the cards from the front of the grid
- Failing to assist an examinee in placing cards if needed

Visual Reproduction

- Displaying the stimulus drawing for more than 10 seconds
- Reexposing the drawings by allowing the examinee to see his or her responses in the response booklet when setting up the response booklet for the delayed condition
- Failing to provide the prompts if an examinee is reluctant to draw or says that he or she does not recall anything

Spatial Addition

- Allowing the examinee to use his or her fingers to mark locations during exposure to the item
- Exposing the pages for more than 5 seconds
- Recording responses from the wrong orientation
- Administering between Designs I and II

Symbol Span

- Exposing the stimulus for more than 5 seconds
- Failing to award partial credit
- Failing to count scores of I on items 3–26 toward the discontinue rule

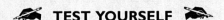

🪶 TEST YOURSELF 🪶

. . . .

1. **In preparing for an evaluation of a 48-year-old man, you find out that he has chronic fatigue and tires easily. You determine that you will need to administer the WMS-IV across two sessions. What must you do to ensure that all the subtest and index scores are available and valid?**

   (a) Administer all the memory subtests in one session and the working memory and BCSE in a second session.

   (b) Administer all conditions for a subtest within a single session, and ensure the appropriate time delay between conditions.

   (c) Administer immediate recall tasks of all the subtests during the first session and the delayed tasks during the second session.

   (d) Administer a partial battery to shorten administration time and decrease the effects of fatigue on results.

2. **The correct responses were removed from the stimulus books to allow a flat presentation of the stimulus books. During testing, where can you easily find the correct responses?**

   (a) *WMS-IV Administration and Scoring Manual*

   (b) WMS-IV Scoring Software

   (c) Record forms

   (d) *WMS-IV Technical and Interpretive Manual*

3. **The administration order for the subtests differs between the Adult battery and the Older Adult battery. How do you determine what order to administer the tests?**

   (a) Follow the order of the subtests presented in the selected record form.

   (b) Follow the order of the subtests presented in the stimulus books.

   (c) Follow the order of the subtests presented in Chapter Three of the *WMS-IV Administration and Scoring Manual.*

   (d) There is not a standard administration order; you may give the subtests in any order.

4. **You must administer all available conditions in a subtest to obtain the index scores.**

   True/False

5. **When you administer a partial battery, what must you consider when reordering the subtests?**

   (a) You should administer all subtests measuring the same domain, such as verbal and visual memory, together.

   (b) Symbol Span cannot be administered between the immediate and delayed conditions of the visual subtests.

   (c) BCSE cannot be administered between the immediate and delayed conditions of the auditory subtests.

   (d) Spatial Addition cannot be administered between Visual Reproduction I and II.

6. **Stimulus items, such as the stories for Logical Memory, can be repeated at the examinee's request.**

   True/False

7. **Testing of the limits should occur following testing or it will affect the validity of obtained scores.**

   True/False

8. **Which subtests contain different memory stimuli in the two batteries?**

   (a) BCSE and VR

   (b) LM and VR

   (c) DE and VR

   (d) LM and VPA

9. **On Symbol Span, discontinue administration following four imperfect scores. An imperfect score on Symbol Span is:**
   (a) A score of 0 for all items
   (b) A score of 0 or 1 on all items
   (c) A score of 0 on items 1 and 2 and 0 or 1 on items 3–26
   (d) A score of 0 or 1 on items 1 and 2 and 0–2 on items 3–26

10. **When providing encouragement to the examinee, praise effort instead of accuracy.**
    True/False

11. **You are scheduled to evaluate a 67-year-old examinee. The examinee has several medical conditions and has known cognitive impairment. Which battery is most appropriate for this examinee?**
    (a) Adult battery
    (b) Older Adult battery

12. **You are scheduled to evaluate a second 67-year-old examinee. The examinee is a doctor who is exhibiting some early symptoms of memory loss. Which battery is most appropriate for this examinee?**
    (a) Adult battery
    (b) Older Adult battery

13. **You are planning to assess an examinee with special needs. Which of the following approaches would best suit this situation?**
    (a) Flexible administration, modifying the subtests and instructions as needed to assist the examinee. Regardless of adaptations, results obtained will be valid and accurately reflect the examinee's ability.
    (b) Rigid approach to testing, stick to the standardized administration directions. The results will accurately reflect the examinee's ability and can be interpreted as such.
    (c) Administer only those subtests that can be administered under standard conditions. The results will not include some areas of memory, but findings will accurately reflect the examinee's ability.
    (d) Flexible administration with some modifications as needed but maintaining administration as close to the standard instructions as possible. Results are interpreted with the modifications indicated in the report.

Answers: 1. b, 2. c, 3. a, 4. False, 5. b, 6. False, 7. True, 8. d, 9. c, 10. True, 11. b, 12. a, 13. d

Chapter Three

HOW TO SCORE THE WMS-IV

L earning to score the Wechsler Memory Scale–Fourth Edition (WMS-IV) is relatively easy for most subtests; however, some subtests take practice to score accurately. After scoring several protocols, you will likely find the scoring to be straightforward and easy to complete. However, it can appear complex to a new user. This chapter provides an overview of scoring the WMS-IV, from obtaining subtest scores to deriving index and contrast scaled scores. Greater detail is provided for new subtests and those requiring subjective judgment.

TYPES OF SCORES

Several types of scores are calculated and derived in the WMS-IV: raw scores, weighted raw scores, cumulative percentages, scaled scores, index scores, and contrast scaled scores. Rapid Reference 3.1 lists the normed score metrics for each type of standard score presented in the WMS-IV. Several scores are available for each subtest. Primary subtest scores describe the main ability measured by the subtest and are used to compute index scores. Primary subtest scores are always scaled scores. Subtest process scores describe specific abilities and skills measured within a subtest and are either scaled scores or cumulative percentages. Process scores are never used to derive index scores.

≣ *Rapid Reference 3.1*

Standard Score Metrics

Type of Standard Score	Mean	Standard Deviation	Range of Values
Scaled Score	10	3	1–19
Index Score	100	15	40–160
Contrast Scaled Score	10	3	1–19

Raw scores are computed for each subtest or process score and are the least informative about the examinee's performance. Raw scores are typically the sum of the scores obtained within the subtest. For example, on Logical Memory (LM) I, the raw score is the total number of points awarded for the details recalled following the administration of the two stories. Raw scores can provide the percentage of information retained or the number of items correctly answered, but they do not provide information about how the examinee's performance relates to similar-aged peers. Normative scores must be derived to relate an individual's performance to that of the normative sample.

On the Brief Cognitive Status Exam (BCSE), item raw scores are converted into weighted raw scores before they are summed to obtain the total raw score. These scores weight performance on an item or set of items relative to the percentage of individuals in the normative sample who obtained specific scores, with higher weighted scores reflecting greater percentages of individuals or better performance. The lowest weighted raw score typically relates to scores obtained by less than 2% of the normative sample. For example, on the time estimation item, less than 2% of the sample was more than 55 minutes off the correct time; therefore, the weighted raw score for >55 minutes is 0, the lowest possible value. The use of weighted raw scores prevents single items from over- or undercontributing to the BCSE total raw score. For example, orientation items are either right or wrong and only a single point can be earned for each; however, an examinee could produce over 20 correct responses to the verbal production item. Therefore, if raw scores were used, the verbal production item would contribute more points to the overall score than the orientation items. Thus, the use of weighted scores ensures that items reflecting various skills are weighted evenly or in a manner that reflects the importance of each cognitive skill.

For several tasks, the majority of individuals obtains perfect or near perfect scores, resulting in a skewed distribution of raw scores. Cumulative percentage ranges are used to describe performance for these scores (i.e., ≤2%, 3–9%, 10–16%, 17–25%, 26–50%, 51–75%, and >75%). Cumulative percentages describe the percentage of individuals who obtained the same or lower score on a task than the examinee. For example, a cumulative percentage range of 51–75 means the examinee scored as well as 51–75 percent of the normative sample. Cumulative percentages are used for several of the process scores, including all the delayed recognition conditions and the copy condition of Visual Reproduction (VR) II. In addition, many of the WMS-IV Additional Scores are presented as cumulative percentages. For some WMS-IV Additional Scores, the highest possible raw score is associated with a relatively low cumulative percentage (e.g., <2%). This reflects a raw score distribution in which nearly all members of the standardization sample obtained a perfect score. When the highest obtainable raw score is not listed in the >75% range, you should include the percentage categories above the highest score. For example, if the highest score is found in the 10–16% range, this does not reflect low average performance but indicates that 90% of the standardization sample obtained perfect scores.

Scaled scores are derived for each subtest condition that contributes to an index score. Scaled scores describe the individual's performance in relation to same-age peers. They are scaled on a metric with a mean of 10, a standard deviation of 3, and a range of 1–19. Scores represent the examinee's rank order of performance relative to age-matched controls. For example, a score of 7 means the examinee scored 1 standard deviation below the mean obtained by same-age peers in the normative sample, which is associated with a percentile rank of 16. The examinee performs better than 16% of same-age peers. Most subtests cover the full range of scaled scores; however, some have truncated floors or ceilings at various age groups. For example, a truncated ceiling is observed in VR I at ages 18–19 reducing the scaled score range to 1–14 (see Table D.1 in the *WMS-IV Administration and Scoring Manual*, p. 127). Alternately, a truncated floor is observed in LM II at ages 85–90 reducing the scaled score range to 3–19 (see Table D.1 in the *WMS-IV Administration and Scoring Manual*, p. 139). In addition to the primary subtest scores, scaled scores are derived for several process scores, including the spatial and content scores for Designs (DE) I and II and the Word Recall condition of Verbal Paired Associates (VPA) II. The ceilings for the process scores are frequently lower than 19.

The scaled scores for the subtests within an index are summed and used to derive the index scores. Index scores are provided for the five indexes and are normed to a metric with a mean of 100, a standard deviation of 15, and a range of 40–160. Just as described for the scaled scores, the index score describes the examinee's rank order of performance relative to individuals in the standardization sample. For example, if an examinee scores between 85 and 115, he or she scored within 1 standard deviation above and below the mean or in the same range as 68% of the population. All index scores contain the full range of scores. The index scores are derived using the full sample because they are calculated using the sum of the age-corrected scaled scores.

A new type of normed score is utilized in the WMS-IV: contrast scaled scores. This type of score originally appeared in the NEPSY-II (Korkman, Kirk, & Kemp, 2007) and is used in place of or in addition to traditional discrepancy analyses. Traditional discrepancy analyses compare two scores by subtracting one score from the other to obtain a difference and then examining the statistical significance of the difference. Base rates of the difference in the normative sample provide information on the clinical significance of the difference. A base rate of 5% means the difference was fairly rare in the standardization sample, occurring in only 5% of the sample. Alternately, a base rate of 75% indicates a relatively common difference in the standardization sample and is unlikely to be clinically meaningful. Several steps are required to complete the traditional discrepancy analyses, and results do not always account for differences in base rates across ability levels. For example, greater differences are more common in individuals with high or low ability.

Contrast scaled scores adjust one score for performance on another score. For example, the Immediate Memory Index versus Delayed Memory Index contrast scaled score creates a new Delayed Memory Index score adjusted for performance on the Immediate Memory Index. The contrast scaled score represents the examinee's normative score when the norm group consists only of examinees with similar immediate memory ability. Similar to the process used to obtain index scores, the score is derived from the entire standardization sample because age is already adjusted for in the contributing scores. Contrast scaled scores are scaled on the same metric as scaled scores, and the full range of 1–19 is included in all the contrast scaled scores. Contrast scaled scores should never be used in place of the scaled scores in deriving index scores. More information on the interpretation of contrast scaled scores is included in Chapter Four of this book.

Changes in the Protocol Forms and Tables

The first four pages of the WMS-IV record form include summary pages for deriving all the scores and completing the discrepancy analyses for the WMS-IV. Raw scores are calculated on the individual subtest pages, with the exception of VR I and II, which are calculated on a scoring page at the back of the record form. The format of the pages has changed to accommodate the new index structure and to imitate the summary page of the WAIS-IV. Subtest scores are now listed by index instead of in administration order. This allows for easy calculation of index scores and accommodates California Verbal Learning Test–Second Edition (CVLT-II) substitution. Derivation of the process and contrast scaled scores, and completion of the ability–memory discrepancy analyses between the WAIS-IV and the WMS-IV are also completed in the summary pages.

The format of the normative tables has changed somewhat from the WMS-III. For each normative age group, all the scaled scores are now included in a single table. In addition, the cumulative percentages are included on the same page in a separate table. This allows for a single page to be located in order to derive all the normed scores. Index scores and contrast scaled scores can be located in Appendixes E and G, respectively, in the *WMS-IV Administration and Scoring Manual*. The normative tables are clearly labeled and the tables are shaded and lined to make finding the appropriate conversions easier.

The WMS-IV Additional Scores discussed in Chapter One are obtained through the completion of the Advanced Clinical Solutions (ACS) Additional Scores Worksheet. Outside of the completion times for VR, all other information needed to obtain these scores is included in the standard WMS-IV record forms. You will need these completed record forms in order to compute the ACS additional subtest, index, and contrast scores.

SCORING THE WMS-IV SUBTESTS

Raw Scores

Scoring begins with the calculation of the subtest-level raw scores. Detailed instructions on how to derive item scores and subtest total raw scores are provided in the *WMS-IV Administration and Scoring Manual*. In general, once the item scores have been calculated, all that is required to obtain the subtest total score is addition. Although the summing is fairly straightforward and easy, it is a good idea to check your work and add the items a second time. Light green shading is used to designate the item scores used to compute the subtest raw scores. Subtest raw scores are designated by a dark green shaded box. The same shade is used to designate the totals for the primary subtest scores and the process scores. For the BCSE, convert the item raw scores to weighted raw scores, then sum the weighted raw scores to obtain the subtest total raw score.

Transfer the totals to either the front or second page of the record form. The primary subtest raw scores used for computing the index scores are transferred to the front page of the record form. The subtests are listed in alphabetical order, by index. This will help you when you are adding the subtest scores to obtain the sum of scaled scores needed to obtain index scores. Process raw scores are transferred to the second page of the record form.

> **CAUTION**
>
> Check your math when summing item scores to ensure that you obtain an accurate total raw score.

Subtests Requiring Additional Training

Brief Cognitive Status Exam

While most items on the BCSE can be readily scored during testing, several items require detailed scoring that needs to be completed following testing. The mental control and inhibition items are relatively easy to administer and score, but attention needs to be paid to the specific instructions for each item. Self-corrections do not count as errors on mental control items but do count as errors on the inhibition item. For the clock-drawing item, use Appendix A in the *WMS-IV Administration and Scoring Manual* to score. Read the initial material in Appendix A to familiarize yourself with the use of the scoring template and the general approach for scoring the clock-drawing item. Each scoring criterion is presented with multiple exemplars and details on how to score atypical responses. You must pay close attention to the criteria to ensure accurate scoring. Finally, the verbal production item may require some judgment to score correctly. Detailed scoring criteria for evaluating responses are provided on page 46 of the manual. Use these criteria to assist in scoring responses.

Logical Memory

The criteria for scoring story details are provided on the record forms and in greater detail in Appendix C of the *WMS-IV Administration and Scoring Manual*. Although scoring can be done during administration, it is recommended that you record the examinee's response verbatim and score after testing is complete. Scoring during testing requires listening to the examinee, reading the scoring criteria, and assigning scores simultaneously. Postponing scoring and recording the response prevents the loss of information as you are searching the scoring criteria to determine scores.

Designs

Scoring the DE subtest is objective but can be somewhat confusing for new examiners. Scoring speed will increase as you become familiar with the steps required to obtain the DE total score. The calculation of three separate scores is required to obtain the total score on DE: content, spatial, and bonus. The easiest way to determine these scores is to treat them as independent scores, even though they are based on the same response and relate to one another.

The content score awards points for recalling the correct images. After recording the response, circle the card numbers in the target (correct) or distracter (incorrect) columns to the right of the response. Each row in the columns lists the related target and distracter card numbers. For example, on Item A the distracter card for card 1 is card 5. Once the card identifiers are circled, you can determine the content score. For each row in which the target card is the only card circled, score 2 points in the content score column. For each row in which only the distracter card is circled, score 1 point in the content score column. For each row in which both the target and distracter cards are circled, score 1 point in the content score column. Finally, for each row in which neither the target nor distracter cards are circled, score 0 points in the content score column. To obtain the item content score, sum the scores in the content score column. A score should be circled in every row. Record the content total in the box at the base of the content score column.

To obtain the spatial score, count the number of responses that were made in a correct location on the grid, indicated with a number in the response grid on the record form. *The number of the response does not need to be the same as the number in the grid for the spatial score; only the correct location needs to be identified.* For example, correct cells for item A are the four corner cells of the grid. Full credit is awarded if cards are placed in all four corners, even if they are the wrong cards. Score 1 point for every correct location. The rows connecting the content and spatial scores are helpful if your examinee chose only one card per row; however, if he or she chose both a target card and distracter, the rows on the record form can be confusing. In this case, simply write the total number of correct location responses in the box at the bottom of the column. You do not need to circle individual scores in the column if this will be confusing. Record the spatial total in the box at the bottom of the spatial score column.

To obtain the bonus score, award 2 points for every target card placed in the correct location. In other words, if the number in the response matches the printed number in the same cell, award 2 points. For the calculation of the bonus score, it does not matter if both the target card and the related distracter card are selected. *Award bonus credit if a target card is placed in the correct location, even if the related distracter card is also placed in the grid.* If either a card is placed in an incorrect location or the wrong card is placed in a correct location, award 0 points. The bonus score for each item is the sum of the bonus scores. Record the bonus total in the box at the bottom of the bonus score column.

The score for each item is the sum of the item content, spatial, and bonus scores. Separate content and spatial scores can be calculated for both DE I and II. Sum the component scores (e.g., item spatial scores for DE I Spatial Raw Score) for the desired scores. Sum the item total scores to obtain the total raw score.

Visual Reproduction

Visual Reproduction (VR) is the most complex test, in terms of scoring, included in the WMS-IV. Each design drawn by the examinee is scored on multiple criteria. The scoring criteria are provided in Appendix B of the *WMS-IV Scoring and Administration Manual*. Read the initial material in Appendix B to familiarize yourself with the general approach for scoring VR items. For each criterion, the full criterion is listed first, followed by clarifications and exceptions. After you become familiar with the criteria, you will only need to read through the exceptions and exemplars for unusual or atypical responses. However, as you are learning the criteria, it is important to evaluate each aspect of the design as described in the criteria as it is easy to overlook portions of a criterion. A short form of the scoring criteria that does not include the details, included in Appendix B, is provided on the *WMS-IV Training CD*.

Subtest-by-Subtest Scoring Guidelines

The BCSE is the most complex subtest in terms of application of a generic scoring rule to the entire subtest due to the variety of items included within the subtest. In addition, for the primary subtests, the point values assigned to items varies among subtests. Most subtest items are scored 0 or 1 point, but some subtests award more points per item. Many of the scoring rules are straightforward, but there are subtle differences between subtests with which you need to be familiar. The Don't Forget box describes the basics for each subtest and provides hints for key scoring concerns. Due to the variety of scoring used within the BCSE, it is not included in this summary.

Primary Scaled Scores

You will need the examinee's chronological age, the raw scores from your record form, and Table D.1 in Appendix D of the *WMS-IV Administration and Scoring Manual* to obtain the primary scaled scores. Norms tables are presented by age group. Use the examinee's exact age as calculated on the front of the record form; do not round. For example, if an examinee is 44 years, 11 months, and 28 days, do not round to 45 years; the lookup table for this examinee is the page for the 35–44 year age group, not the page for the 45–54 year age group. Locate the appropriate age group norm in Table D.1; ages are provided in bold at the top of the table. For ages 65–69, ensure that you are using the correct table for the battery administered; separate tables are provided for the Adult and Older Adult battery norms.

> ## CAUTION
> ....
> For ages 65–69, ensure that you are using the norm table for the correct battery.

DON'T FORGET

Subtest-by-Subtest Scoring Keys

Subtest	Item Definition	Item Score Ranges	Helpful Hints
Logical Memory I and II; Recall	Story detail	0–1	Record response for scoring later.
Logical Memory II; Recognition	Item	0–1	Score during testing.
Verbal Paired Associates I and II; Recall	Word pair	0–1	Record incorrect responses, score during testing.
Verbal Paired Associates II; Recognition	Item	0–1	Score during testing.
Verbal Paired Associates II; Word Recall	Word	0–1	Record all responses, score later.
Designs I and II; Recall	Card	Content: 0–2 Spatial: 0–1 Bonus: 0 or 2 Total: 0–5	Record response, score later.
Designs II; Recognition	Item	0–2	Score during testing. One point is awarded for each response.
Visual Reproduction I and II; Recall	Item criterion	0–1	Score after testing session.
Visual Reproduction II; Recognition	Item	0–1	Score during testing.
Visual Reproduction II; Copy	Item criterion	0–1	Score after testing session.
Spatial Addition	Item	0–1	Record response, score during testing.
Symbol Span	Item	0–2	Record sequence of response, score during testing. Partial credit is awarded.

Subtests are presented in the same order on the front of the record form and in Table D.1. However, in Table D.1, primary and process scaled scores are presented together for VPA and DE, so be careful to derive the correct scaled score for each raw score. Rapid Reference 3.2 lists the steps to convert raw scores to scaled scores.

≡ *Rapid Reference 3.2*

Steps to Convert Raw Scores to Scaled Scores

1. Transfer the raw scores to the appropriate raw score column on the summary pages of the record form.

2. Find the page of Table D.1 that corresponds to the examinee's chronological age.

3. Find the appropriate column in Table D.1 for each score. Read down the column to find the examinee's raw score. Once you find the raw score, read across the row to the extreme left or right column labeled SS (scaled score) to find the examinee's scaled score.

4. Record this score in the scaled score column(s) on the front page of the record form. The empty squares under the scaled score header designate the scaled scores used in each index score. Most scaled scores are used in the calculation of two index scores. For example, VR I is included in both the Visual Memory Index and the Immediate Memory Index. Be sure to record scaled scores in all appropriate columns.

CVLT-II Equated Scores

If you substitute CVLT-II scores for VPA scores, you will need to obtain the VPA Equivalent Scores. It should be noted that if both VPA and CVLT-II scores are available, the VPA scores should be used in calculating index scores. Substitute CVLT-II scores only if VPA is not given or VPA scores are invalid. Transfer the CVLT-II Trials 1–5 T Score and Long Delay z score to the raw score column of the WMS-IV record form. Use Tables D.2 and D.3 from the *WMS-IV Administration and Scoring Manual* to obtain the VPA I and II Equivalent scaled scores, respectively. Find the examinee's CVLT-II Trials 1–5 T score in Table D.2 and read across to the left to find the examinee's VPA I Equivalent scaled score. Repeat this process with Table D.3 to convert the Long Delay z score to the VPA II Equivalent scaled score. Note that these tables are not presented by age group because the CVLT-II scores are already age adjusted.

Some caution is warranted when obtaining equivalent scores for VPA II. The equivalent score range for the VPA II Equivalent scaled scores is greater than the VPA II scaled score range available for each age group. If the obtained equivalent score is higher than the maximum VPA II scaled score for the age of your examinee, adjust the equivalent to the maximum score for that age group. For example, for an examinee aged 27, the maximum VPA II scaled score is 13; however, VPA II Equivalents extend to 19. If a VPA II Equivalent of over 13 is obtained, adjust the equivalent to 13 to match the maximum score available for this age group. Similarly, for ages 80–90, the minimum scaled score available for VPA II is 2. If a VPA II Equivalent score of 1 is obtained in one of the two affected age groups, adjust the score to 2 to match the minimum score available. Record the VPA II Equivalent in the empty squares in the scaled score columns on the record form. The boxes contain parentheses to indicate that the scores are substituted for VPA scores. Rapid Reference 3.3 lists the minimum and maximum scaled scores for VPA II for each age group.

≡ *Rapid Reference 3.3*

Maximum VPA II Scaled Score Available for CVLT-II Equivalent, by Age Group

Age Group	Minimum Scaled Score	Maximum Scaled Score
16–17	1	12
18–19	1	12
20–24	1	13
25–29	1	13
30–34	1	14
35–44	1	14
45–54	1	15
55–64	1	15
65–69 (Adult battery)	1	16
65–69 (Older Adult battery)	1	15
70–74	1	16
75–79	1	17
80–84	2	17
85–90	2	18

Converting Scaled Scores to Index Scores

Once all the primary subtest scaled scores have been derived and entered into the empty boxes in the scaled score conversion table, the index scores can be calculated. If you are substituting CVLT-II scores for VPA scaled scores, use the VPA Equivalent scores in the calculation of the index scores. Each scaled score column on the record form corresponds to one of the five indexes available in the WMS-IV. For example, the Auditory Memory Index (AMI) column contains the scaled scores for LM I and II and VPA I and II.

CAUTION

Ensure that the VPA II Equivalent scaled score is within the range of possible scores for the examinee's age group.

To obtain the index score for each index, you will need the record form and Appendix E from the *WMS-IV Administration and Scoring Manual.* Sum the subtest scaled scores in each column to obtain the sum of scaled scores for each index score. Record this total for each index in the box at the bottom of each column. Turn to the appropriate table in Appendix E. Locate the sum of scaled scores in the light green shaded column and read to the left to obtain each index score, percentile rank, and confidence interval for the examinee. Record each value in the appropriate box on the record form. Confidence intervals are provided for the 90% and 95% confidence levels. You will need to select and indicate the chosen level on the record form in order to obtain the desired confidence interval.

You can plot the subtest and index scores on the profiles located on the cover of the record form. This provides a visual display of the examinee's strengths and weaknesses and can be used to provide feedback to examinees following the test sessions. A horizontal green bar appears on each profile to indicate the mean for each score.

BCSE Descriptive Category

The BCSE subtest total raw score is not converted to a scaled score, but instead produces a classification of the examinee's performance. This classification is derived in a table provided at the end of the BCSE subtest. In order to derive this classification, you will need the examinee's chronological age and years of education, and the BCSE total raw score and conversion table from the record form. In the table, find the examinee's age in the ranges provided. Note that the age groups included in the BCSE classification table are not the same as the normative age groups for the primary subtests. Then, find the examinee's years of education within the appropriate age group. Read right across the identified row to find the examinee's BCSE total raw score. The raw score ranges in this table are listed from highest to lowest so be careful when selecting the correct range. Once you find the correct range, follow the column up to the header to determine the examinee's classification level and circle this on the record form.

The BCSE classification levels reflect the percentage of individuals in the normative sample who obtained similar raw scores. Scores in the Very Low and Low range are atypical and represent less than 2% and 5% of the normative sample, respectively. The Borderline, Low Average, and Average ranges reflect 10%, 25%, and >75% of the sample, respectively.

Process Scores

Process scores are derived on the second page of the record form. Process scaled scores are calculated in the same manner described for the primary subtest scaled scores. Simply transfer the raw score to the conversion table and use the appropriate page of Table D.1 to obtain the scaled score. Record the scaled scores in the scaled score column. For several process scores, cumulative percentages are provided. For these scores, use the second table located at the bottom of the appropriate page of Table D.1. The table is designed in the same presentation as the scaled score conversion table. Find the appropriate column in Table D.1 for each raw score. Read down the appropriate column to find the examinee's raw score. Once you find the raw score, read across the row to the extreme left or right column labeled Cumulative Percentage to find the examinee's cumulative percentage range. Record this range in the cumulative percentage column in the conversion table. The empty squares under the scaled score or cumulative percentage header designate which type of score is available for each process score.

ACS Additional Scores

The steps required to calculate the ACS process and index scores are included in the *ACS Administration and Scoring Manual* and *Additional Scores Booklet*. All the required tables are also included in the ACS manuals. Although these scores were listed in Chapter One and will be discussed in later chapters, the scoring will not be described. The steps to derive the ACS additional scaled scores, cumulative percentages, and index scores are the same as described for the WMS-IV, although the referenced tables will differ. Calculate only the additional scores you need to answer the examinee's specific clinical questions. If you administer a partial battery, only those scores that are related to the subtests you administer will be available.

Computer Scoring Procedures

A computerized scoring assistant is available for the WMS-IV from Pearson. For the majority of subtests, you will need to enter the total raw scores, so you will still need to calculate these. However, for the DE subtest, you will enter the grid responses directly, and the program will calculate the total raw scores for the content, spatial, and total scores. The scoring assistant derives the cumulative percentages and the scaled, index, and contrast scaled scores. The major benefits of using the scoring program are the increased accuracy of scoring and decreased scoring time overall. The scoring assistant produces a score report that includes the following tables and graphs:

- Summary table for the BCSE, including the raw score, classification level, and base rate in the normative sample.
- Summary table for the index scores, including the index scores, confidence intervals, percentile ranks, and qualitative descriptors. A profile of the index scores is also provided that incorporates standard error of measurement (SEM).
- Summary table for the primary subtest scaled scores, including the raw scores, scaled scores, and percentile ranks. A profile of the primary subtest scaled scores is also provided with scores presented within domain.
- Summary tables for process scores, by domain, for the auditory memory and visual memory domains. The tables include raw scores, scaled scores or cumulative percentages, and percentile ranks.
- Subtest-level differences within indexes for AMI, VMI, IMI, and DMI. Individual subtest scaled scores are compared to the mean index scaled score for their respective index. The tables include scaled scores, the index mean score, differences, critical values, and base rates from the normative sample.
- Subtest discrepancy comparisons table for SA and SSP. Only one discrepancy is provided at the subtest level. The table includes the

subtest scaled scores and the difference, critical value, and base rate from the normative sample.

- Subtest-level contrast scaled scores table, including subtest scaled scores or cumulative percentages and the contrast scaled scores. The table includes the contrast scaled scores for LM, VPA, DE, and VR.
- Index-level contrast scaled scores table, including index scores and the contrast scaled scores for all index-level comparisons.
- Summary table of raw scores for the primary subtest scores and process scores. The table includes the ranges of raw scores available in the Adult and Older Adult batteries and the examinee's raw scores.

Research on Scoring Errors

Although the scoring criteria have been improved, scoring errors are still likely to occur during administration and scoring of the WMS-IV. Several studies have examined examiner errors in earlier versions of the WMS. The scoring process can be divided into four phases: item score assignment, summing item scores to calculate the total raw scores, transcribing the raw scores to the summary pages, and derivation of index scores. Errors can occur at any of these stages and can involve mathematical errors, judgment errors, or transcription errors. Sullivan (2000) examined scoring errors in graduate students who completed a WMS-R scoring training. She found no scoring errors for subtests with relatively objective scoring, like VPA. However, scoring errors were frequently made on LM and VR. The scoring errors resulted in discrepancies of up to 13 points between the graduate student and the expert scorer. Most discrepancies could be attributed to inconsistent judgment in applying the scoring criteria, but mathematical and transcription errors also occurred.

Kozora, Kongs, Hampton, and Zhang (2008) examined scoring errors on the WMS-III LM subtest in examiners who participated in an ongoing training program on test administration but who had no experience in clinical assessment. They noted that LM scoring errors were present in a large number of cases. Scoring errors decreased with training, but errors were still made frequently. In both studies, many of the scoring errors resulted in different classifications of performance that would likely impact test interpretation. Given the clinical consequences of incorrect scoring, it is imperative that you check your scoring. As you learn the test, it may be a good idea to have a second person score the subtests and to compare results. This is the best way to reduce judgment errors in scoring.

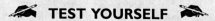

✎ TEST YOURSELF ✎

1. **Why are weighted raw scores used on the BCSE?**
   (a) Weighted raw scores allow a greater range of possible scores, improving the psychometric properties of the subtest.
   (b) Weighted raw scores allow distribution of scores to reflect the importance of individual skills in the overall score.
   (c) Weighted raw scores adjust one score based on performance on another score, enhancing interpretation of differences.
   (d) Weighted raw scores reflect the percentage of correct responses, while raw scores reflect percentage of individuals obtaining similar scores.

2. **You choose to administer the CVLT-II in place of VPA. Your 43-year-old examinee obtains a VPA-II Equivalent of 18. What final value do you use for the VPA-II Equivalent?**
   (a) 18
   (b) 16
   (c) 14
   (d) 12

3. **Why are some scores presented as cumulative percentages instead of as scaled scores?**
   (a) Distribution of raw scores is skewed.
   (b) Distribution of raw scores is flat.
   (c) Cumulative percentages are easier for examinees to understand.
   (d) Scaled scores are used only to obtain index scores.

4. **A base rate of 5% means that the score difference is fairly common in the normative sample and is not likely to be clinically meaningful.**
   True/False

5. **When scoring the Designs subtest:**
   (a) Consider the card identifier when obtaining the spatial score.
   (b) Consider the location of the card when obtaining the content score.
   (c) Consider the presence of a distracter card when obtaining the bonus score.
   (d) Consider both the card identifier and the location of the card when obtaining the bonus score.

6. **All ACS WMS-IV Additional Scores can be calculated from performance on the standard WMS-IV administration.**
   True/False

7. **When transferring subtest scores to the summary pages of the record form, the subtests in the summary table are listed in administration order.**
   True/False

8. The **BCSE** descriptive classification ranges reflect the percent of cases in the normative sample who obtained similar scores.
True/False

9. There is little reason to recheck your scoring, as few errors have been reported in studies on examiner error and the WMS.
True/False

Answers: 1. b, 2. c, 3. a, 4. False, 5. d, 6. True, 7. False, 8. True, 9. False

Chapter Four

INTERPRETATION

The Wechsler Memory Scale–Fourth Edition (WMS-IV) is a flexible instrument that can be interpreted in degrees of complexity and detail based on the clinician's needs and the referral question to be answered. While the WMS-IV may be interpreted in isolation from other cognitive measures, several other instruments are relevant to its interpretation. The WMS-IV was codeveloped with the Wechsler Adult Intelligence Scale–Fourth Edition (WAIS-IV) to enable examiners to answer sophisticated hypotheses about memory functioning within the context of other cognitive functions. In addition, Advanced Clinical Solutions (ACS) for the WAIS-IV and WMS-IV enhances the evaluation of memory functions measured by the WMS-IV through a variety of new scores. This chapter provides a general framework for interpreting scores from the WMS-IV at the index and subtest level. In addition, when appropriate, information from the ACS is included for a more sophisticated analysis of memory functions. The use of the WAIS-IV and WMS-IV together is covered in Chapter Six.

KEY CONCEPTS

When interpreting the WMS-IV, several theoretical and practical issues need to be considered. The WMS-IV was developed with the underlying assumption that there are no "pure memory or working memory" tests (Heilbronner, 1992; Weiss, Saklofske, Prifitera, & Holdnack, 2006). There are language-based tasks that have a memory or working memory component and there are visual–perceptual tasks that have a memory or working memory component. Even relatively simple verbal memory tests (e.g., list learning for first-grade-level words) can be failed by an examinee for non-memory-related problems, such as aphasia, severe language delays, or limited language proficiency (i.e., English as a second language). Therefore, during the development of the WMS-IV, confounding factors in the assessment of memory or working memory were accepted; however, emphasis was placed on developing tasks that minimized the impact of precursor abilities and providing statistical methods to control for overlapping abilities. While attempts were made to limit the degree to which additional cognitive factors influenced memory performance, these factors need to be considered when interpreting WMS-IV results.

When interpreting results obtained on the WMS-IV or any other battery of tests, consider the performance of normally developing individuals. Normal, healthy adults obtain low scores on cognitive tests (Brooks, Holdnack, & Iverson, Submitted; Brooks, Iverson, Holdnack, & Feldman, 2008) for a variety of reasons other than poor ability, such as lapses in attention, poor motivation, or random variance. While some low scores are common in healthy examinees, a large number of low scores can be unusual. The rate at which low scores occur on a given measure varies by education and ability. Comparing an examinee's performance to base rates commensurate with the examinee's background may improve diagnostic accuracy (Brooks et al., Submitted; Brooks, Iverson, Feldman, & Holdnack, 2009). In addition, always look for patterns of low scores across measures to confirm results.

Deciding what constitutes a low score on the WMS-IV is a challenge. Using a restrictive cutoff, such as 1.5 or more standard deviations below the mean (i.e., scaled scores of less than 6 or index scores below 78), results in lower rates of false positives (e.g., identifying normal memory functioning as abnormal); however, only the most impaired individuals will be identified. For instance, in the WMS-IV clinical studies, only the most severely impaired examinees obtained mean subtest scaled scores below the 1.5 standard deviation cutoff. Subtest scores for those with dementia or mild intellectual disability were in the range of 3.9 to 6.5 and index scores ranged from 63.6 to 71.7 (Wechsler, 2009). However, even in these groups, individuals obtained some scaled scores above 5. Moderate levels of memory impairment, such as those observed in moderate to severe traumatic brain injury (TBI) and schizophrenia, resulted in mean subtest scaled scores in the range of 5–8 and mean index scores in the 77–85 range (Wechsler, 2009) both above the –1.5 standard deviations cutoff. Using a restrictive cutoff may fail to identify memory difficulties in patients with less severe memory impairments such as those with moderate levels of memory impairment (e.g., moderate TBI, Temporal Lobe Epilepsy) or in patients with mild memory weaknesses (e.g., attention-deficit/hyperactivity disorder, learning disorder). These clinical groups have mean memory scores at or above 1 standard deviation below the mean; therefore, half or more of the individuals in these clinical groups will be above this cutoff.

In the context of effect sizes, a 0.8 effect size is considered large by research standards (Cohen, 1988). Translated into scaled score units, a 0.8 large effect size is equivalent to a mean scaled score of 7.6 and a mean index score of 88;

an effect size near 0.5 equals a mean of 8.5 at the subtest level and 92.5 at the index level. Therefore, when examinees achieve scores in the low average to average ranges, it does not indicate a problem with the test or the normative data; rather, it reflects the moderate effect sizes observed between many clinical and control groups.

In selecting a cutoff score to maximize sensitivity and specificity, it is recommended that you use a moderately restrictive criterion (e.g., 1–1.25 standard deviations below the mean) and require multiple measures to fall below the cutoff. The selected cutoff should accommodate an examinee's background characteristics or specific clinical questions. For example, a dementia evaluation would require a more restrictive cutoff than an evaluation for mild cognitive impairment to account for the greater memory impairment observed in dementia. No single cutoff can be effectively applied to every assessment; select an appropriate cutoff for each evaluation based on clinical experience, relevant research, and specific needs of a particular examinee.

 *Rapid Reference 4.1*

Key Concepts

There Are No Pure Memory Tests

Language ability affects verbal memory measures.

Visual–perceptual abilities affect visual memory measures.

Motor skills can affect memory tests requiring drawing or constructing.

Low Scores Are Commonly Observed in Healthy People

One low score is unlikely to be pathological.

Base rates of low scores vary by ability level.

While one or two low scores may not indicate pathology, it may signal a weakness in a specific aspect of memory functioning.

Cutoff Scores Are Difficult to Set

Only severely impaired examinees perform below 1.5 standard deviations from the mean.

Most disorders show mild to moderate memory deficits, and restrictive cutoffs may not identify memory difficulties in these groups.

Requiring multiple moderately low scores may maximize sensitivity and specificity.

Cutoffs should vary by clinical question and the ability level of the patient.

SCORE TYPES

There are multiple types of normed scores on the WMS-IV, most of which will be familiar to clinicians who have used the Wechsler scales. All of these scores are expressions of normative data, but each score is derived and expressed differently.

≡ Rapid Reference 4.2

WMS-IV Score Types

Scaled score: Age-adjusted standardized score used for subtests with a mean of 10 and a standard deviation of 3. Scores are derived by age group.

Index score: Summary score of multiple subtest scaled scores with a mean of 100 and standard deviation of 15. Scores are derived from entire normative sample by battery (i.e., Adult, Older Adult).

Cumulative percentages: Age-adjusted scores presented in bands based on cumulative percentages of scores within an age group. These scores are used for optional measures with very skewed distributions.

Contrast scaled score: Scaled score that adjusts one score based on performance on another score. The adjusted score is normed by ability band of the control variable. The resulting score partials out the common variance between the two scores.

Combined score: Combined scores are found in the ACS and combine two variables with non-normal distributions. Each variable contributes equally and is age-adjusted before being combined and transformed into a standardized score.

Subtest Scaled Scores

At the subtest level, all the primary scores and some process and additional scores are expressed in scaled score units. Scaled scores have a mean of 10 and a standard deviation of 3. Scaled scores are derived from the distribution of scores within the 100 cases in a specific normative age band. They represent the rank order of the individual compared to a representative sample of individuals of similar age. Scaled scores are derived using a form of inferential norming (Gorsuch, 2003) that yields raw to scaled score conversions that closely align to a normalized z-transformation of the raw midpoint percentiles but is less affected by sampling errors than traditional z-normalization methods. These scores should be interpreted as the rank order of the individual within their age band and not necessarily as the unit distance from the mean (i.e., one standard deviation from the mean). When the raw score distribution is perfectly normal, the linear transformation of the mean and standard deviations aligns perfectly to the percentile distributions of the normal z-distribution and thus can be interpreted in standard deviation units (see Anastasi & Urbina, 1997, for review). Otherwise, using linear transformation of skewed distributions will yield a mismatch between the standardized score and the individual's actual percentile rank (e.g., a scaled score of 7 misaligns with a percentile of 23 rather than the theoretical percentile of 16). Subsequently, scores across measures cannot be directly compared, as they do not align to the same rank order. Applying methods that yield a normalized z-distribution avoids this problem. Therefore, a scaled score has the same meaning across scores (e.g., a scaled score of 6 is always equal to the ninth percentile). Table 4.1 presents the standard deviations from the mean, percentile rank, and level of performance descriptor corresponding to each scaled score.

Table 4.1 Index and Subtest Percentile Ranks and Performance Descriptors

Standard Score	Scaled Score	Number of SDs from the Mean	Percentile Rank	Qualitative Descriptor
160		$+4$	> 99.9	Very Superior
155		$+3\frac{2}{3}$	> 99.9	Very Superior
150		$+3\frac{1}{3}$	> 99.9	Very Superior
145	19	$+3$	99.9	Very Superior
140	18	$+2\frac{2}{3}$	99.6	Very Superior
135	17	$+2\frac{1}{3}$	99	Very Superior
130	16	$+2$	98	Very Superior
125	15	$+1\frac{2}{3}$	95	Superior
120	14	$+1\frac{1}{3}$	91	Superior
115	13	$+1$	84	High Average
110	12	$+\frac{2}{3}$	75	High Average
105	11	$+\frac{1}{3}$	63	Average
100	10	0	50	Average

(*continued*)

Table 4.1 (Continued)

Standard Score	Scaled Score	Number of SDs from the Mean	Percentile Rank	Qualitative Descriptor
95	9	$-\frac{1}{3}$	37	Average
90	8	$-\frac{2}{3}$	25	Average
85	7	-1	16	Low Average
80	6	$-1\frac{1}{3}$	9	Low Average
75	5	$-1\frac{2}{3}$	5	Borderline
70	4	-2	2	Borderline
65	3	$-2\frac{1}{3}$	1	Extremely Low
60	2	$-2\frac{2}{3}$	0.4	Extremely Low
55	1	-3	0.1	Extremely Low
50		$-3\frac{1}{3}$	< 0.1	Extremely Low
45		$-3\frac{2}{3}$	< 0.1	Extremely Low
40		-4	< 0.1	Extremely Low

Index Standard Scores

In most cases, the index-level scores represent a primary score for WMS-IV measures, although some additional scores are presented in index standard score units. Index standard scores are derived from subtest-level age-adjusted scaled scores; thus, index scores are not adjusted by age a second time. The index standard score represents the examinee's rank order within the normative sample for a particular index. For examinees 16–69 years of age, the normative sample is the 900 cases that completed the Adult battery. In older adults ages 65–90, the index scores are derived from the 500 cases from the Older Adult normative sample. At the index score level, the examinee's performance is considered relative to the entire normative sample. The metric for the index standard score is a mean of 100 and a standard deviation of 15. Due to the greater range of values used to derive index scores, the index scores provide a finer gradation of performance and higher reliability than individual subtest scaled scores. It is important to note that due to the inclusion of multiple skills, an examinee's index score may be lower than the specific subtest level scores. For example, an examinee may obtain four scaled scores of 7 (1 standard deviation below the mean) on the Auditory Memory Index

(AMI) subtests and obtain an AMI of 82 (more than 1 SD below the mean). Additionally, there may be some variability in the scores that contribute to the index. Although the index includes multiple skills, it represents an average of the examinee's overall abilities. If the examinee has a specific strength or weakness within the skills measured in an index, the index score can be interpreted; however, it is important to report the variation of performance within that cognitive domain. For example, if an examinee obtains a low average AMI but performs better on Verbal Paired Associates (VPA) than on Logical Memory (LM), you would state that the examinee scored within the low average range on auditory memory with an observed strength in multitrial learning relative to single-trial learning. Table 4.1 presents the standard deviations from the mean, percentile rank, and level of performance descriptor corresponding to each index score.

Cumulative Percentages

Some scores on the WMS-IV have very skewed distributions and are presented as cumulative percentages. Attempting to scale these scores on a normal distribution yields a measure with a poor raw to scaled score gradient. Small raw score changes yield large jumps in the scaled score distribution, making the scaled score units unstable when factoring in measurement error. These scores typically represent skills that are almost always performed perfectly or near perfectly by healthy controls; therefore, missing a small number of points yields a score that is considered well below average. Although most of these tasks are performed almost perfectly by healthy controls, the scores vary by age group, and age-adjustments are provided. For highly negatively skewed distributions, it is not possible to show superior abilities. Nearly all scores will fall at or below the mean. The scaling of the scores focuses primarily on the lower end of the distribution to enable the examiner to identify weaknesses in functioning.

The cumulative percentages are presented in bands that represent commonly interpreted levels of performance. The percentage bands are: $\leq$ 2, 3–9, 10–16, 17–25, 26–50, 51–75, and > 75 and are interpreted as extremely low, borderline, low average, low average, average, average, and high average, respectively. The scores are presented as bands rather than specific cumulative percentages to account for measurement error in the scores. The cumulative percentage represents the percentage of cases in the normative sample who obtained the same or lower score than the examinee.

The clinician should set cutoff scores consistently across measures using the various score metrics. For a cutoff scaled score of 7, the 10–16 cumulative percentage range is roughly equivalent. The 3–9 percentage range covers scaled scores of 5 and 6, and the cumulative percentage range of ≤ 2 is roughly equivalent to a scaled score of 4 or less.

Contrast Scaled Scores

Contrast scaled scores are derived to aid in the interpretation of an examinee's performance. The contrast scaled scores are best understood from the perspective of Bayesian probabilities. In Bayes theorem, the likelihood that an event occurs is related not only to the probability that the event itself occurs, but also to the likelihood that the event occurs in the presence of other factors or events. In other words, the likelihood of a specific result varies depending on context (e.g., prior events). In WMS-IV, the examiner may pose the question, what is the likelihood of obtaining a scaled score of 6 on LM II? Using the normal curve, roughly 9 in 100 cases would be expected to obtain a score of 6. However, the likelihood of obtaining a 6 on LM II varies depending on how well the examinee encoded information during LM I. Thus, the examiner may ask, what is the probability of obtaining a LM II score of 6 if the examinee obtains a scaled score of 15 on LM I? The probability of obtaining a scaled score of 6 on LM II when the immediate scaled score was 15 is 1 in 100; however, if the immediate scaled score was 5, then the probability of having a 6 on delayed recall is 50 in 100. Contrast scaled scores describe the rank order of an examinee on one variable, within the sample of similarly scoring individuals on a second variable.

In the contrast scaled score model, there are two variables of interest. The first is the "dependent" variable or the cognitive skill of interest. The second is the "control" variable, which represents some precursor ability to the dependent measure or in some way shares variance with the dependent measure. The control variable represents the "context" in which the dependent measure occurs. For example, a delayed memory score is the dependent variable, and the related immediate memory score is the control variable. The contrast score is derived by dividing the control variable into varying ability levels. Within each ability level, the age-adjusted scaled scores of the dependent variable are evaluated. The age-adjusted scaled scores for the dependent variable are adjusted to represent the rank order of performance within the ability level of the control variable. There is no difference between the age-adjusted scaled score and the contrast scaled score when the mean of the dependent variable was 10, the standard deviation was 3, and the distribution was normally distributed within an ability level. However, in most cases, the mean, variance, and skew are different for each level of ability. For example, for examinees with LM I scaled scores of 4, the mean performance on delayed memory is 5, not 10. The contrast scaled score adjusts the dependent variable based on the distribution of scores within the specific ability level of the control variable.

Contrast scaled scores answer a different question than the age-adjusted scaled score. The age-adjusted scaled score answers the question of whether the score is atypical for the person's age (e.g., does the examinee have poor delayed recall in comparison to the general population of 16- to 17-year-olds?). The contrast scaled score shows whether a score is atypical given the examinee's ability on the control variable (e.g., given the examinee's above-average immediate memory, is the delayed recall score unexpectedly low?). In this example, the examinee is not being compared to the general population but rather to individuals with the same level of immediate memory encoding.

Contrast scaled scores are derived using a similar procedure as age-adjusted scaled scores. The primary difference is that the grouping variable for contrast scaled scores is not age but ability on a specific measure, and the score that is adjusted is not the subtest raw score but the subtest scaled score. The contrast scaled score is expressed in scaled score units that are easily interpreted into the examinee's rank order of performance on the dependent variable. For instance, the LM Immediate Recall versus Delayed Recall contrast scaled score provides information on the examinee's delayed recall ability for stories when you control for the initial level of encoding. A scaled score of 5 on this contrast score indicates the examinee's delayed recall is at the fifth percentile compared to individuals with similar ability on immediate story recall. A contrast scaled score of 5 could be derived from different combinations of subtest scaled scores, such as an immediate story memory of 15 and a delayed recall of 11 or an immediate recall of 6 and a delayed recall of 4. However, each combination is interpreted exactly the same way; the examinee's delayed story recall is at the fifth percentile when compared to individuals with similar immediate story recall. Notice in this example the numerical difference between the scores is not the same (i.e., 4 scaled score points and 2 scaled score points). This exemplifies the main advantage of using the contrast score method—it accounts for regression to the mean effects and for variation in score differences due to ability level (i.e., the tendency of scores near the upper end of the distributions to have larger differences and scores at the lower end to have smaller differences).

At the index score level, contrast scaled scores return similar results as the traditional predicted difference method. However, when the relationship between the two variables is either nonlinear or when the standard deviation of the dependent variable is not homogeneous across the regression line, (i.e., heteroscedasity) results may not be identical. For example, individuals with high general ability have more variability in memory functioning than individuals with low general ability. In these situations, the contrast scaled score is more accurate, as it does not depend on a linear relationship between the variables, nor does it require a homogeneous standard deviation across levels of the predictor variable.

Contrast scaled scores represent the rank order of the individuals within the specified ability group of the control variable. Therefore, the score itself is similar to the base rate of a discrepancy between an actual score from a predicted score (e.g., delayed memory predicted from general ability). The percentile rank of the contrast scaled score informs the clinician of the atypicality of the achieved scaled score within a specified ability level. Set the cutoff score in a manner similar to other scores; however, it is recommended that the highest cutoff, to show a specific weakness in cognitive functioning, should be no greater than 7. The reliability of a contrast score is difficult to estimate. In the absence of a specific reliability coefficient, you may wish to apply a general rule of only interpreting scaled scores of 7 (e.g., a base rate of about 15%) or a more restrictive value of 5 (e.g., a base rate of about 5%) as low. You may want to use different cutoffs for index scores versus subtest scaled scores with index level contrast scores having a less restrictive cutoff such as 7 and subtest level contrast scores a more restrictive cutoff such as 5. This is due to the higher reliability and the greater range of data points within each ability band at the index level.

It is important to remember that the contrast scaled scores will yield very different results as a function of the correlation between the two variables in question. For example, only very small differences are required to obtain an atypical result when you compare immediate and delayed memory. However, very large score differences may not yield atypical results when you compare auditory and visual working memory. The contrast scaled scores account for the level of association between the variables. This can be confusing initially, as the same numerical difference can be atypical in one contrast scaled score, while in another it does not yield an atypical result.

The contrast scaled score approach works well when there is a clear control versus dependent measure hierarchy, for example, immediate versus delayed memory or visual working memory versus visual memory. In each of these cases, the control variable is an obvious precursor skill to the dependent variable in question. However, the contrast scaled scores may yield unexpected results when there is no true hierarchy between the control and contrast variable. For example, the auditory versus visual memory contrast scaled score does not have a clear hierarchy. The contrast score could have easily been visual versus auditory, with the visual memory score as the control variable. When no true hierarchy exists, scores at the extremes of the distribution may be difficult to interpret. For example, a low auditory memory score (e.g., AMI = 74) requires a score of 99 on visual memory to show that visual memory is unusually better than auditory memory. This is due to the relatively low correlation between visual and auditory memory and to regression to the mean effects in which control scores below the mean have relatively higher scores on the dependent measure. In contrast, if visual memory was 74, then any value on auditory memory would yield a scaled score of 7 or less. When scores are below the mean, the contrast scaled score is more likely to identify weaknesses in visual memory but not strengths in visual memory. When evaluating differences between cross-modal measures, it is important to also use the simple differences level of statistical significance and base rates. These comparisons do not account for changes in the base rates of differences at the extremes of the distribution, but they can help identify differences in performance between auditory and visual memory when the contrast scores do not seem to make clinical sense.

Combined Scores

The WMS-IV does not use combined scores; however, combined scores are used to generate alternate indexes in the ACS. Combined scores were introduced in the NEPSY-II as a method for combining two scores with different metrics (e.g., combining performance on a scaled score and a cumulative percentile) or two cumulative percentile scores. Combined scores avoid the problem of combining unadjusted raw scores with very different statistical distributions. For example, combining a score based on time with an error rate score on the same test results in a score that is 90% based on time due to the larger distribution of the time score. Subtracting a point or two for errors makes almost no impact on the overall distribution. Thus, speed may be rewarded over accuracy. Additionally, the variables in question may vary dramatically by age such that multiple errors may be very common in one group but quite rare in another; simply combining the raw scores may result in misleading results.

In the WMS-IV, the combined score methodology allows the combination of recognition trials for the auditory or visual measures into index-level scores. The combined score method also allows scores with very different distributions (e.g., Visual Reproduction [VR] recognition and Designs [DE] recognition) without overly weighting one of the scores due to differences in score distributions. Combined scores can be directly compared to other index scores to identify relative strengths and weaknesses in memory functioning.

SUBTEST-LEVEL INTERPRETATION

This section describes general principles for interpreting the WMS-IV subtest scores. First, each subtest is briefly described and all primary scores are discussed.

Alternate hypotheses for poor performance are also presented. For subtests that vary across the Adult and Older Adult batteries, each version is discussed individually. Second, the process conditions and scores, and contrast scores for the subtest are described. Finally, the ACS additional scores for the subtest are briefly discussed.

Logical Memory (LM) I and II

LM is a story recall subtest. The examinee is read a story and asked to repeat the contents immediately after presentation and after a 20- to 30-minute delay. In general, this subtest is a measure of auditory memory. Specifically, it is an assessment of memory for orally presented verbal information that is semantically and sequentially organized. Additional interpretative considerations for LM scores are discussed in the following pages. Rapid Reference 4.3 summarizes the interpretation of the LM subtest scores.

Rapid Reference 4.3

Interpreting Logical Memory Performance

General Level of Interpretation

Measure of auditory immediate and delayed memory

Specific Level of Interpretation

Encoding and retrieval of orally presented verbal information that is semantically and sequentially organized

Logical Memory Scores

Primary measures:

LM I: Scaled score measuring working memory and initial encoding and retrieval of organized verbal information

LM II: Scaled score measuring encoding and retrieval of organized verbal information from long-term memory

Process measures:

LM II Recognition: Cumulative percentage reflecting ability to recognize encoded organized verbal information in long-term memory stores

LM II Recognition versus Delayed Recall Contrast Scaled Score: Scaled score evaluating encoding versus retrieval deficits for organized verbal information in long-term memory stores

LM Immediate Recall versus Delayed Recall Contrast Scaled Score: Scaled score testing the hypothesis that delayed memory for organized verbal information is unexpectedly low or high compared to initial encoding

Additional scores in ACS:

Individual Story Norms: Scaled scores and cumulative percentages enabling use of a single story to evaluate organized verbal memory.

LM I Story A First Recall versus Story A Second Recall Contrast Scaled Score: Scaled score (Older Adult battery only) measuring learning from first story presentation to second story presentation

LM II Cue Given: Cumulative percentage measuring the examinee's need to be prompted in order to provide any information on delayed free recall and an indicator of retrieval difficulties

Additional Cognitive Functions Affecting Performance

Expressive Language: Ability to effectively repeat story details.

Receptive Language: Ability to process sentences in the story and understand what has been said; meaning-based encoding may allow for better retrieval.

Auditory Working Memory: Ability to temporarily hold, process, and manipulate sentences as the text is too long to encode instantly; efficient processing in working memory facilitates encoding.

Auditory Attention: Brief focused auditory attention and freedom from distraction enable the examinee to hear and process all the information being presented.

General Intellectual Ability: General deficits in processing information limit the ability to preprocess information for effective storage and retrieval.

Hearing Acuity: Poor hearing may result in missed or misheard information, resulting in a loss of points.

Articulation: Severe impairments in articulation may make it difficult for the clinician to correctly hear and score responses.

Attention/Concentration: Lapses in brief focused attention or sustained attention may moderately impact performance, as the examinee only gets one chance to learn material.

Executive Functioning: Impairments in organization may result in story recall that interferes with the examinee's ability to use the intrinsic semantic and sequential structure of the test and may impact test results.

Primary Scores (Adult Battery Ages 16–69)

Chapters 2 and 3 presented detailed information regarding the administration and scoring of the LM subtest. The primary scores derived are LM I and II scaled scores. These scores represent the examinee's ability to *recall details* about a story immediately after presentation and after a 30-minute delay. It is important to note that LM I and II do not measure the examinee's ability to retell a story. The scoring rules do not account for the examinee's ability to provide a coherent, sequentially accurate, retelling of the story. The examinee is awarded credit for remembering details of the story, and most details are scored in isolation of other aspects of the story content (e.g., "Anna Thompson is a rocket engineer" still gets credit for "Anna Thompson" even though she's actually a cook). Additionally, the details are not weighted by their relative importance to the story content such that remembering the detail that "a woman was robbed" is given the same credit as recalling the detail that she "worked in a school cafeteria."

The *LM I scaled score* is interpreted as the examinee's ability to immediately recall details from orally presented information with meaningful content that is semantically and sequentially related. LM I also measures working memory span such that information in working memory may get repeated immediately but may not get encoded into long-term memory stores. The *LM II scaled score* represents the examinee's ability to retrieve semantically and sequentially related information that has meaningful content from long-term memory stores. LM II represents the amount of information that was *encoded* into memory that the examinee was able to *retrieve* following a delay. An important component of LM is the sequential and semantic organization of the information. This may facilitate retrieval of the information from memory. For example, the examinee may recall that "there was a woman and something bad happened to her." Recalling this information then helps the examinee search for relevant information related to the story even if it is not initially recalled.

The semantic basis of LM allows for the interaction of newly acquired information with semantic knowledge. The logical progression of the stories enables the examinee to evaluate the probability that a response is more or less correct. For example, most people will "know" at some level that when a person is robbed they will contact the police. They would also have an idea that a school cook is unlikely to have a lot of money and therefore would experience some hardship from having even a small amount of money taken. This prior knowledge can facilitate the encoding and retrieval processes, unlike other verbal memory measures which are not semantically organized. Therefore, a breakdown in semantic memory functions or in language functioning could impact efficiency of storage and retrieval on LM I and LM II.

It is important to note that on the Adult battery, neither story is repeated. Therefore, performance on this test is a measure of single-trial learning. Examinees that have difficulty learning information based on a single presentation will have difficulty on this test compared to measures that allow for repetition of the stimuli. A single exposure to the stimuli is adequate for healthy adults to retain story information over a 30-minute delay.

Primary Scores (Older Adult Battery Ages 65–90)

The LM subtest for older adults is different in content and administration from the Adult battery. The first story (Story A) in the Older Adult battery is linguistically less complex and shorter than the stories found in the Adult battery. In a key difference between the batteries, Story A is repeated one time after the first presentation. The second story presented to the older adults is the same as the first story presented to the younger adults, providing continuity between the Older Adult and Adult batteries.

Just like in the Adult battery, LM is a measure of an examinee's ability to store and retrieve details related to orally presented, semantically and sequentially organized verbal information. In general, the same interpretation guidelines apply to LM in both batteries, with some caveats. The primary differences include repetition of the first story, shorter length of the first story, and the lower linguistic complexity of the first story. Interpretation of the older adult version should account for the differences in content and presentation. First, repetition of the first story enables healthy older adults to better encode the story details and improves delayed memory performance. However, it also changes LM to multitrial learning for the first story. A second factor that needs to be considered is the lower level of linguistic complexity of the first story relative to the second story. While this reduces any confounding of performance with verbal skills, it may also limit the use of semantic memory to facilitate the storage and retrieval of the information. A third factor to consider when interpreting the Older Adult battery is the shorter length of the first story. A shorter story may allow working memory span to contribute more to immediate recall than it can with a longer story and thus reduces the need to encode details of the story. Thus, delayed recall may be impacted if the level of encoding during immediate memory is compromised due to a heavy reliance on working memory.

WMS-IV Process Scores

Each of the stories has an associated optional delayed recognition trial. In the Adult battery, the recognition trials have 15 items for each story, for a total of 30 points. The Older Adult battery recognition trials have 8 and 15 items, respectively, for a total of 23 points. The recognition trials do not differ in administration, scoring, or interpretation; only the content differs between the Adult and the Older Adult batteries. Therefore, the interpretation of the recognition trial is consistent across both batteries.

The recognition trials ask the examinee yes/no questions about the content of the stories. The examinee must recognize whether the content of the question matches information from the story. As noted previously, this is an optional procedure used when the examiner has a question about the examinee's ability to recognize versus freely recall information from long-term memory. The recognition trial enables the clinician to determine if the examinee has adequately encoded the story information by providing clues to aid in retrieving the information. In cases where the examinee has demonstrated average or above-average performance on the free recall trial, the clinician may choose not to administer the recognition trial. In this situation, the examinee has already demonstrated adequate encoding and retrieval, and the recognition trial will not provide much additional information about the examinee's memory functioning. Alternately, when the examinee has a low score on LM II, performance on the recognition trial may help determine if the examinee failed to encode the information (e.g., low score on both LM II and recognition) or encoded the information but failed to retrieve it (e.g., low LM II score and average or better score on recognition).

The recognition trial measures the examinee's ability to recognize specific details from the story. Recognition assesses a subset of the story content; the total number of recognition items is less than the total number of scored details in the free recall condition. Therefore, the scores are not equivalent in the amount of information required but represent the examinee's relative performance compared to age peers. The recognition trial is presented as a cumulative percentage, so it is possible to identify very low, borderline, low average, average, and high average performance. Comparing scores on LM II and recognition will help determine whether the examinee is relatively better at recognition than free recall. Better performance on recognition suggests that memory encoding functions are intact, but the examinee has difficulty accessing their knowledge (i.e., retrieval deficit). Alternately, the recognition trial requires less effort than the free recall condition. For examinees with significant problems initiating and sustaining effort, performance will likely be better on the recognition task; however, it may not be due to a specific problem with memory retrieval but rather to better performance on tasks requiring less cognitive exertion.

In some cases, examinees may have better free recall than recognition. This is an unusual finding as LM II has elements of both encoding and retrieval so to show adequate encoding and retrieval on one variable and then to show poor encoding on a second variable is difficult to explain. Some hypotheses might be language-based issues (e.g., not understanding the recognition questions adequately), response bias (e.g., all "yes" or "no" responding on the recognition trial), variable attention (e.g., not fully attending to the recognition questions), variable effort (e.g., not putting forth consistent effort), or a failure to improve performance during the recognition trial. In the normative sample, examinees recalled more information during recognition than delayed free recall. If the examinee recognizes only the information recalled during LM II, it is likely that his or her LM II score will be higher than his or her recognition score. For example, for a 68-year-old, an LM II raw score of 17 points is equal to a scaled score of 9, while 17 points on LM recognition would be at the second cumulative percentage. It is good to compare the information recalled freely versus in the recognition trial when trying to understand an examinee's performance. If no additional information is recalled during recognition, cuing is not helping retrieval.

Contrast Scores

The LM subtest provides two contrast scores to help the clinician further describe the examinee's memory functioning. The first score is the *LM II Recognition versus Delayed Recall* contrast scaled score. This contrast score enables the clinician to determine if the examinee's delayed free recall ability is consistent with his or her level of recognition memory. The score represents the examinee's rank order on LM II compared to examinees with a similar level of delayed recognition. A low score (e.g., score of 7 or less) indicates that the examinee's LM II score is below average compared to others with similar delayed recognition ability. This suggests that the ability to retrieve semantically and sequentially organized material is below expected levels given the examinee's encoding ability.

The contrast score is interpreted in the same manner regardless of the level of recognition performance; in other words, if the examinee has above-average recognition or below-average recognition, the contrast score of 7 is interpreted the same. This is important to understand because when describing the examinee's memory performance you will need to report both age-adjusted scaled scores and contrast scaled scores. The contrast scaled score does not replace the LM II scaled score. The overall interpretation of an examinee's memory functioning will differ if the examinee has an average LM II scaled score and a low average LM II Recognition versus Delayed Recall score in comparison to an examinee with an extremely low LM II score and a low average contrast scaled score.

As stated previously, having better free recall compared to recognition is an unusual finding. High scores on this contrast score suggest that the examinee has unexpectedly good free recall for semantically and sequentially organized verbal material compared to individuals with similar levels of recognition memory. Factors other than memory functioning may need to be considered during interpretation of results (e.g., language, attention, effort, response bias). Evaluate the items the examinee received credit for in the recall and recognition conditions. If the examinee recognized only the information he or she recalled during free recall, this contrast scaled score will likely be elevated.

The second contrast score is *LM Immediate versus Delayed Recall.* This score provides the clinician with data regarding the relative performance on delayed recall of semantically and sequentially organized verbal information relative to immediate recall ability. It provides an estimation of information loss or gain from initial encoding into long-term storage. Some forgetting of information between immediate and delayed recall is observed in healthy adults, and the observed rate of forgetting increases with age. In the Adult battery, the comparison between LM I and LM II can be interpreted as "forgetting rate"; however, for older adults, the immediate memory score has a multitrial learning component. Therefore, the immediate memory and delayed memory scores are not directly comparable in terms of the number of raw data points. The contrast scaled score indicates how well the examinee's delayed recall is functioning relative to his or her immediate learning but is not conceptually the same as forgetting rate.

The LM Immediate versus Delayed Recall contrast scaled score is best conceptualized as the variance in delayed recall for semantically and sequentially organized verbal information that is not attributable to performance during initial encoding. Alternately, it can be viewed as the examinee's delayed recall ability in comparison to individuals with similar levels of immediate memory ability. Low scores indicate that delayed recall for organized verbal information is unexpectedly low considering initial recall performance. A low score suggests that the examinee has lost more information from memory than expected. A high score indicates that the examinee's delayed memory performance is better than expected given their initial level of recall. This could indicate that the examinee benefits from additional time for memories to be consolidated into long-term stores.

Additional Scores in the ACS

The *ACS Administration and Scoring Manual* provides additional normative data for the LM subtest. Most of the normative information is related to the administration of a single story. Situations in which you might use only a single story include an administration error in one of the stories, insufficient time to administer both stories, or one of the stories appears to be invalid for a specific reason (e.g., content caused examinee to get upset). The additional scores provided in the ACS are individual story norms for recall and recognition, including norms for the first and second recall of Story A in the Older Adult battery, contrast scores for the first versus second recall of Story A and immediate and delayed recall for each story, and a cumulative percentage for cuing on delayed memory.

The single-story norms should be interpreted using the same strategy as the standard two-story administration. However, the clinician should be more cautious in the conclusions he or she draws from one story given the smaller sample of behavior on which the examinee's performance is based. Also, consider that score reliabilities are lower for a single story than for multiple stories.

LM I Story A First Recall versus Story A Second Recall describes the examinee's performance on the second recall of Story A, controlling for the initial level of encoding. This is similar to a learning slope for story recall. Low scores indicate that the examinee's performance after hearing the story a second time was lower than expected compared to individuals with similar levels of initial recall. This suggests that the examinee did not benefit from the repetition of the story to the same degree as others with similar single-trial recall. High scores on this measure indicate the examinee's performance improved more than expected. These individuals benefit more from repetition than other individuals with similar levels of initial recall.

The administration of LM delayed recall requires the clinician to provide a memory cue for individuals who say they cannot remember anything from the story. The examiner can note the use of prompts to facilitate retrieval from long-term memory stores. The ACS provides a cumulative percentage to determine if the examinee's need for prompting falls within normal limits. If the number of cues required is atypical, this may signal difficulties with retrieval from long-term memory. If the examinee is cued and then shows good recall for the information, it suggests some difficulties with accessing encoded information. If the examinee is prompted and still shows poor recall, it may reflect either more significant problems with retrieval or poor encoding of material into long-term memory. Administration of recognition trials may help clarify the problem.

Additional Cognitive Functions Affecting Performance

Logical Memory is a language-based task; therefore, any disturbance in language functioning is likely to impact performance. Since the examinee must listen to and process moderately complex sentences and then recall what was said, both receptive and expressive language abilities are required. In addition to language skills, LM requires auditory working memory in order to process information in conscious awareness and to facilitate effective storage and retrieval. Moreover, general intellectual functioning will impact the examinee's ability to encode and retrieve information from long-term memory stores. Brief auditory attention, adequate hearing acuity, and sufficient articulation are additional basic abilities that could influence results on this subtest.

Verbal Paired Associates (VPA) I and II

VPA is an associative learning task. Unlike standard list-learning tasks, VPA measures the examinee's ability to learn new connections between pairs of words. In standard list-learning tasks, the examinee recalls all the words he or she can from the list presented. In VPA, the recall of information is controlled by the clinician. The clinician requests the associated words one at a time and corrects any errors and provides any forgotten words. In general, this subtest is a measure of auditory memory. Specifically, the test is an assessment of cued recall of associative learning for semantically related and unrelated words. The content of the test varies slightly between the Adult and Older Adult batteries. However, the differences in content are not sufficient to warrant a change in interpretation between the batteries. Additional interpretative considerations are discussed in the following pages. Rapid Reference 4.4 summarizes the interpretation of the VPA scores.

 *Rapid Reference 4.4*

Interpreting Verbal Paired Associates Performance

General Level of Interpretation

Measure of auditory immediate and delayed memory

Specific Level of Interpretation

Encoding and cued recall of associative learning for semantically related and unrelated words

Verbal Paired Associates Scores

Primary measures:

VPA I: Scaled score measuring initial learning and encoding for semantically related and unrelated word pairs

VPA II: Scaled score measuring encoding and retrieval of semantically related and unrelated word pairs from long-term memory stores

Process measures:

VPA II Recognition: Cumulative percentage reflecting ability to recognize associations between semantically related and unrelated word pairs in long-term memory

VPA II Word Recall: Scaled score measuring ability to encode and retrieve words from verbal memory

VPA II Recognition versus Delayed Recall Contrast Scaled Score: Scaled score evaluating encoding versus retrieval deficits for semantically related and unrelated word pairs in long-term memory

VPA Immediate Recall versus Delayed Recall Contrast Scaled Score: Scaled
score testing the hypothesis that delayed memory for associative verbal
learning is unexpectedly low or high compared to initial encoding

Additional scores in ACS:

VPA I Recall A: Scaled score measuring single-trial associative learning for
semantically related and unrelated words

VPA I Recall D: Scaled score measuring recall of associations between related
and unrelated words after multiple learning trials

VPA I Recall A versus Recall D Contrast Scaled Score: Scaled score measuring
single-trial versus multitrial recall abilities providing estimation of the degree
to which repetition improves recall

VPA I Easy Items: Scaled score measuring total learning for associations
between semantically related words

VPA I Hard Items: Scaled score measuring total learning for associations
between semantically unrelated words

VPA I Easy Items versus Hard Items Contrast Scaled Score: Scaled score
evaluating learning ability for semantically related versus unrelated word
associations

VPA I Intra-List Intrusions: Cumulative percentage of total errors in recall during initial learning of the word associations related to incorrect
associations between words

VPA I Extra-List Intrusions: Cumulative percentage of total errors in recall
during initial learning of the word associations related to both incorrect
recall of words and incorrect associations

VPA I Intrusions: Scaled score measuring total number of intrusion errors
made during initial learning trials for associations between semantically
related and unrelated words

VPA II Easy Items: Cumulative percentage of recall of associations between
semantically related words from long-term memory

VPA II Hard Items: Cumulative percentage of recall of associations between
semantically unrelated words from long-term memory

VPA II Intra-List Intrusions: Cumulative percentage of total errors in recall during delayed recall of the word associations related to incorrect
association between list words

VPA II Extra-List Intrusions: Cumulative percentage of total errors in recall
during delayed recall of the word associations related to both incorrect
recall of words and incorrect associations

VPA II Intrusions: Cumulative percentage of total number of intrusion errors
made during initial learning trials for associations between semantically
related and unrelated words   (*continued*)

VPA II Recognition Easy Items: Cumulative percentage of recognition of associations between semantically related words from long-term memory

VPA II Recognition Hard Items: Cumulative percentage of recognition of associations between semantically unrelated words from long-term memory

VPA II Recognition Hits: Cumulative percentage of examinee's ability to recognize newly learned verbal associations in long-term memory

VPA II Recognition False Positives: Cumulative percentage of the rate at which the examinee erroneously recognizes verbal information in long-term memory

VPA II Recognition Discriminability: Cumulative percentage of total accuracy of recognition of information in long-term memory

VPA II Word Recall Repetitions: Cumulative percentage of the rate at which the examinee recalls redundant information from long-term memory

Additional Cognitive Functions Affecting Performance

Expressive Language: Minimal to moderate as test requires only single word response; however, patients with word finding difficulty may struggle with this task

Receptive Language: Requires moderate degree of receptive language to understand directions and be able to take advantage of semantic relationships between words

Auditory Working Memory: Moderate degree of working memory is required during initial learning trials

General Intellectual Ability: General deficits in processing information limit the ability to preprocess information for effective storage and retrieval

Hearing Acuity: Poor hearing may result in missed or misheard words, resulting in a loss of points

Articulation: Severe impairments in articulation may make it difficult for the clinician to correctly hear and score responses

Attention/Concentration: Lapses in brief focused attention or sustained attention may have a small impact; however, multiple repetitions provide the examinee multiple chances to learn information

Executive Functioning: Impairments in cognitive flexibility may interfere with the examinee's ability to learn semantically unrelated word pairs.

Primary Scores

The clinician reads a series of word pairs to the examinee (i.e., 14 pairs for ages 16–69; 10 pairs for ages 65–90). The examinee is presented the list of word pairs four times during the initial learning phase. The items are presented in different serial orders in order to eliminate primacy and recency effects on recall. After a

20- to 30-minute delay, the examinee is again presented with the cue words and asked to provide the target words. In the immediate learning condition, the clinician corrects all erroneous or missing responses, but in the delayed condition no feedback is provided. After the delayed cued recall, two optional conditions (i.e., delayed recognition and delayed free recall) may be administered.

The primary scores for VPA are the VPA I and VPA II scaled scores. These scores represent the amount of information the examinee learned to associate during immediate learning and delayed cued recall conditions. The VPA I and VPA II scores represent a combination of semantically related and semantically unrelated recall. The *VPA I scaled score* is interpreted as the examinee's ability to learn novel and semantically related and unrelated associations between words. This score does not measure free recall as the recall is prompted, and the order in which information may be recalled is under the control of the clinician, not the examinee. Initial learning and encoding of the word pairs may be influenced by working memory skills; however, due to the cued recall, the ability to quickly recall information during initial processing is not required for this test. Therefore, immediate auditory span may not influence performance as greatly as observed on free recall memory tests.

The *VPA II scaled score* represents the examinee's ability to retrieve semantically related and unrelated word associations from long-term memory. VPA II represents the examinee's ability to access specific information when prompted. The delayed cued recall performance is influenced by the initial presentation of information in a learning format. Since a cue is provided to elicit the examinee's responses, it is difficult to discern retrieval versus encoding deficits. If an examinee has a minor retrieval issue, performance on VPA may not be affected; however, if an examinee has a significant retrieval deficit, then prompting may be insufficient to facilitate retrieval. Moreover, semantically related items (e.g., boy–girl) facilitate recall by linking new learning to prior knowledge. The examinee may invoke semantic memory to provide reasonable response alternatives when he or she is uncertain of the correct response. In cases where semantic memory or language functioning is compromised, the examinee may have difficulty learning and recalling the semantically associated items.

WMS-IV Process Scores

VPA II Recognition evaluates the examinee's ability to recognize the previously presented word pairs. The examinee is presented a pair of words and asked to indicate if the pair was previously presented. The examinee must correctly identify the correct word pairs and the distracters. The distracter pairs are comprised of two novel words (i.e., neither word was included in any of the original word pairs), one novel word and one word from the original pairs, or two words from the original pairs that are mismatched. The examinee must recognize both the correct words and the correct associations between words to perform well. Most healthy individuals achieve a perfect or near perfect score.

The recognition condition enables the clinician to determine if the examinee is having difficulty retrieving information from memory or difficulty with encoding information into memory. An examinee with low free recall scores but average recognition may be having difficulty accessing encoded information. Alternately, if the examinee has both low cued recall and recognition scores, this suggests difficulties encoding the information into long-term memory. You may also wish to review the specific types of false positive errors made by the examinee. For example, some examinees make errors related only to associations between the words, saying "yes" to correct words that are incorrectly matched. Others may only partially encode the information and recognize one of the words as correct but not the second word as incorrect. These examinees endorse more items where one word is from the list and the other is not. Finally, examinees with poor encoding frequently respond to word pairs where neither word appeared on the list.

For *VPA II Word Recall*, the examinee is asked to say all the words he or she can recall from the list of word pairs; the examinee does not have to remember the correct association. This condition should be administered only following the recognition trial in order to apply the normative data. This condition functions like a traditional word list recall task; however, it is not a true delayed recall condition, because the examinee is reexposed to all the target words during the cued recall task and all the correct words during the recognition trial before completing word recall.

This score measures the overall amount of information encoded and retrieved from memory. Examinees who perform poorly on cued recall and recognition but do well on the free recall condition may be having difficulties with association memory rather than global difficulties with verbal memory. Alternately, examinees who perform well on cued recall but poorly on free recall may have difficulty retrieving information from memory without prompting or cuing. Examine the results from VPA and LM to determine the consistency of verbal memory retrieval problems.

Contrast Scores

The *VPA II Recognition versus Delayed Recall* score compares performance on the recognition trial to performance on cued recall. This comparison is not as direct an indicator of encoding versus retrieval difficulties as the LM contrast score due to the cued recall nature of VPA. This score describes the impact of increasing retrieval help on information recall. For this score, the recognition trial is the control variable and the cued recall condition is the dependent measure.

Low scores indicate retrieval deficits. The examinee is better able to recognize word pairs than produce correct responses when prompted. Therefore, more structure is required for retrieval than simple cuing provides. High scores on this measure are unexpected and suggest that the examinee performs better when receiving only the target word prompt than the whole pair. For high scores, it is important to evaluate errors on the recognition trial. Perhaps on the recognition trial, the examinee missed items where both words were correct but were incorrectly associated, suggesting poor association memory but good general memory. It takes very few errors on recognition to obtain a low percentile rank; therefore, poor encoding could influence performance on recognition more than on cued recall. For example, if an examinee recalls 10 items during cued recall and only remembers those items on delayed recall, he or she would obtain a scaled score of 11 on VPA II. However, recalling only those 10 items on recognition results in a percentage of 17 to 25 and a contrast score of 14. Always review an examinee's item-level performance when unexpected results are obtained.

The *VPA Immediate Recall versus Delayed Recall* contrast scaled score compares performance on immediate versus delayed cued recall. The control variable is VPA I, and the dependent variable is VPA II. This score represents the examinee's delayed cued recall ability controlling for initial level of learning. It is not specifically a measure of forgetting; a forgetting measure would compare performance on the last trial of immediate recall versus delayed recall. This score uses overall learning on trials 1–4 as an indicator of immediate encoding. Therefore, this score measures the examinee's ability to access association memory from long-term memory stores controlling for overall initial encoding.

A low score indicates difficulty accessing verbal associations from long-term memory relative to initial encoding ability. A high score indicates that the examinee has better-than-expected delayed cued recall compared to initial encoding level. In either case, you will want to evaluate the specifics of the performance. Examine performance on the final initial recall trial compared to the delayed trial to determine if there is information loss (i.e., loss of information from immediate to delayed recall). Conversely, the examinee may recall a low but consistent amount of information across trials, giving them a relatively high score on immediate recall and a low delayed recall score. However, no obvious loss of information occurred from the last learning trial to delayed recall.

Additional Scores in the ACS

The ACS provides additional data designed to enhance the interpretation of VPA scores. The ACS scores include error scores, process scores, and contrast scores and are presented as either scaled scores or cumulative percentages.

Two error scores are provided for both VPA I and VPA II: intra-list and extra-list intrusions. An intra-list intrusion occurs when the examinee responds with a word from the list of word pairs but associates the word with the wrong cue. This type of error is relatively common among normal controls. It represents poor encoding of the association and/or a willingness to put forth effort on the test even when the examinee is not certain of the correct answer. A modest number of intra-list errors is expected during the encoding phase and represents a normal learning pattern. Very high rates of intra-list errors suggest the examinee is able to remember the correct words, correctly encoding some of the information, but has significant difficulty linking the words in memory. This score is presented as a cumulative percentage for VPA I and VPA II. This allows you to determine if errors occur primarily during learning, delayed recall, or both, indicating the difficulties are with initial acquisition of associative learning or with accuracy of delayed recall, or both, respectively.

An extra-list intrusion occurs when the examinee responds to the cue word with a novel word. This error represents an error of association and an intrusion of information not presented to the examinee. This error type indicates poor encoding of the association and the verbal material. The examiner should note whether the errors represent high probability semantic errors (e.g., a response with a high degree of association with the cue word). The extra-list intrusion is a relatively more serious type of memory error as it represents a breakdown in the encoding and retrieval of both the association and the verbal information. This type of error occurs within the normative sample but at a lower rate than intra-list intrusions. Extra-list errors are available for VPA I and VPA II and are presented as cumulative percentages.

A third intrusion variable, *total* intrusions, is obtained by summing the raw intra-list and extra-list errors. This score measures the examinee's overall error rate. The interpretation of the total intrusions score must take into account the nature of the memory errors (e.g., extra-list and intra-list). If one type of error is over-represented in the total intrusions score, consider not reporting total intrusions. The primary advantage of the total intrusion score is its presentation as a scaled score for the immediate condition, making it more comparable to other cognitive skills. For VPA II, total intrusions is presented as a cumulative percentage.

Memory errors represent a breakdown in memory encoding functions and/or in the retrieval process. For verbal memory measures, consider the impact of language functioning, particularly when language difficulties are present but not severe enough to exclude the use of verbal memory measures (e.g., dysnomia or developmental language disorder). Memory errors can occur due to inadequate self-monitoring during memory retrieval. If an examinee fails to appreciate that a response is incorrect or does so only after providing an incorrect response, this suggests poor self-monitoring. Memory errors are complex and you will need to use multiple sources of information to confirm hypotheses about which cognitive functions may be producing high rates of memory errors by the examinee. Look for consistency of errors across memory tests. For example, does the examinee have high rates of intrusions on other memory measures (e.g., VR, LM, California Verbal Learning Test–Second Edition [CVLT-II])? Are memory errors confined to one modality (e.g., verbal)? Does the examinee have impaired memory functioning in general, specific to auditory modality, or is memory functioning relatively normal except for high error rates? You may also want to review performance on language tests to determine if language deficits are contributing to errors on VPA. In particular, you need to ensure that the examinee understood the task. Some examinees do not understand VPA and say, "But gold doesn't go with west, it goes with silver," or a similar comment and tend to have a response bias toward semantically related but erroneous responses. Evaluation of executive functioning may help clarify the nature of the difficulty, particularly performance on language-based tasks such as verbal fluency and Stroop-type tasks, as well as general impulsive responding across executive function measures.

The ACS also provides error rates for VPA II Recognition and Word Recall. The error score for the recognition trial is for *false positives*—responses in which the examinee identifies an incorrect word pair as one of the target word pairs. Just as with recall errors, you may wish to identify specific types of errors the examinee makes (e.g., incorrect associations, incorrect words). A high false-positive rate indicates that the examinee does not accurately recognize information in long-term memory and/or does not effectively monitor memory for accuracy.

For the free recall task, you can identify intrusion and repetition errors. In this trial, there are no association errors since the examinee simply recalls any word from the list one at a time. Repetition errors occur when the examinee repeats the same items without noticing he or she has already provided the information and represents a breakdown in the examinee's ability to filter out redundant information. Errors on free recall indicate problems with encoding, retrieval, or self-monitoring in memory functions. The error scores should be used in conjunction with one another to identify the consistency and nature of memory errors.

Process scores describe a particular aspect of memory performance, enabling the clinician to better understand how the examinee approached a task and providing finer descriptions of memory performance. The VPA I process scores for cued recall include Recall A, Recall D, Easy Items, and Hard Items. All of these scores are presented in scaled score units. The scores for VPA II are Easy and Hard Items and are presented as cumulative percentages. Recognition trial scores include Easy Items, Difficult Items, Hit Rate, and Discriminability and are presented as cumulative percentages.

While VPA I measures the total amount of learning across *all* four learning trials, *VPA I Recall A* measures single-trial learning of the word pairs. VPA I Recall A provides information about initial encoding of verbal information following a single exposure to the stimuli. Comparing this score to LM I for ages 16–69 or either LM Story A First Recall or Story B for ages 65–90 provides an estimation of the effects of organized versus unorganized presentation of information on memory functioning.

VPA I Recall D describes the amount of associative verbal information encoded and retrieved on the final learning trial. While VPA I includes total learning across the four trials, Recall D represents the amount of information retained after having heard the word pairs four times. This is a multitrial learning score that can be compared to the second recall of Story A in older adults. This comparison enables the clinician to determine the impact of multiple learning trials on memory for organized versus unorganized verbal information. Comparing VPA Recall A and Recall D shows the level of improvement in memory functioning associated with repeating information (see the VPA I Recall A versus Recall D contrast scaled score later in this chapter).

Four of the word pairs in VPA are considered "easy" because they are semantically related, such as "boy–girl." The degree of association between the words is about 30%. In other words, examinees saying the first thing that comes to mind when hearing the cue word say the target word 30% of the time. This is a relatively low level of association to prevent examinees from getting points for correctly guessing the word associated with the cueing word. The other word pairs are considered "hard," as the pairs are semantically unrelated.

The *Easy Items* scores for immediate and delayed VPA represent the examinee's ability to recall items that are semantically related. For most examinees, these items have a previous association in long-term semantic memory that should facilitate encoding and retrieval of those items. If the examinee has a language deficit, he or she might not be able to take advantage of the preexisting linguistic association. The *VPA I Easy Items* score represents the examinee's ability to recall the semantically related items during the initial learning phase, while *VPA II Easy Items* describes the examinee's ability to recall the semantically related items from long-term memory stores. Low scores on easy items scores indicate difficulty taking advantage of the semantic relationship of the items to facilitate memory encoding and retrieval.

The *Difficult Items* scores for immediate and delayed VPA reflect purer measures of verbal associative learning than the easy items scores. The difficult items have no intrinsic semantic relationship; therefore, there is no prior associative knowledge in semantic memory to facilitate encoding and retrieval. This score describes the examinee's ability to learn and recall novel verbal associations. The *VPA I Difficult Items* scaled score represents the examinee's immediate associative learning for unrelated verbal information. The *VPA II Difficult Items* cumulative percentage represents the examinee's ability to retrieve novel verbal associations from long-term memory stores. The comparison between performance on easy and difficult items indicates the degree to which the examinee is able to use the structure of existing semantic associations to facilitate encoding and retrieval of verbal associations. This comparison is discussed in the contrast score section.

The process scores for the recognition condition reflect the examinee's ability to identify learned information and provide an indication of encoding versus retrieval problems. The *Hit Rate* indicates the number of target word-pairs the examinee correctly identifies. Having a high hit rate score indicates that the examinee recognizes the correct information. That is not to say he or she has good recognition overall, but at least he or she recognizes the correct information. Low scores on hit rate indicate that the examinee has not effectively encoded the target information. This could occur in the presence of an adequate score on the standard recognition measure, which is more heavily weighted toward rejecting incorrect word pairs than identifying the correct information.

The *Discriminability* measure for the recognition trial evenly weights the ability to accurately identify the targets and correctly reject the distracters. This limits the influence of response bias and enables the clinician to identify difficulties with VPA recognition. Discriminability represents the percentage of accurate responding to both targets and distracters. Low scores on this measure indicate problems recognizing correct associations in long-term memory and indicate encoding problems for this type of verbal information. Discrepancies may occur between the standard scoring of recognition and the Discriminability score if there is a response bias in which the examinee misses more targets (i.e., says "no" to correct pairs) than makes false positives (i.e., says "yes" to incorrect pairs) or vice versa.

Easy items on the recognition trial measure the level of encoding for the semantically related word pairs. It must be considered that the Easy Items Recognition score has only four data points. It is important when interpreting this score to understand that a perfect score of four may fall in the 17–25 cumulative percentage range. This does not mean that getting a perfect score is low average but that the score of four includes all ranges from 17–25 to >75%. In other words, 83% of examinees get all of the scores correct. For a score of 4, include all the ranges above that the range listed for 4. Missing any of the easy items is unusual in healthy controls, so having a low score here reflects a problem with encoding these semantically related items after multiple exposures.

The Difficult Items Recognition score reflects the examinee's ability to encode the unrelated word pairs. The difficult items represent a more pure associative learning, and low scores on this measure may indicate difficulties learning new associations. If easy items are within the normal range, it may be a specific problem with novel associative learning. If both easy and difficult item scores are low, there is a general deficit in associative learning.

The *VPA I Recall A versus Recall D* contrast scaled score provides an estimation of learning rate for VPA I. The control variable in this contrast is the VPA I Recall A scaled score, and the dependent measure is the VPA I Recall D scaled score. This score represents the relative amount of improvement in performance due to repeated exposure to the information. The clinician has to be aware that a high score on this variable can be achieved when the Recall D scaled score is lower than the Recall A scaled score. This result appears counterintuitive; if the examinee is benefiting from repetition of the information, his or her performance after multiple trials should be higher than following a single exposure. However, if initial encoding is very good (e.g., Recall A > 13), average performance is slightly lower on Recall D (e.g., for a Recall A score of 15, the mean Recall D score is 13.5). This is a statistical artifact due to the restricted range of Recall D (i.e., highest SS < 18). When interpreting this score, consider that very high initial encoding will limit the amount of additional learning that can occur. Low scores indicate lower-than-expected encoding after multiple exposures to the stimuli controlling for initial level of encoding; the examinee does not benefit from having information repeated. High scores indicate higher-than-expected performance subsequent to multiple exposures to the stimuli controlling for initial levels of encoding. This indicates significantly improved performance when information is repeated versus single-trial learning.

The *VPA I Easy Items versus Difficult Items* contrast scaled score measures the examinee's ability to learn novel verbal associations controlling for his or her ability to learn semantically related verbal associations. In this contrast score, the Easy Items scaled score is the control variable and the Difficult Items score is the dependent measure. Low scores indicate that the examinee's ability to recall novel associations is unexpectedly low given his or her ability to recall semantically related items. The more pure associative learning task poses greater difficulty for the examinee and may represent a breakdown in verbal memory functioning that is masked in the total score by the examinee performing well on the easy items. A high score indicates that the examinee performed better than expected on the novel associations considering his or her score on semantically related items. If the Easy Items score is low, a high score suggests the individual is not able to take full advantage of the semantic association to facilitate encoding, which could indicate a semantic memory or language problem. If the Easy Items score is high, this suggests that the examinee may have focused on learning the hard items or missed a few easy items during initial encoding stages. Evaluate the actual item-level performance to best understand the high score.

Additional Cognitive Functions Affecting Performance

VPA is a language-based task; therefore, any disturbance in language functioning is likely to impact this subtest. The recall of words is facilitated by knowledge of and familiarity with the words (e.g., trying to remember a word list from a foreign language would be much harder than recalling a word list from your native language). The words selected for VPA are at the first- to third-grade level, so most adolescents and adults should have knowledge of the words on the list; however, individuals with language problems may experience some difficulty encoding and retrieving the information. The expressive and receptive language demands on VPA should be lower than on LM since the examinee responds with a single word and does not hear complex sentences, only simple word pairs.

In addition to language skills, VPA requires auditory working memory in order to process information in conscious awareness and to facilitate effective storage and retrieval. General intellectual functioning will also impact the examinee's ability to encode and retrieve information from long-term memory stores. Brief auditory attention, adequate hearing acuity, and sufficient articulation are additional basic abilities that could influence results on this subtest. Executive functioning may play a role in the examinee's ability to understand the task of learning to pair two words together that are not normally associated. Very concrete examinees may state that the words do not go together, interfering with the ability to remember the association.

CVLT-II Substitution for VPA

The WMS-IV enables CVLT-II users to substitute the immediate learning and delayed free recall trials of the CVLT-II for the VPA I and VPA II scaled scores, respectively, in the computation of the Auditory Memory Index (AMI), Immediate Memory Index (IMI), and Delayed Memory Index (DMI). However, using the CVLT-II changes the specific content of these indexes. The CVLT-II is not an associative learning task; it is a free recall task for words. Like VPA, the words are semantically related and unrelated; however, for the CVLT-II the examinee must recognize which words are semantically related and organize the information in order to use the semantic categories to facilitate storage and retrieval.

The CVLT-II and WMS-IV were normed at different times and use different score metrics. A linking sample of 380 adults and older adults were administered both the WMS-IV and the CVLT-II. This sample was used to derive VPA equivalent scores for the CVLT-II Trials 1–5 T-Score and Long Delay z score.

The CVLT-II scores are converted into VPA Scaled Score equivalents, which can be entered into the sum of scaled scores for the appropriate indexes. The scores are derived using equipercentile equating. This will equate level of performance between the two tests and adjust for any normative drift in the CVLT-II compared to the WMS-IV. The new index scores were compared when using the standard VPA scores and the equated VPA scores. There was very little difference in performance (average difference of approximately 1.5 points higher) when using the CVLT-II substitution. Tables D.2 and D.3 of the *WMS-IV Administration and Scoring Manual* provide the CVLT-II to VPA equivalent conversions.

Interpretation of the CVLT–II scores is beyond the scope of this text. The clinician should be familiar with the CVLT-II before using the substitution rules. Also, it is important to remember that the CVLT-II kit is not part of the WMS-IV; it must be purchased separately. Moreover, the CVLT-II software does not interact with the WMS-IV software so the clinician will need the CVLT-II software to generate the T and z scores before entering these scores into the WMS-IV software to derive the equivalents. Do not substitute CVLT-II for VPA when both are administered; VPA is the most appropriate subtest to include when deriving index scores.

CAUTION

The use of the CVLT-II substitution changes the composition of the Auditory, Immediate, and Delayed Memory Indexes, which needs to be considered when interpreting these scores.

The clinician should be familiar with the CVLT-II before using the substitution rule.

The CVLT-II is not part of the WMS-IV and must be purchased separately.

Do not substitute CVLT-II for VPA when both tests are given.

Visual Reproduction (VR) I and II

VR is a geometric design recall task. The examinee sees a series of pages with one or two designs on each page presented for 10 seconds. In general, VR is a measure of visual memory. Specifically, the subtest is an assessment of memory for details of geometric designs. Additional interpretative considerations are discussed in the following pages. Rapid Reference 4.5 summarizes the interpretation of the VR subtest.

≡ *Rapid Reference 4.5*

. . . .

Interpreting Visual Reproduction Performance

General Level of Interpretation

Measure of visual immediate and delayed memory

Specific Level of Interpretation

Encoding and retrieval of visual details and spatial relations of geometric designs

Visual Reproduction Scores

Primary measures:

VR I: Scaled score measuring initial encoding and retrieval of visual details and spatial relations of geometric designs

VR II: Scaled score measuring encoding and retrieval of visual details and spatial relations of geometric designs from long-term memory stores

Process measures:

VR II Recognition: Cumulative percentage reflecting ability to recognize details and spatial relations of geometric designs in long-term memory

VR II Copy: Cumulative percentage reflecting ability to draw details and spatial relations of geometric designs

VR II Recognition versus Delayed Recall Contrast Scaled Score: Scaled score evaluating encoding versus retrieval deficits for visual details and spatial relations of geometric designs in long-term memory stores

VR Immediate Recall versus Delayed Recall Contrast Scaled Score: Scaled score testing the hypothesis that delayed memory for visual details and spatial relations of geometric designs is unexpectedly low or high compared to initial encoding

VR Copy versus Immediate Recall Contrast Scaled Score: Scaled score testing the hypothesis that memory functioning is relatively high or low compared to the examinee's ability to simply draw the designs

Additional scores in ACS:

VR I Additional Design Elements: Cumulative percentage reflecting intrusion errors during initial recall for details of geometric designs

VR II Additional Design Elements: Cumulative percentage reflecting intrusion errors during recall from long-term memory for details of geometric designs

VR I Average Completion Time: Scaled score measuring the speed at which the examinee drew the designs from immediate memory

VR II Average Completion Time: Scaled score measuring the speed at which the examinee drew the designs from long-term memory

(continued)

VR I Average Completion Time versus Immediate Recall Contrast Scaled Score: Scaled score evaluating if immediate memory performance is high or low controlling for speed at which the designs were drawn

VR II Average Completion Time versus Delayed Recall Contrast Scaled Score: Scaled score evaluating if delayed memory performance is high or low controlling for speed at which the designs were drawn

Additional Cognitive Functions Affecting Performance

Visual Perceptual Skills: Moderate degree of visual perceptual and spatial reasoning abilities to process, store, retrieve, and execute designs from memory.

Language: Moderate degree of language to concurrently use verbal labels to help encode and retrieve the visual details from memory.

Visual Working Memory: Moderate degree of working memory is required during initial and delayed encoding, retrieval, and execution of design memory.

General Intellectual Ability: General deficits in processing information limit the ability to preprocess information for effective storage and retrieval.

Visual Acuity: Poor vision may result in inaccurate perception of design details resulting in errors in encoding and retrieval.

Fine/Gross Motor Skill: Severe impairments may make it difficult to execute drawing the designs resulting in loss of points or making the subtest unusable.

Visual Scanning: Significant impairments in visual scanning, particularly hemineglect, may result in poor encoding of the design.

Executive Functioning: Impairments in organization and planning may interfere with effective storage, retrieval, and execution of drawings from memory, which may have a small impact on obtained scores.

Primary Scores

Chapters 2 and 3 presented detailed information regarding the administration and scoring of VR. The clinician shows the examinee five pages of designs, with the last two pages each having two designs on the page. After the examinee sees each design, he or she is asked to draw the design from memory. In general, the scoring is based on recalling specific features/details of the designs. There is no overarching score for each individual design. Therefore, the examinee gets credit for recalling correct components of the design. Some details require the presence of other details to get credit, while others do not. The scoring focuses on recall rather than precise drawing criteria. Therefore, the recall is not based on a precise mechanical recreation of the design but on the correct recall of specific elements of the design. In some cases, scoring requires measuring angles, but these angles are not measured for precision but as an indication that the examinee has accurately recalled the design's orientation in space.

After a 20- to 30-minute delay, the examinee is asked to draw the designs again from memory. VR also includes optional recognition and copy conditions. Unlike the verbal recognition conditions, VR II Recognition does not have a 50% guess rate. The examinee must select the correct design from six possible designs, which yields a guess rate of 17%. In the copy condition, the examinee draws the designs while the stimuli are displayed. This provides an estimate of the degree to which constructional or motor problems may have interfered with VR performance.

The primary scores for VR are the VR I and VR II scaled scores. These scores represent the examinee's ability to retrieve details of designs from immediate and delayed memory stores. VR is not a measure of constructional abilities or the ability to accurately reproduce images from memory, although these abilities can impact performance. In addition, some of the scoring criteria measure aspects of spatial memory such as rotated or misplaced designs or placement of design elements relative to other design elements. Individual scoring criteria are not normed separately so the total score reflects the combined impact of recall for visual details and spatial relations. In general, VR is weighted toward the recall of visual details more than spatial components of memory.

Process Scores

VR II Recognition measures retrieval versus encoding deficits for visual details. This measure is scaled as a cumulative percentage and represents the examinee's ability to recognize visual details and to a lesser degree visual spatial information in long-term memory. This score can be compared to the VR II scaled score to determine whether the examinee is able to encode information but has difficulty retrieving it (i.e., good recognition and low VR II) or poor encoding in general (i.e., low recognition and low VR II).

VR II Copy measures the examinee's ability to copy the designs without any memory demands. This measure is only needed when testing examinees with known or suspected construction problems or motor impairments. For examinees with good drawing skills, it is not necessary to administer the copy condition. The VR II Copy cumulative percentage can be used to determine if the examinee's VR I or VR II scores were impacted by constructional or motor abilities. Low scores suggest poor drawing or constructional abilities may have influenced lower scores on the recall conditions. If the examinee has very poor drawing ability, the test may not adequately capture the examinee's visual memory ability. The *VR Copy versus Immediate Recall* contrast scaled score provides a good estimate of the degree to which drawing ability impacted performance.

Contrast Scores

VR offers three optional contrast scores to provide a more refined description of memory functioning. For the *VR II Recognition versus Delayed Recall* contrast scaled score, the recognition trial cumulative percentage is the control variable and the VR II scaled score is the dependent variable. The score reflects the examinee's free recall of visual details controlling for his or her ability to recognize visual details. The recognition trial represents the general level of encoding of the information, while delayed recall represents retrieval of information from memory. Low scores suggest that given the examinee's recognition ability, free recall is unexpectedly low. That is, delayed recall is not consistent with the exhibited level of encoding on recognition, indicating a possible retrieval deficit. High scores are unusual but may represent better recall for individual design details rather than recall of the whole design.

For *VR Immediate Recall versus Delayed Recall* contrast scaled score, VR I is the control variable and VR II is the dependent variable. This score represents the examinee's ability to recall information from delayed memory controlling for initial level of memory encoding. Low scores indicate that the examinee has lower than expected long-term memory recall for visual details considering initial encoding and retrieval ability. High scores indicate better than expected recall of visual details from delayed memory relative to initial levels of encoding and retrieval. Specifically, low scores suggest a higher-than-expected forgetting rate, while high scores indicate improvement in memory functioning when given additional time for memory consolidation.

Finally, for the *VR Copy versus Immediate Recall* contrast scaled score, VR II Copy cumulative percentage is the control variable and VR I is the dependent measure. This score measures the examinee's immediate memory in relation to his or her ability to draw the design. A low score indicates memory performance is low even when you control for difficulties with drawing. A high score suggests good memory performance despite some drawing problems. In the presence of adequate drawing skills, a high score indicates good memory for visual details in general.

Additional Scores in the ACS

The ACS provides error, process, and contrast scores for the VR subtest. The two error scores provided are *VR I and VR II Additional Design Elements*. The scores are referred to as additional design elements because they represent visual details added to the designs by the examinee during recall that are not present in the original design. These additional design elements represent an incorrect recall of information; specifically, an intrusion into the recall of visual details. The scores are presented as cumulative percentages. High rates of errors indicate difficulty monitoring recall of visual details for accuracy in immediate and/or delayed recall conditions. This may represent a form of memory dysfunction or a breakdown in the executive control of retrieval and/or monitoring of recall. In some cases, these errors may represent impairment of visual–perceptual processing and the additional element is a misrepresentation of a real design element. These hypotheses need to be evaluated by examining test results from other visual–perceptual measures or other sources of information.

The two process scores in the ACS are *VR I and VR II Average Completion Time*. These scores represent the speed at which the examinee draws the designs. Observationally, an examinee may draw the designs very slowly and carefully or quickly without obvious concern to the quality of the drawing. The Average Completion Time scaled scores enable the clinician to validate observations on the speed at which the examinee completed the items. Examinees who draw very quickly run the risk of losing points due to careless mistakes, while very slow examinees may forget specific design details while completing his or her response because a longer period of time passes before he or she accesses memory for that detail. Conversely, speed may not be related to memory performance at all; rather, it represents general issues with processing speed or impulsivity. High scores indicate much faster response time than expected while low scores indicate a slower-than-expected drawing time. The score is based on an average completion time so consider any outliers in your interpretation (e.g., a long completion time for one design among relatively fast completion times). The interpretation of the score should consider other skills such as construction ability, overall processing speed, impulsivity, and general memory ability.

The two additional contrast scores available on the ACS are *VR I Average Completion Time versus Immediate Recall* and *VR II Average Completion Time versus Delayed Recall*. In these contrast scores, the control variable is the VR I or VR II Average Completion Time scaled score, and the dependent variable is the VR I or VR II scaled score, respectively. These contrast scores allow you to determine if the achieved memory score is relatively low or high compared to how quickly the designs were drawn. This score is used only when the clinician believes that the examinee's performance may have been affected by the speed at which the examinee drew the designs. A low score indicates lower than expected memory scores controlling for how quickly the examinee completed the designs. A high score indicates good memory performance controlling for how quickly the examinee completed the designs.

Additional Cognitive Functions Affecting Performance
VR is a visual–perceptual and constructional task; therefore, any disturbance in visual–perceptual processing or constructional abilities is likely to affect

performance. In addition, multiple systems are required to encode the geometric designs in the 10-second exposure. During this brief exposure, the examinee must evaluate the specific details and the relative spatial relationship among the elements of the design, visually scan the page to make sure he or she has identified all the salient pieces of information, and hold the information in working memory, while it is processed for visual–perceptual and visual–spatial features and stored into long-term memory. Moreover, the designs contain elements that can be verbalized (e.g., flags, boxes, circles, dots); thus, language ability may affect performance. Finally, executive functioning may play a role in the examinee's ability to organize and encode the visual information efficiently and aid in the motor planning required for responding.

Designs (DE) I and II

DE is a recognition memory measure for spatial and visual content for individuals ages 16–69. The examinee is shown a varying number of designs on a 4-by-4 grid and asked to recall the design features and the design's spatial location in the grid immediately after presentation and after a 20- to 30-minute delay. In general, this subtest is a measure of visual memory. Specifically, the test is an assessment of memory for spatial locations and visual details. This subtest, unlike VR, specifically measures spatial recall independent of memory for visual details. Additional interpretive considerations are discussed in the following pages. Rapid Reference 4.6 summarizes the interpretation of the DE subtest.

Rapid Reference 4.6

Interpreting Designs Performance

General Level of Interpretation

Measure of visual immediate and delayed memory

Specific Level of Interpretation

Encoding and retrieval of visual details and visual–spatial locations of geometric designs

Designs Scores

Primary measures:

DE I: Scaled score measuring initial encoding and retrieval of visual details and spatial locations

DE II: Scaled score measuring encoding and retrieval of visual details and spatial locations from long-term memory

Process measures:

DE I Content: Scaled score measuring immediate encoding and retrieval for visual details

DE I Spatial: Scaled score measuring immediate encoding and retrieval for visual–spatial locations

DE II Content: Scaled score measuring encoding and retrieval for visual details from long-term memory

DE II Spatial: Scaled score measuring encoding and retrieval for visual–spatial locations from long-term memory

DE II Recognition: Cumulative percentage reflecting examinee's ability to recognize visual–spatial locations and details in long-term memory

DE Recognition versus Delayed Recall Contrast Scaled Score: Scaled score evaluating encoding versus retrieval deficits for visual details and spatial locations in long-term memory stores

DE Immediate Recall versus Delayed Recall Contrast Scaled Score: Scaled score testing the hypothesis that delayed memory for visual details and spatial locations is unexpectedly low or high compared to initial encoding

DE I Spatial versus Content Contrast Scaled Score: Scaled score testing the hypothesis that immediate memory for visual details is relatively high or low compared to immediate spatial memory

DE II Spatial versus Content Contrast Scaled Score: Scaled score testing the hypothesis that long-term memory for visual details is relatively high or low compared to long-term spatial memory

Additional scores in ACS:

DE Rule Violation: Cumulative percentage reflecting the frequency at which an examinee places more designs in the grid than requested indicating an atypical response style, lack of understanding of the test, and/or significant memory problems

Additional Cognitive Functions Affecting Performance

Visual–Perceptual Skills: Moderate degree of visual perceptual and spatial reasoning abilities to process, store, and recall designs from memory.

Visual Working Memory: Moderate degree of working memory required during initial and delayed encoding and retrieval.

General Intellectual Ability: General deficits in processing information limit the ability to preprocess information for effective storage and retrieval.

Visual Acuity: Poor vision may result in inaccurate perception of design details resulting in errors in encoding and retrieval.

(continued)

Fine/Gross Motor Skill: Severe impairments may make it difficult to place cards in the grid, but the clinician may help if this occurs.

Visual Scanning: Significant impairments in visual scanning, particularly hemineglect, may result in poor encoding of the design.

Executive Functioning: Impairments in organization and planning may interfere with effective storage and retrieval of designs from memory, which may have a small impact on obtained scores.

Chapters 2 and 3 presented detailed information regarding the administration and scoring of the DE subtest. The examiner shows the examinee a page with 4–8 designs on a 4-by-4 grid for 10 seconds. Immediately after the stimulus page is removed, the examinee is given cards and asked to identify the correct designs by placing the correct cards in the correct location in the grid. There are four sets of designs to recall. After a 20- to 30-minute delay, the examinee is asked to select the correct designs and place them in the grid again for each set of designs. Following the delayed recall condition, the examiner may also administer a recognition trial. For each set of designs, the examinee is scored on correctly recalled spatial locations without consideration of the selected design (e.g., credit is awarded for each correct location regardless of the card placed in the location). In addition, a score is given for the number of designs correctly recognized regardless of the location in which the design is placed. The examinee is awarded bonus points for each correct design placed in its correct location.

DE differs from VR in several ways. The recall trials for VR are completely free recall while DE is primarily a recognition measure. The examinee must recognize which design is correct and recognize the correct location in the grid for the design. VR scoring is based primarily on remembering visual details and to a much lesser degree the spatial relationship within a single design or between two designs. In DE, scoring is based on distinguishing correct designs from distracters with changes in one or more details to the correct design. In DE, more information is required at one time, which makes it very difficult to use verbal cues to aid storage and retrieval of the visual information; this may also increase working memory demands as visual detail and spatial span may play a larger role in immediate memory functioning. Although DE may be affected by motor issues, it is to a lesser degree than in VR. To eliminate the impact of motor issues on DE, you may assist the examinee by having him or her point at a card and then point at a location in the grid and then you may place the card in the grid for the examinee. In VR, the clinician cannot draw the design for the examinee.

The primary scores for the DE subtest are DE I and DE II scaled scores. These scores represent the combined memory for spatial location, visual details, and exact recall for correct designs in correct locations. The DE I score indicates initial encoding ability for visual details and spatial locations and DE II represents the ability to recall visual and spatial information from long-term memory.

Process Scores

DE provides an optional recognition trial that may be used to determine if memory ability improves with more recognition structure than in the standard condition. In the recognition condition, the examinee must select two designs from a grid that are both the correct design and in the correct location. The recognition trial is used when the clinician believes the examinee has difficulty retrieving spatial and/or visual details from long-term memory. This score is scaled as a cumulative percentage, with high scores indicating good recognition memory for visual information and low scores indicating difficulty recognizing visual information in memory.

DE allows the clinician to score spatial recall and recall for visual details separately. For both immediate and delayed recall, two optional scaled scores, Spatial and Content, can be computed. The *DE I Spatial* scaled score measures the examinee's ability to recall spatial locations from immediate memory, while *DE I Content* measures the examinee's ability to recognize visual details in immediate memory. *DE II Spatial* measures the examinee's ability to recall visual–spatial information from long-term memory and *DE II Content* measures the examinee's ability to recognize visual details in long-term memory.

DE offers four contrast scores to describe visual memory functioning. *DE II Recognition versus Delayed Recall* evaluates recall ability for visual–spatial information from long-term memory relative to the ability to recognize visual–spatial information. Low scores indicate lower than expected recall from memory considering recognition performance and suggest difficulties retrieving visual–spatial information encoded in memory. High scores indicate good recall from delayed memory.

The *DE Immediate Recall versus Delayed Recall* contrast scaled score evaluates the examinee's recall of visual–spatial information from long-term memory controlling for performance on immediate recall. Low scores indicate unexpectedly low delayed recall considering initial encoding ability. This suggests greater forgetting of visual–spatial information than expected. A high score indicates good long-delay recall relative to the initial level of encoding, which suggests good memory consolidation ability over time.

The remaining contrast scores allow the examiner to determine if memory for visual details is relatively good when controlling for visual–spatial memory.

DE I Spatial versus Content measures the examinee's immediate recall for visual details controlling for visual–spatial memory abilities. A low score indicates unexpectedly low memory for visual details compared to visual-spatial recall. A high score suggests better-than-expected immediate visual recall for details compared to spatial memory. The *DE II Spatial versus Content* score provides the same comparison but for the delayed memory conditions. The interpretation is the same except the scores reflect long-term memory for visual details and spatial memory.

Additional Scores in the ACS

The ACS provides one additional score for DE, *DE Rule Violation* cumulative percentage. This score reflects the number of items on which the examinee places more cards in the memory grid than required. For each item, only one rule violation is scored, for a maximum of eight possible rule violations across the immediate and delayed conditions. This is an unusual type of error as the examiner states how many cards should be placed in the grid for each item. Low scores may reflect a lack of understanding of the task, a lapse in attention or motivation, or perhaps an atypical approach to the task. It may also indicate a rather significant memory problem.

Additional Cognitive Functions Affecting Performance

DE is a visual–spatial/perceptual task; therefore, any disturbance in visual–spatial processing or visual–perceptual reasoning may affect performance. Just as on VR, multiple systems are required to encode multiple geometric designs in a spatial array during the 10-second exposure. In that time, the examinee must evaluate the specific design details and the location of each detail within the 4-by-4 grid, visually scan the page to make sure he or she has identified all the salient pieces of information, and hold the information in working memory while it is processed for visual–perceptual and visual–spatial features and stored into long-term memory. Unlike VR, it is very difficult to use verbalization to facilitate encoding and retrieval of the visual–spatial information. Therefore verbal abilities should not strongly influence performance on this test. Executive functioning may play a role in the examinee's ability to organize and encode the visual information efficiently.

Spatial Addition (SA)

SA is a spatial working memory test for ages 16–69. In general, SA is a measure of visual working memory. Specifically, it is an assessment of spatial working memory. SA is designed as a visual analog to the WAIS-IV Arithmetic subtest.

≡ Rapid Reference 4.7

Interpreting Spatial Addition Performance

General Level of Interpretation

Measure of visual working memory

Specific Level of Interpretation

Measure of visual working memory for spatial span, mental manipulation of spatial locations, and freedom from competing information

Spatial Addition Scores

Primary measure:

SA: Scaled score measuring visual–spatial working memory

Additional Cognitive Functions Affecting Performance

Visual–Perceptual Skills: Moderate degree of visual–perceptual and spatial reasoning abilities is needed to process spatial information.

General Intellectual Ability: General deficits in processing information limit the ability to encode and mentally manipulate information.

Visual Acuity: Poor vision may result in inaccurate perception of design locations resulting in errors in encoding and manipulating spatial locations.

Fine/Gross Motor Skill: Severe impairments may make it difficult to place cards in the grid, but the clinician may help the examinee if this occurs.

Visual Scanning: Significant impairments in visual scanning, particularly hemineglect, may result in poor encoding of the spatial locations due to misperception or failure to perceive the locations.

Executive Functioning: Impairments related to distractibility and/or impulsivity could interfere with proper location encoding due to competing information.

Additional interpretative considerations are discussed in the following pages. Rapid Reference 4.7 summarizes the interpretation of the SA subtest.

Primary Score

The *SA scaled score* is the only interpreted score for this subtest. SA taps several key skills associated with working memory. Spatial span, the number of spatial locations that can be held in working memory, is assessed by the increasing number of locations to be recalled. Mental manipulation of objects in working memory is required to maintain one image in mind while integrating it with a second image to create a third new mental image. The ability to ignore irrelevant information, a component process of the central executive of the working memory system proposed by Baddeley (2000), is also required. It is important to note that red dot errors, made when a red dot is placed in the grid, occurred very rarely in the normative sample and in clinical populations including individuals diagnosed with intellectual disability. This behavior represents an atypical response style that can be noted in the evaluation. If red dot errors occur, you may need to evaluate the examinee's understanding of the instructions.

Additional Cognitive Functions Affecting Performance

SA is a visual–spatial/perceptual task; therefore, any disturbance in visual–spatial processing or visual–perceptual reasoning may affect performance on this subtest. For SA, spatial memory is very important, as the examinee must remember the exact locations of the blue dots on the page. If he or she has difficulty correctly identifying the precise location of the dots on the grid, he or she will not be able to complete the working memory component of the test. In addition, impairments in executive functioning may result in the examinee having difficulty ignoring the red dots. This typically results in misplaced blue dots in the response but rarely in the use of red dots, as discussed previously.

Due to the brief exposure time of the stimuli, processing speed and attention may impact performance. The examinee must visually scan the page to identify all the salient pieces of information during the 5-second exposure. Visual scanning and attention may also impact performance. Although this subtest is difficult to verbalize, good verbal skills may facilitate comprehension and retention of the subtest rules.

Symbol Span (SSP)

SSP is a working memory task for visual details. The examinee is shown a series of designs for 5 seconds and asked to recall and select the correct designs in sequence from a large array of designs. Partial credit is awarded for correct recall of details that are out of sequence. In general, SSP is a measure of visual working memory. Specifically, it is a measure of working memory for visual details. It was developed as a visual analog to the WAIS-IV Digit Span subtest. Additional interpretative considerations are discussed in the following pages. Rapid Reference 4.8 summarizes the interpretation of SSP.

≡ *Rapid Reference 4.8*

Interpreting Symbol Span Performance

General Level of Interpretation

Measure of visual working memory

Specific Level of Interpretation

Measure of visual working memory for span and mental manipulation of visual details

Symbol Span Scores

Primary measure:

SSP: Scaled score measuring visual-detail working memory

Additional Cognitive Functions Affecting Performance

Visual–Perceptual Skills: Moderate degree of visual–perceptual skills is needed for processing visual information.

General Intellectual Ability: General deficits in processing information limit the ability to encode and mentally manipulate information.

Visual Acuity: Poor vision may result in inaccurate perception of design details, resulting in errors in encoding and manipulating visual details.

Visual Scanning: Significant impairments in visual scanning, particularly hemi-neglect, may result in poor encoding of the designs or their sequence due to missed details.

Executive Functioning: Impairments related to distractibility and/or impulsivity could interfere with proper encoding and subsequent sequencing of the designs.

Primary Score

The *SSP Scaled Score* is the only interpreted score from this subtest. SSP taps several key skills associated with working memory. Visual span, the number of visual designs that can be held in working memory, is assessed by the increasing number of designs to be recalled. Mental manipulation of objects in working memory is required to maintain the recall of the order of the items before responding by selecting designs in the correct order.

Additional Cognitive Functions Affecting Performance

SSP is a visual–perceptual task; therefore, any disturbance in visual–perceptual reasoning may affect performance. Visual attention may also impact performance, particularly attention to details and visual scanning. The stimuli on SSP are difficult to verbalize; therefore, language functioning is not expected to affect performance.

Brief Cognitive Status Exam (BCSE)

The BCSE measures the mental status of the patient and functions similarly to the Mini-Mental State Examination (MMSE; Folstein, Folstein, & McHugh, 1975). The BCSE evaluates several cognitive domains that may indicate either specific or diffuse cognitive problems. The BCSE is not intended to diagnose dementia, delirium, or other serious cognitive disorders. Rather, the BCSE indicates if there are general, significant, cognitive impairments that could be associated with many clinical disorders. It was derived from multiple sources, including subtests previously found on the WMS-III. Additional novel tasks and measures frequently used to evaluate severe cognitive impairment were also included. The BCSE is divided into multiple sections that measure specific aspects of cognition.

The weighted raw scores obtained on the BCSE are derived from the performance of the entire WMS-IV normative sample. The maximum score reflects the number of points obtained by at least 75% of the sample. Lower scores reflect increasingly lower percentages of cases achieving that score. In most cases, the weighted raw scores reflect the percentages of <2, 3–5, 6–10, 11–25, and >25 for values of 0–4. Some scores are more heavily weighted in the total score and range from 0–8. In other cases, there are more or less than five gradations of performance. In these cases, the raw score ranges were better suited to fewer or more data points.

The first sections are comprised of temporal orientation and estimation questions. The questions reflect both knowledge of immediate time frame and current reference points such as the name of the president. There are no questions that reflect orientation to place, self, or others since this information is frequently obtained as part of a standard interview. Temporal orientation items account for up to 12 points of the BCSE total.

The second section administered measures incidental memory. The examinee names pictures of stimuli without being instructed to remember the items. Later, the examinee is asked to remember the pictures that he or she had seen previously. This measures the examinee's incidental recall for visual–verbal information. In addition, you may wish to note if the examinee has specific difficulties naming the objects in the picture. If the examinee is unable to name any of the pictures correctly, a further evaluation of confrontation naming and language skills is recommended. The incidental recall items account for 8 points of the BCSE total score.

The third item set administered assesses processing speed and cognitive control. The examinee must quickly recite overlearned information in reverse sequence. The task requires working memory and access to long-term semantic memory. The mental control tasks account for 12 points of the BCSE total score.

The fourth task is clock drawing. Clock drawing has a long history of use for identifying cognitive impairments, particularly in dementia evaluations (Morris et al., 1994). This is a complex cognitive task requiring intact visual–perceptual skills, intact visual attention, adequate motor planning and control, and executive functioning. The scoring rules used in the BCSE are very basic to allow for quick assessment of overall cognitive functioning. More complex scoring and interpretation of clock drawing can be obtained elsewhere (Morris et al., 1994). Close observation of the examinee's performance is useful in determining if poor performance on this task is due to poor planning skills, impaired visual–spatial functioning, attention, or motor control. The clock-drawing test accounts for 4 points of the BCSE total score.

The fifth task is the inhibition test. In this task, the examinee must inhibit the overlearned response of naming a shape that is presented (i.e., a rectangle) and respond with the name of an alternate shape that is present (i.e., a triangle). The inhibition task has three scores: completion time, omission errors, and commission errors. Performance on this test is affected by processing speed, visual scanning, visual attention, and inhibitory control. The inhibition task contributes 16 points to the BCSE total score, with inhibition errors equally weighted with processing speed (i.e., completion time) and visual scanning and attention (i.e., omission errors).

The final task is verbal productivity. The test is a semantic fluency measure in which the examinee names as many objects from the specified category as possible within 30 seconds. This score measures access to semantic memory stores, verbal production, and cognitive flexibility. Verbal productivity accounts for 6 points of the BCSE total score.

Low BCSE scores can be evaluated for deficits in specific cognitive functions. For example, examinees with slow processing speed will have low scores on both mental control and inhibition. Executive functioning impairments will be evident on inhibition, clock drawing, and verbal productivity. Impairments in language functioning will likely impact multiple scores, and naming difficulties on incidental memory, difficulties with rapid naming on inhibition, and low scores on verbal productivity, in particular, may signal problems with language functioning.

INDEX LEVEL OF INTERPRETATION

This section describes general principles for interpreting the WMS-IV index scores. Each WMS-IV index score will be described and discussed, followed by the WMS-IV index-level contrast scaled scores. A brief description of the ACS Additional Index Scores and contrast scaled scores completes the section.

The index-level scores reflect more complex memory functioning than observed at the subtest level; therefore, all the caveats regarding the interpretation of the subtests that contribute to an index apply to interpreting the index itself. The caveats will not be repeated in this section but the examiner is referred back to the subtest section for determining additional cognitive factors and specific aspects of memory associated with each index.

WMS-IV Index Scores

The WMS-IV is comprised of four memory indexes and a working memory index. The index level is the primary level for interpreting WMS-IV results. Even if subtest score variability is present within an index, the index score is still a strong estimate of the examinee's general memory functioning. The WMS-IV indexes are Auditory Memory, Visual Memory, Immediate Memory, Delayed Memory, and Visual Working Memory. These indexes are composed of the primary subtest scores from the WMS-IV; no optional or contrast scaled scores contribute to any WMS-IV index.

Auditory Memory Index (AMI)

The AMI is derived from the LM I and II and VPA I and II primary subtest scaled scores. This index measures both immediate and delayed recall for verbally presented information. In general, AMI measures encoding and recall of verbal information. More specifically, it measures multiple aspects of verbal memory, including memory for semantically related and unrelated information, sequentially related and unrelated information, multitrial and single-trial learning, and retrieval from immediate and long-term memory stores. If CVLT-II scores are substituted for VPA scores, the interpretation of this index needs to be modified to account for the different subtest composition of the index.

Visual Memory Index (VMI)

The VMI is derived from VR I and II and DE I and II primary scores for the Adult battery. In the Older Adult battery, the VMI contains only VR I and II. In general, both the Adult and Older Adult VMI scores are interpreted as the examinee's ability to encode and retrieve visual details and spatial information from immediate and long-term memory. More specific interpretation will differ between the two batteries. In the Older Adult battery, VMI indicates the examinee's ability to encode and recall visual details and the spatial relations among those details from immediate and long-term memory. In the Adult battery, the VMI represents the examinee's ability to encode, recall, and recognize visual details, spatial relationships, and spatial locations from immediate and long-term memory. When interpreting the results of the VMI, the Older Adult battery will focus only on the impact of additional cognitive skills on VR; however, in the Adult battery, the additional cognitive skills influencing performance on both the DE and VR subtests will need to be considered.

Immediate Memory Index (IMI)

The IMI is derived from the immediate recall conditions of LM, VPA, VR, and DE for the Adult battery, and of LM, VPA, and VR for the Older Adult battery. In the Adult battery, the IMI is equally balanced between verbal and visual subtests and therefore is not influenced by one modality more than the other. For the Older Adult battery, the IMI will be more affected by auditory memory difficulties than visual memory problems. In general, the IMI is interpreted the same for both batteries. It represents the examinee's ability to encode and recall information immediately after presentation. More specifically, the index is quite complex, reflecting differences in modality of memory, multitrial and single-trial learning, related and unrelated stimuli, and spatial and visual detail memory. The interpretation of the specific aspects of memory functioning will differ between the Adult battery and the Older Adult battery based on the difference in the scores making up the IMI. When making specific comments regarding immediate memory functioning, the clinician will need to consider the cognitive factors that influence subtests that contribute to the index. If CVLT-II scores are substituted for VPA scores, the interpretation of this index needs to be modified to account for the different subtest composition of the index.

Delayed Memory Index (DMI)

The DMI is derived from the delayed conditions of LM, VPA, VR, and DE for the Adult battery and of LM, VPA, and VR for the Older Adult battery. In the Adult battery, the DMI is equally balanced between verbal and visual subtests and therefore is not influenced by one modality more than the other. For the Older Adult battery, it is important to keep in mind that the DMI will be influenced more by specific auditory memory difficulties than visual memory problems. In general, the DMI is interpreted the same for both batteries. It represents the examinee's ability to encode and recall information from long-term memory. More specifically, the index is quite complex, reflecting differences in modality of memory, multitrial and single-trial learning, related and unrelated stimuli, and spatial and visual detail memory. The interpretation of the specific aspects of memory functioning will differ between the Adult battery and the Older Adult battery based on the difference in the scores making up DMI. When making specific comments regarding delayed memory functioning, the clinician will need to consider the subtest factors that contribute to the index. In addition to reviewing the contributing subtest scores, it is important to note that the DMI will be affected by the examinee's initial encoding ability. Delayed recall will be constrained to some degree by the amount of information encoded during the immediate encoding and recall condition. Therefore, delayed memory ability needs to be considered within the context of initial memory functioning. If CVLT-II scores are substituted for VPA scores, the interpretation of this index needs to be modified to account for the different subtest composition of the index.

Visual Working Memory Index (VWMI)

VWMI is only available in the Adult battery. It is derived from the SA and SSP subtest scaled scores. In general, this index measures visual working memory. More specifically, it measures visuospatial working memory span, mental manipulation of spatial information and visual details, and aspects of executive control over working memory functions. When interpreting this index, consider the specific aspects of visual working memory functioning as indicated by the contributing subtests as well as the cognitive skills influencing performance described within the subtest interpretation section.

WMS-IV Index-Level Contrast Scaled Scores

The WMS-IV includes three optional contrast scaled scores at the index level. These contrast scores enable the clinician to control for overlapping variance among the memory measures and more precisely define memory processes for a specific examinee. The three contrast scaled scores are *Auditory Memory Index versus Visual Memory Index, Immediate Memory Index versus Delayed Memory Index*, and *Visual Working Memory Index versus Visual Memory Index.*

Auditory Memory Index Versus Visual Memory Index Contrast Scaled Score

The *Auditory Memory Index versus Visual Memory Index* contrast scaled score is one method for comparing auditory versus visual memory functioning on the WMS-IV. For this score, the control variable is the AMI, and the dependent variable is the VMI. Therefore, this score represents the examinee's visual memory ability controlling for auditory memory functioning. Low scores represent low visual memory functioning considering the examinee's level of auditory memory. High scores represent better-than-expected visual memory functioning controlling for auditory memory functioning. Caution must be used in interpreting this index when both scores are at the low end of the distribution. In this case, the contrast scaled score will indicate that visual memory is unexpectedly below auditory memory when in fact the scores are equivalent or nearly equivalent. In this scenario, the examinee does not have a material specific deficit in memory but poor memory functioning in general. The low score is noting that when auditory memory is low, visual memory tends to be a little better. However, from a practical standpoint, it may not make sense to interpret this contrast score when both indexes are very low. This caveat is specific to this score because there is not a well-defined control versus dependent measure. The score could be derived in the opposite direction, with visual memory controlling for auditory memory, unlike the other WMS-IV contrast scores.

CAUTION

When both the AMI and VMI are low, the Auditory Memory Index versus Visual Memory Index will return a low score, which suggests that visual memory is unexpectedly low compared to auditory memory. If this occurs, evaluate the simple difference between the two indexes and interpret the results based on both data points. A low score may suggest general memory problems rather than a specific deficit in auditory or visual memory.

Immediate Memory Index Versus Delayed Memory Index Contrast Scaled Score

The *Immediate Memory Index versus Delayed Memory Index* contrast scaled score is one method used to determine if delayed memory performance is different from immediate memory performance. For this contrast, the control variable is the IMI, and the dependent variable is the DMI. Therefore, this contrast score is interpreted as the examinee's delayed memory functioning controlling for his or her initial level of encoding. Low scores reflect unexpectedly low delayed memory performance relative to immediate encoding ability. In general, it is an indicator of information loss between immediate and delayed recall. A high score reflects improved memory performance between immediate and delayed recall. This indicates that delayed memory is better than expected considering initial levels of encoding. This score is composed of multiple modalities and memory functions. One or more specific types of memory may show more loss of information than others and unduly influence the contrast score. Therefore, you should examine the subtest level contrast scaled scores to make more specific interpretations.

Visual Working Memory Index Versus Visual Memory Index Contrast Scaled Score

The *Visual Working Memory Index versus Visual Memory Index* contrast scaled score is available in the Adult battery only. The control variable in this score is VWMI, presumably because having good working memory improves the ability to encode and retrieve information from long-term memory. However, in Baddeley's (2000) model, it is suggested that episodic memory can support working memory functioning. This occurs when the amount of information in immediate memory exceeds the working memory buffer and results in interplay between working memory span, episodic memory, and the central executive in order to retain the information. For the purposes of this contrast score, the association is treated as unidirectional with the influence of working memory functioning on episodic memory functioning being partialed out. Low scores indicate that visual memory functioning is lower than expected given visual working memory ability. High scores indicate better-than-expected visual memory functioning in comparison to visual working memory skills.

> **DON'T FORGET**
> ....
> Contrast scaled scores represent a within-person evaluation of cognitive functioning. These scores do not replace age-adjusted scaled scores and do not necessarily indicate how well an examinee will function in the general population. These optional scores help refine hypotheses and interpretation of memory functioning.

Additional Index Scores in the ACS

The ACS provides additional WMS-IV indexes that further describe memory functioning. These indexes are similar to those found in the WMS-III. The additional indexes are based on scaled scores or cumulative percentages obtained during the WMS-IV assessment. No additional tests are needed to obtain these additional index scores; however, to use all of the indexes, the optional recognition trials and DE process scores will need to be available. Like the primary indexes, the additional indexes have a mean of 100 and a standard deviation of 15. The additional indexes available in ACS are: Auditory Immediate, Auditory Delayed, Auditory Recognition, Visual Immediate, Visual Delayed, Visual Recognition, Designs Spatial, and Designs Content. For the Older Adult battery, only the Auditory Immediate, Auditory Delayed, and Auditory Recognition Indexes can be derived. The ACS also provides additional index-level contrast scaled scores utilizing the alternative index structure.

Auditory Immediate Index (AII)

The AII is derived from the LM I and VPA I scaled scores. In general, this index is a measure of the examinee's ability to immediately encode and recall verbal information. More specifically, this score represents immediate memory for semantically and sequentially related and unrelated verbal information, and single-trial and multitrial learning. It is a subcomponent of the AMI, and you may wish to report this score if auditory immediate memory is significantly better or worse than auditory delayed memory to compare immediate and delayed auditory memory functioning at the index level.

Auditory Delayed Index (ADI)

The ADI is derived from the LM II and VPA II scaled scores. In general, this index is a measure of the examinee's ability to recall verbal information from long-term memory. More specifically, this score represents delayed free and cued recall for semantically and sequentially related and unrelated verbal information, and single-trial and multitrial learning. It is a subcomponent of the AMI, and you may wish to report this score if auditory delayed memory is significantly better or worse than auditory immediate memory to compare immediate and delayed auditory memory functioning or auditory delayed recall and recognition at the index level.

Auditory Recognition Index (ARI)

The ARI is comprised of the LM II Recognition and VPA II Recognition combined score derived from the *ACS Administration and Scoring Manual*. The combined score uses the age-adjusted cumulative percentages to create a sum of scaled scores equivalent score. This new score is converted into an index score based on standard norming procedures. In general, this index is a measure of the examinee's ability to recognize verbal information in long-term memory. More specifically, this score represents delayed recognition for semantically and sequentially related and unrelated verbal information, and single-trial and multitrial learning. You may wish to report this score in order to compare auditory recognition memory to other indexes, particularly the ADI, on the same standard score metric.

Visual Immediate Index (VII)

The VII is derived from the VR I and DE I scaled scores. In general, this index is a measure of the examinee's ability to immediately encode, recall, and recognize visual information. More specifically, this score represents immediate memory for visual details, the relationship among the visual details, and spatial locations. It is a subcomponent of the VMI and you may wish to report this score if visual immediate memory is significantly better or worse than visual delayed memory to compare immediate and delayed visual memory functioning at the index level.

Visual Delayed Index (VDI)

The VDI is comprised of the VR II and DE II scaled scores. In general, this index is a measure of the examinee's ability to recall visual information from long-term memory. More specifically, this score represents delayed recall and recognition memory for visual details, the relationship among the visual details, and spatial locations. It is a subcomponent of the VMI and you may wish to report this score if visual delayed memory is significantly better or worse than visual immediate memory to compare immediate and delayed visual memory functioning or visual delayed recall and recognition at the index level.

Visual Recognition Index (VRI)

The VRI is derived from the VR II Recognition and DE II Recognition combined score derived in the *ACS Administration and Scoring Manual.* The combined score uses the age-adjusted cumulative percentages to create a sum of scaled scores equivalent score. This new score is converted into an index score based on standard norming procedures. In general, this index is a measure of the examinee's ability to recognize visual information in long-term memory. More specifically, this score represents delayed recognition for visual details, the relationship among the visual details, and spatial locations. You may wish to report this score in order to compare visual recognition memory to other index scores, particularly the VDI on the same standard score metric.

Designs Spatial Index (DSI)

The DSI is derived from the DE I Spatial and the DE II Spatial scaled scores. This index measures encoding and recall of spatial information after immediate presentation and after a 20- to 30-minute delay. You may wish to use this index to obtain a more reliable measure of spatial memory than obtained with individual subtest scores. Also, the index-level contrast scaled scores may provide a more robust comparison between memory for spatial locations and visual details than the subtest-level comparisons.

Designs Content Index (DCI)

The DCI is comprised of the DE I Content and the DE II Content scaled scores. This index measures encoding and recall for visual details after immediate presentation and after a 20- to 30-minute delay. You may wish to use this index to obtain a more reliable measure of memory for visual details than obtained with individual subtest scores. Also, the index-level comparisons may provide a more robust comparison between memory for visual details and spatial locations than the subtest-level comparisons.

Additional Index-Level Contrast Scaled Scores in the ACS

The ACS provides additional index-level contrast scaled scores to test specific hypotheses about memory functioning. The contrast scaled scores provided include: *Auditory Immediate Index versus Auditory Delayed Index; Auditory Recognition Index versus Auditory Delayed Index; Visual Immediate Index versus Visual Delayed Index; Visual Recognition Index versus Visual Delayed Index;* and *Designs Spatial Index versus Designs Content Index.* These contrast scaled scores provide additional information about the examinee's performance across the alternate indexes.

Auditory Immediate Index Versus Auditory Delayed Index Contrast Scaled Score

The *Auditory Immediate Index versus Auditory Delayed Index* contrast scaled score compares the examinee's relative performance on delayed recall to initial encoding ability. On this contrast score, the AII is the control variable, and the ADI is the dependent measure. Therefore, this contrast score reflects the examinee's delayed recall ability for auditory information controlling for initial encoding ability. A low score indicates lower-than-expected delayed recall considering performance on initial recall. The low score suggests more forgetting of information than expected. Alternately, a high score indicates better-than-expected delayed recall for auditory information relative to initial encoding. The high score suggests better consolidation of information in memory relative to initial recall.

Auditory Recognition Index Versus Auditory Delayed Index Contrast Scaled Score

The *Auditory Recognition Index versus Auditory Delayed Index* contrast scaled score compares the examinee's relative performance on auditory delayed recall to performance on delayed recognition. On this contrast score, the ARI is the control variable, and the ADI is the dependent measure. Therefore, this contrast score reflects the examinee's delayed recall ability for auditory information controlling for the ability to recognize that information. A low score indicates lower-than-expected delayed recall considering ability to recognize that information in long-term memory. The low score suggests difficulties with retrieval of auditory information. Alternately, a high score indicates better-than-expected delayed recall relative to recognition and is relatively unusual. This can occur due to the truncated range of the recognition trial or to carelessness by the examinee on the recognition trial. On the auditory recognition trials, even a few errors can result in a low age-adjusted score. When high scores are obtained on this score, it is important to evaluate the raw scores obtained on the recognition trials to determine if there is an unusually low number of correct responses.

Visual Immediate Index Versus Visual Delayed Index Contrast Scaled Score

The *Visual Immediate Index versus Visual Delayed Index* contrast scaled score compares the examinee's relative performance on delayed recall to initial encoding ability. On this contrast score, the VII is the control variable and the VDI is the dependent measure. Therefore, this contrast score reflects the examinee's delayed recall ability for visual information controlling for initial encoding performance. A low score indicates lower-than-expected delayed recall considering initial recall level. The low score suggests more forgetting of information than expected. Conversely, a high score indicates better-than-expected delayed recall for visual information relative to initial encoding. The high score suggests better consolidation of information in memory relative to initial recall.

Visual Recognition Index Versus Visual Delayed Index Contrast Scaled Score

The *Visual Recognition Index versus Visual Delayed Index* contrast scaled score compares the examinee's relative performance on visual delayed recall and delayed recognition. On this contrast score, the VRI is the control variable and the VDI is the dependent measure. Therefore, this contrast score reflects the examinee's delayed recall ability for visual information controlling for the ability to recognize that information. A low score indicates lower-than-expected delayed recall considering the ability to recognize that information in long-term memory. The low score suggests difficulties with retrieval of visual information. Conversely, a high score indicates better-than-expected delayed recall relative to recognition for visual information. A high score is unusual and may occur due to the truncated range of the recognition trial or in some cases carelessness during the recognition trial. When high scores are obtained on this score, it is important to evaluate the raw scores obtained on the recognition trials to determine if there is an unusually low number of correct responses.

Designs Spatial Index Versus Designs Content Index Contrast Scaled Score

The *Designs Spatial Index versus Designs Content Index* contrast scaled score compares the examinee's spatial memory performance and memory for visual details. In this contrast score, the DSI is the control variable and the DCI is the dependent variable. Therefore, this contrast score reflects the examinee's ability to recall visual details controlling for spatial memory ability. A low score indicates relatively poor memory for visual details relative to the ability to recall spatial designs. Conversely, a high score indicates relatively good visual memory considering spatial recall skill.

As was noted for the Auditory Memory Index versus Visual Memory Index, there is no specific way to select the control and dependent variables for this contrast. As a result, the scores tend to reflect the examinee's performance on the dependent measure more than performance on the control variable. When both contributing scores are low, this score may still return a low value, suggesting lower performance on memory for visual details than on visual spatial recall. However, in this scenario, the low score actually represents poor visual memory in general and memory for visual details may not necessarily be worse than spatial recall.

INTERPRETING WMS-IV RESULTS USING VARIOUS LEVELS OF DETAIL

The following section uses a case example to illustrate the use of the WMS-IV at various levels of detail. The level varies as follows: WMS-IV primary scores only; WMS-IV primary and process scores; all available WMS-IV and ACS scores; and selected WMS-IV subtests used for a brief evaluation. This section illustrates the types of information available from the various scores and provides some general guidelines for when to report additional scores. Ultimately, you must decide how much detail is required to answer the clinical or referral question for a specific examinee.

Background

Mr. Johnson is a 68-year-old white man with 18 years of education. He is currently retired from his job as director of engineering at a machine manufacturer. Mr. Johnson is a widower and lives alone. His adult children visit him frequently but are concerned about his ability to care for himself. Mr. Johnson denies any significant problems with memory or self-care. He reports that he is "just a little depressed and just doesn't feel like doing much." Mr. Johnson denies having problems caring for himself but his family observed that he has not been paying his bills consistently and that he has lost weight. Mr. Johnson was referred for neurological evaluation due to his family's concerns about his forgetfulness, lack of interest in activities he previously enjoyed (e.g., reading, cooking, watching television, participating in social events), and potential problems managing his finances and self-care. Neurological exam was generally unremarkable but indicated decreased mental status; subsequently, further radiological and neuropsychological studies were recommended. Neuropsychological evaluation was performed and included the Adult battery of the WMS-IV. The results of the WMS-IV are discussed here using multiple levels of detail to illustrate how the WMS-IV may be used.

WMS-IV Primary Index and Subtest Scores

When evaluating the WMS-IV primary index and subtest scores, it is recommended that the index scores be described first. Figure 4.1 presents the results for Mr. Johnson. Based on the index-level scores alone, the clinician may be able to conclude that Mr. Johnson appears to be having some difficulty with delayed recall in particular and that both auditory and visual modalities are in the borderline range. Interpreting the index-level scores, the clinician could report, "Mr. Johnson's memory performance is characterized by borderline ability to encode and retrieve both auditory and visual information from immediate and long-term memory stores. His ability to remember auditory and visual information immediately after hearing or seeing the information is in the low average range, while his ability to access that information following a delay is in the extremely low range. Mr. Johnson's ability to temporarily hold both visual–spatial information and visual details in memory while performing mental operations on that information is in the low average range."

Figure 4.1 Index Score Summary for Mr. Johnson

Index	Sum of Scaled Scores	Index	Score	Percentile Rank	95% Confidence Interval	Qualitative Description
Auditory Memory	24	AMI	77	6	72–84	Borderline
Visual Memory	25	VMI	78	7	73–85	Borderline
Visual Working Memory	15	VWMI	85	16	79–93	Low Average
Immediate Memory	28	IMI	80	9	75–87	Low Average
Delayed Memory	21	DMI	67	1	62–76	Extremely Low

The *WMS-IV Administration and Scoring Manual* provides statistical significance levels and base rates for simple differences between WMS-IV index scores. For Mr. Johnson, at the $p < 0.05$ level, the DMI is significantly lower than the IMI and the VWMI (note that the DMI is not compared to the AMI or VMI because they share common subtests). The base rate of the differences between the DMI and IMI indexes is 5.9% and 11.0%, compared to the VWMI, indicating that the difference is both statistically significant and atypical among individuals in the normative sample. The clinician would conclude that delayed memory is a relative weakness.

The next step in interpretation involves evaluating subtest scores to determine specific areas of memory difficulties that should be further elaborated. Figure 4.2 presents Mr. Johnson's subtest scaled scores and the within-index subtest-level differences. This figure illustrates how subtest differences may be determined within each memory index and provides additional information for deeper interpretation of the index level scores. For the AMI, the VPA immediate recall score is significantly higher than the average of the subtest scaled scores that contribute to the index, although the base rate of 25% is not particularly rare. The *WMS-IV Administration and Scoring Manual* provides statistical significance levels and base rates for specific subtest-level comparisons. In this instance, the clinician may wish to note specific pairwise comparisons that are significantly different between the auditory measures. For Mr. Johnson, only the VPA I versus VPA II difference of 4 points was statistically significant. Among visual memory measures, the VR II subtest was significantly lower than the average of the visual subtest scores in

Figure 4.2 Subtest Level Comparisons Within Index for Mr. Johnson

Subtest-Level Differences Within Indexes

Auditory Memory Index

Subtest	Scaled Score	AMI Mean Score	Difference from Mean	Critical Value	Base Rate
Logical Memory I	6	6.00	0.00	2.64	>25%
Logical Memory II	6	6.00	0.00	2.48	>25%
Verbal Paired Associates I	8	6.00	2.00*	1.90	25%
Verbal Paired Associates II	4	6.00	−2.00	2.48	25%

Statistical significance (critical value) at the .05 level.

* Statistically significant difference.

(continued)

Figure 4.2 (Continued)

Visual Memory Index

Subtest	Scaled Score	VMI Mean Score	Difference from Mean	Critical Value	Base Rate
Designs I	7	6.25	0.75	2.38	>25%
Designs II	7	6.25	0.75	2.38	>25%
Visual Reproduction I	7	6.25	0.75	1.86	>25%
Visual Reproduction II	4	6.25	−2.25*	1.48	25%

Statistical significance (critical value) at the .05 level.
*Statistically significant difference.

Immediate Memory Index

Subtest	Scaled Score	IMI Mean Score	Difference from Mean	Critical Value	Base Rate
Logical Memory I	6	7.00	−1.00	2.59	>25%
Verbal Paired Associates I	8	7.00	1.00	1.82	>25%
Designs I	7	7.00	0.00	2.42	>25%
Visual Reproduction I	7	7.00	0.00	1.91	>25%

Statistical significance (critical value) at the .05 level.

Delayed Memory Index

Subtest	Scaled Score	DMI Mean Score	Difference from Mean	Critical Value	Base Rate
Logical Memory II	6	5.25	0.75	2.44	>25%
Verbal Paired Associates II	4	5.25	−1.25	2.44	>25%
Designs II	7	5.25	1.75	2.44	>25%
Visual Reproduction II	4	5.25	−1.25	1.57	>25%

Statistical significance (critical value) at the .05 level.

Subtest Discrepancy Comparison

Comparison	Score 1	Score 2	Difference	Critical Value	Base Rate
Spatial Addition-Symbol Span	8	7	1	2.74	85.9

Statistical significance (critical value) at the .05 level.

the VMI; although, the base rate was not rare. Additionally, the VR II scaled score was significantly lower than the VR I subtest.

For the IMI, none of the subtest scores were significantly different from the IMI mean of the subtest scaled scores. No pairwise comparisons were significantly different, either. Similarly, the DMI yielded no significant subtest differences from the DMI mean subtest score. However, a significant pairwise difference between VR II and DE II is observed. Be careful not to overinterpret pairwise comparisons when a large number of comparisons are made because the chance of finding a difference by chance is increased (Binder, Iverson, & Brooks, 2009). The comparison between SA and SSP can also be evaluated, and in Mr. Johnson's case there was no significant difference between these scores.

Based on the observed subtest-level performances, the clinician may wish to elaborate on the earlier interpretation of Mr. Johnson's memory functioning. "Significant variability was observed on the subtests comprising the AMI. Mr. Johnson's overall auditory memory functioning was in the borderline range; however, he exhibited a relative strength on a multitrial learning task for semantically related and unrelated word associations. On this same measure, he displayed average immediate learning but borderline ability to recall that information following a 20- to 30-minute delay. Mr. Johnson also displayed some variability in his visual memory functioning. He had a relative weakness in his ability to recall visual details and spatial relations from long-term memory compared to his immediate recall and memory ability for the same information. Variability in performance on recall of visual information was also observed on the DMI."

When using only the primary WMS-IV subtest and index scores, you could conclude that the examinee has extremely low to low average memory functioning. Four index scores were at or below the ninth percentile, which is unusual when you consider using the WMS-IV in isolation (Brooks et al., submitted; Iverson, Brooks, & Holdnack, 2008) for an examinee with more than 16 years of education. You may also conclude that delayed memory is a significant weakness compared to immediate. More specifically, Mr. Johnson has a weakness associated with drawing designs from long-term memory and remembering novel and related word associations. In the auditory domain, repeating information improves Mr. Johnson's immediate memory performance but does not improve his long-term memory functioning.

Considering the overall findings, particularly deficient long-term memory functioning and a relatively high number of obtained low scores, Mr. Johnson's performance is likely indicative of memory difficulties. Can the clinician diagnose Mr. Johnson with dementia based on the test results? No, the clinician must consider all evidence in an evaluation, including clinical interview, background history, and other test results. Although the WMS-IV provides one piece of evidence fitting such a diagnosis, it is not diagnostic in and of itself.

WMS-IV Process Scores

The case of Mr. Johnson is expanded upon by using the process and contrast scaled scores available in the WMS-IV. The additional procedures included were the BCSE, the recognition trials for all four delayed memory conditions, VPA II Word Recall, and VR Copy. The index-level and subtest-level contrast scaled scores were also included.

The contrast scaled scores test specific hypotheses in contrast to pairwise comparisons that may or may not relate to a specific hypothesis. Figure 4.3 displays Mr. Johnson's index-level contrast scaled scores. The contrast scores, particularly at the index level, are interpreted when the scaled score is 7 or less or 12 and greater. For Mr. Johnson, each of the contrast scores would be interpreted.

The Auditory Memory Index versus Visual Memory Index scaled score of 7 indicates that Mr. Johnson's VMI is at the 16th percentile in comparison to individuals with borderline auditory memory (i.e., the same auditory memory ability level as Mr. Johnson). This reflects general memory problems, since slightly higher visual memory scores are expected when auditory memory scores are below average and there is no true memory hierarchy between auditory and visual memory skills. The Visual Working Memory Index versus the Visual Memory Index score indicates that Mr. Johnson's visual memory functioning is unexpectedly low given his visual working memory functioning. Therefore, his low visual memory scores are not likely related only to problems with low visual working memory. It is important to note that no difference was observed between these index scores using the

Figure 4.3 Index-Level Contrast Scaled Scores for Mr. Johnson

Index-Level Contrast Scaled Scores

Score	Score 1	Score 2	Contrast Scaled Score
Auditory Memory Index versus Visual Memory Index	77	78	7
Visual Working Memory Index versus Visual Memory Index	85	78	7
Immediate Memory Index versus Delayed Memory Index	80	67	3

simple difference method. The simple difference method does not take into account where in the score distribution Mr. Johnson's scores fall. For scores that fall below the mean, smaller score differences frequently have a lower observed base rate than the same score difference in scores above the mean. The Immediate Memory Index versus Delayed Memory Index confirmed the previous finding that delayed memory is unexpectedly low given immediate memory performance.

The optional conditions provide additional information about Mr. Johnson's performance on specific subtests. Figure 4.4 presents the subtest-level contrast scaled scores for Mr. Johnson. On LM, Mr. Johnson performed in the average range (51–75%) on recognition. The LM II Recognition versus Delayed Recall score indicates that delayed recall performance is well below expected considering his average performance on the recognition trial. Mr. Johnson appears to have difficulties retrieving semantically and sequentially related verbal information from long-term memory. The LM Immediate Recall versus Delayed Recall score of 9 indicates average delayed memory performance considering initial level of encoding of the stories. On VPA Recognition, Mr. Johnson performed in the low average range (17–25%) for delayed recognition. His performance on VPA II Word Recall was in the deficient range (ss = 2). The VPA contrast scaled scores indicate that Mr. Johnson's delayed recall was unexpectedly low both for his level of recognition (ss = 5) and for his immediate encoding ability (ss = 2).

Mr. Johnson's auditory memory functioning is notable for retrieval deficits related to recall of semantically related and unrelated word associations, and semantically and sequentially organized verbal information. In addition, he not only has difficulty recalling word associations from long-term memory, but he is also unable to recall the individual words from memory.

In the visual domain, additional scores and procedures are available for DE and VR. On DE II Recognition, Mr. Johnson performed in the deficient range ($\leq 2\%$) on the recognition trial. The process scores showing memory for spatial locations and memory for visual details are all in the average range with the exception of delayed memory for visual details which is low average (DE II content = 6). The DE contrast scores indicate that delayed memory for visual details is unexpectedly low compared to delayed memory for spatial locations. Also, Mr. Johnson's delayed recall is better than expected considering his poor performance on the recognition trial. Inspection of his responses to the recognition trial shows difficulties identifying the correct visual details.

The VR optional conditions indicate that Mr. Johnson has low average recognition (10–16%) for the visual designs. His ability to copy the designs is in the average range (26–50%). The Recognition and Immediate Recall versus Delayed Recall contrast scaled scores indicate that delayed free recall is unexpectedly

Figure 4.4 Subtest-Level Contrast Scores for Mr. Johnson

Subtest Level Contrast Scaled Scores

Logical Memory

Score	Score 1	Score 2	Contrast Scaled Score
LM II Recognition versus Delayed Recall	51–75%	6	4
LM Immediate Recall versus Delayed Recall	6	6	9

Verbal Paired Associates

Score	Score 1	Score 2	Contrast Scaled Score
VPA II Recognition versus Delayed Recall	17–25%	4	5
VPA Immediate Recall versus Delayed Recall	8	4	2

Designs

Score	Score 1	Score 2	Contrast Scaled Score
DE 1 Spatial versus Content	8	8	9
DE II Spatial versus Content	10	6	5
DE II Recognition versus Delayed Recall	≤ 2%	7	13
DE Immediate Recall versus Delayed Recall	7	7	8

Visual Reproduction

Score	Score 1	Score 2	Contrast Scaled Score
VR II Recognition versus Delayed Recall	10–16%	4	6
VR Copy versus Immediate Recall	26–50%	7	7
VR Immediate Recall versus Delayed Recall	7	4	6

low compared to both recognition and immediate encoding ability. Mr. Johnson shows difficulties with encoding and retrieval of visual details and spatial relations among the details. The VR Copy versus Immediate Recall score shows that his immediate memory performance was lower than expected given his ability to directly copy the design. Thus, his low scores on this subtest are not likely attributable to poor motor control.

The BCSE was also administered. The weighted raw score of 48 was in the borderline range for his age and education. Borderline scores on BCSE occur in 10% or less of the general population and may signal general problems with cognitive functioning. Mr. Johnson had the most difficulty on the mental control, inhibition, and incidental memory items of the BCSE; orientation items were within normal limits.

Using the optional procedures and contrast scores, you may elaborate on the interpretation of the primary subtest and index scores. At the index-score level, the clinician could add, "Mr. Johnson exhibits visual memory deficits even when controlling for relatively low visual working memory skills." The additional findings of differences between auditory and visual memory and between immediate and delayed memory do not need further elaboration, since low functioning in both modalities and a significant weakness in delayed memory was reported previously.

At the subtest level, the optional procedures and scores help elaborate specific aspects of memory functioning. "Among auditory memory measures, Mr. Johnson performed in the average range on recognition of orally presented stories, indicating greater difficulties with retrieval than encoding of complex semantically and sequentially organized verbal information. Similarly, his recognition for semantically related and unrelated verbal information is low average and is better than his cued recall for this information indicating both retrieval and encoding difficulties. Mr. Johnson's performance on VPA II Word Recall was in the extremely low range, indicating that he has difficulty with general encoding and retrieval of semantically related and unrelated words, and thus his difficulties are not restricted to associative memory."

On visual memory measures, the additional scores and procedures also provide useful information about Mr. Johnson's memory performance. "On VR, Mr. Johnson showed average ability to copy designs so his low memory scores are not likely due to motor or constructional difficulties. His VR II Recognition performance was in the low average range. Controlling for his performance on recognition, his delayed recall was lower than expected. This suggests difficulties with encoding and retrieval of visual details and the spatial relations among visual details." In this case, the score difference between immediate and delayed memory was identified using the simple differences and the contrast score would not add to the interpretation. The process scores for DE were notable for average performance on immediate and delayed spatial memory and average immediate memory for visual details but low average performance on delayed recall. "Mr. Johnson showed deficient recognition on the Designs subtest, and further evaluation of his responses indicated difficulties recognizing correct visual details. His delayed recall was better than expected given his deficient recognition memory performance, suggesting that his intact spatial memory assisted his performance on delayed memory in comparison to performance on recognition. Mr. Johnson's visual memory is notable for encoding and retrieval issues related specifically to visual details, while spatial memory appears relatively intact."

The use of the optional scores and procedures does not change the overall impression that Mr. Johnson is having memory deficits. However, the scores identified specific deficits and abilities. In the verbal domain, delayed recognition memory is more preserved than free recall. Therefore, Mr. Johnson is able to encode more verbal information than he is able to retrieve. This information could be used to help Mr. Johnson adapt to his memory problems. Also, the verbal learning deficits are not restricted to associative memory but to encoding of verbal information more generally. In the visual domain, visual construction problems can be ruled out as causing poor performance on visual memory tests. His visual memory problems are related to visual details more so than spatial memory. In addition, administration of the BCSE suggests memory difficulties are not the only cognitive difficulties present and further evaluation of processing speed and executive functioning is indicated.

Additional Subtest and Index Scores in the ACS

The ACS provides the clinician with additional scoring options for the WMS-IV indexes and subtests. Not all scores are relevant to every evaluation, and it is helpful to familiarize yourself with the available scores. For example, LM additional scores are suggested when one of the stories is invalid for some reason or if there is insufficient time to administer both stories. For Mr. Johnson, all the additional index scores and relevant contrast scaled scores are presented.

The additional index scores and comparisons are presented in Figure 4.5. The index scores range from Extremely Low to Average with three index scores below the 5th percentile and six scores below the 16th percentile. Using the simple difference method to compare scores, the only significant difference is observed between the ADI and ARI. Based on these results, it appears that there is no difference between immediate and delayed memory or between memory for visual details and spatial memory. The contrast scaled scores for the key index-level comparisons indicate that delayed memory is unexpectedly low controlling for initial encoding for both verbal and visual indexes. Also, the ADI is unexpectedly low given performance on ARI. Finally, memory for visual details is unexpectedly low controlling for spatial memory ability.

The additional verbal subtest scores enable the clinician to identify verbal memory issues not identified using the standard WMS-IV scoring. Mr. Johnson

Figure 4.5 Additional WMS-IV Index Scores for Mr. Johnson

WMS-IV Additional Index Score Summary

Index	Sum of Scaled Scores	Index Score	Percentile Rank	Confidence Interval	SEM	Qualitative Description
Auditory Immediate	14	83	13	77–91	4.5	Low Average
Auditory Delayed	10	71	3	66–83	5.41	Borderline
Auditory Recognition	20	91	27	82–105	8.08	Average
Visual Immediate	14	83	13	77–92	4.74	Low Average
Visual Delayed	11	72	3	67–81	4.24	Borderline
Visual Recognition	11	61	0.5	63–86	8.87	Extremely Low
Designs Spatial	18	95	37	86–106	6.71	Average
Designs Content	14	84	14	77–95	6.54	Low Average

WMS-IV Additional Index Comparisons

Comparison	Score 1	Score 2	Difference	Critical Value	Significant Difference	Base Rate
AII - VII	83	83	0	12.81	N	
ADI - VDI	71	72	−1	13.47	N	47.7%
AII - ADI	83	71	12	13.79	N	5.9%
ADI - ARI	71	91	−20*	19.06	Y	3.0%
VII - VDI	83	72	11	12.46	N	16.2%
VDI - VRI	72	61	11	19.27	N	21.2%
VII - VWMI	83	85	−2	12.46	N	46.3%
DSI - DCI	95	84	11	18.37	N	23.7%

Statistical significance (critical value) at the .05 level.
*Statistically significant difference.

(*continued*)

Figure 4.5 (Continued)

WMS-IV Additional Index-Level Contrast Scaled Scores

Score	Score 1	Score 2	Contrast Scaled Score
Auditory Immediate Index versus Auditory Delayed Index	83	71	4
Auditory Recognition Index versus Auditory Delayed Index	91	71	3
Visual Immediate Index versus Visual Delayed Index	83	72	6
Visual Recognition Index versus Visual Delayed Index	61	72	9
Designs Spatial Index versus Designs Content Index	95	84	7

needed to be cued to recall both of the LM stories. The LM II Cue Given score of 2 is in the low average range (10–16%); therefore, Mr. Johnson requires more prompting from delayed memory than is expected for his age.

Compared to most subtests, VPA has a large number of additional scores. It is recommended that the clinician organize the interpretation of these scores into error scores and process scores. Error scores reflect the examinee's ability to screen recall for incorrect information while process scores describe specific aspects of the examinee's memory such as memory ability for semantically related items. Figure 4.6 presents Mr. Johnson's additional VPA scores. On error measures, he performed in the extremely low to average ranges. His performance was notable for low average association errors for immediate learning (VPA I Intra-List Intrusions 10–16%) and average errors for delayed recall (VPA II Intra-List Errors 26–50%). Mr. Johnson's ability to screen for intrusion errors during recall was in the borderline range for immediate learning (VPA I Extra-List Intrusions 3–9%) and in the extremely low range for delayed recall (VPA II Extra-List Errors ≤ 2%). His overall error rate for both incorrect words and incorrect associations was in the extremely low range for immediate learning (VPA I Intrusions ss = 3) and in the borderline range for delayed recall (VPA II Intrusions 3–9%). Mr. Johnson had a high number of errors on delayed word recall (VPA II Intrusions 3–9%), but he did not repeat information more than was expected (VPA II Word Recall Repetitions 26–50%). While cued and free recall measures showed high rates of memory errors, Mr. Johnson had an average rate of delayed recognition errors (VPA II Recognition False Positives 26–50%).

The VPA process scores provide more descriptive information regarding Mr. Johnson's ability. His ability to learn the associations after a single exposure

Figure 4.6 Additional Scores for Verbal Paired Associates

WMS-IV Verbal Paired Associates Additional Score Summary

Score	Raw Score	Scaled Score	Percentile Rank	Cumulative Percentage
VPA I Recall A	3	9	37	—
VPA I Recall D	6	7	16	—
VPA I Easy Items	8	6	9	—
VPA I Hard Items	11	9	37	—
VPA I Extra-List Intrusions	18	—	—	3–9%
VPA I Intra-List Intrusions	10	—	—	10–16%
VPA I Intrusions	28	3	1	—
VPA II Easy Items	2	—	—	10–16%
VPA II Hard Items	0	—	—	≤ 2%
VPA II Extra-List Intrusions	7	—	—	≤ 2%
VPA II Intra-List Intrusions	2	—	—	26–50%
VPA II Intrusions	9	—	—	3–9%
VPA II Recognition Easy Items	4	—	—	17–25%
VPA II Recognition Hard Items	7	—	—	3–9%
VPA II Recognition Hits	11	—	—	10–16%
VPA II Recognition False Positives	2	—	—	26–50%
VPA II Recognition Discriminability	0.9	—	—	26–50%
VPA II Word Recall Intrusions	4	—	—	3–9%
VPA II Word Recall Repetitions	1	—	—	26–50%

was in the average range (VPA I Recall A ss = 9), while his recall after four repetitions was in the low average range (VPA I Recall D ss = 7). His recall after four exposures to the list was lower than expected compared to his single-trial learning (VPA I Recall A versus Recall D ss = 7). His immediate learning for semantically related word pairs was low average (VPA I Easy Items ss = 6); however, his learning for unrelated items was in the average range (VPA I Hard Items ss = 9). His immediate recall for difficult items was better than expected controlling for his ability to learn semantically related items (VPA I Easy Items versus Hard Items ss = 13). On delayed recall, Mr. Johnson had low average recall for semantically related items (VPA II Easy Items 10–16%) and extremely low recall for unrelated items (VPA II Hard Items ≤ 2% percentage). His recognition for both semantically related and unrelated items was in the low average range (VPA II Recognition Hits 10–16%), as was his overall performance on the recognition trial when hits and false-positive responses are equally weighted (VPA II Recognition Discriminability 26–50%). His ability to recognize semantically related items was low average (VPA II Recognition Easy Items 17–25%) and borderline for recognition of unrelated items (VPA II Recognition Hard Items 3–9%).

The visual memory subtests offer a few additional scores that enable the clinician to more fully elaborate aspects of memory functioning. The additional time scores on VR are useful if the clinician believes the examinee completed the designs very quickly with little attention to quality, which might result in lower memory scores. "Mr. Johnson performed in the low average range for VR Immediate (VR I Average Completion Time ss = 6) and Delayed (VR II Average Completion Time ss = 7) Average Completion Time. His immediate (VR I Average Completion Time versus Immediate Recall ss = 7) and delayed (VR II Average Completion Time versus Delayed Recall ss = 3) recall are below expected levels controlling for the speed at which he drew the designs. It is unlikely that the speed at which the designs were completed resulted in the low memory scores. In addition to low recall scores, Mr. Johnson had more visual memory intrusions at immediate (VR I Additional Design Elements ≤ 2%) and delayed (VR II Additional Design Elements ≤ 2%) recall than expected. This suggests he has difficulty screening his responses for accuracy." On the Designs rule violations measure, he had zero rule violations. The raw score of zero yields a classification level of 10th–16th percentage; however, it is important to remember that this score will include all higher percentage groups and therefore technically represents 10–100% of cases.

In this case, it is worthwhile to summarize the additional information garnered by using the ACS additional scores. At the index level, the use of visual and auditory immediate and delayed scores did not provide any additional information beyond the standard indexes (i.e., delayed memory is a weakness compared to immediate memory and visual and auditory memory do not differ from one another). The visual and auditory recognition indexes indicated a retrieval deficit for auditory memory but for visual memory the memory impairment was most evident on the recognition index. This information was also observed at the subtest level on all subtests except DE; a tendency existed for relatively better recognition than free recall, so in some ways the use of the index scores masked the more accurate description of memory performance. The DE indexes indicated that memory for spatial information is intact, while memory for visual details is significantly lower. This was also identified at the subtest level, and the additional indexes did not yield more detailed information. Index scores are more reliable than subtest scores, so using the additional index scores may at times be desirable; however, in many cases the same information may be derived using the index scores available on the standard WMS-IV.

The ACS additional subtest scores provided information regarding Mr. Johnson's memory performance that was not obtained on the standard WMS-IV. One critical piece of information obtained from these additional scores was the high rate of memory intrusions for both verbal and visual information. Memory errors may represent a breakdown in memory functions, executive functions, or language processes. In Mr. Johnson's case, the presence of memory intrusions in both visual and verbal domains suggests that language impairments are not the primary cause of incorrect recall from memory. Executive functioning would need to be evaluated further to determine if poor executive functioning was contributing to recall errors. Additionally, his error rate during recognition was average, so he encodes information correctly and recognizes correct versus incorrect information. It is important to note that Mr. Johnson had better immediate recall for semantically unrelated items than for semantically related words, so he was not able to take advantage of prior associations to enhance memory performance; however, after the 20- to 30-minute delay, his recall was better for the related versus unrelated items. Although results are somewhat inconsistent, linking information to previously acquired knowledge would not likely be an effective memory tool for Mr. Johnson. However, repeating information resulted in relatively better memory functioning, although he acquired less information during repetition than was expected for his initial level of learning. Although he recalls more information after repetition, he does not benefit to the same degree as age-peers or individuals with similar levels of single-trial learning. Mr. Johnson's low scores on VR were not due to drawing too quickly, and the scores confirm slower processing speed noted on the BCSE. On story recall,

Mr. Johnson required cueing in order to initiate retrieval, further confirming retrieval difficulties noted previously.

The ACS additional scores provide memory information that is not necessarily required to identify the presence of memory problems. However, the scores help identify memory retrieval problems associated with memory intrusions and can help rule out competing factors such as speed of drawing for VR or comprehension of the instructions on DE. Base the use of additional scores on the needs of the examinee and the clinical question being answered. When choosing to use more scores, be aware that the likelihood that a low score will be observed by chance increases with the addition of scores; therefore, there is a need to be cautious and not overinterpret a few obtained low scores that are inconsistent with the examinee's performance on other measures.

Using an Abbreviated WMS-IV Assessment: Logical Memory and Visual Reproduction

In some circumstances, you may not wish to administer the entire WMS-IV due to limited testing time, reimbursement restrictions, examinee's health or cognitive status, the nature of the referral question, or the use of WMS-IV for screening purposes. As noted in Chapter Two, when using a partial battery, it is recommended that VR be administered first. If VR is not administered, then the examiner must remember to inform the examinee after the first memory test that he or she will be asked "to remember the (stories, word pairs, designs) because I will be asking you about it again in a little while."

During development of the WMS-IV, users of the WMS-III were polled to identify how they used the tests and which subtests they were most likely to use. Many clinicians reported primarily using the VR and LM subtests from the WMS-III and less frequently the entire battery. There are advantages and disadvantages to using a subset of subtests from within the entire battery. The main advantage of a partial battery is the reduced amount of time required to assess memory functioning. The primary disadvantages include loss of reliability, fewer observations on which to generalize behavior, and less information to describe memory functions in detail. When selecting subtests to create a shorter battery, it is important to consult the *WMS-IV Technical and Interpretation Manual.* Not all the subtests are equally sensitive to specific clinical disorders (e.g., VPA and DE are more sensitive to traumatic brain injury than are LM and VR), and subtests vary in the types of cognitive processes that affect performance. For example, for an examinee with a significant tremor, DE might be a better choice than VR to assess visual memory.

As an example of how using a shorter battery may be implemented, Mr. Johnson's data will be presented applying just LM and VR scores. This allows for the comparison of conclusions that may be drawn from shorter and longer batteries. A shorter battery may include optional recognition procedures for the subtests in question. The recognition trials typically require only a few additional minutes for administration, so they can be used without significantly increasing the administration time of a short battery. As reported earlier, Mr. Johnson performed in the low average range on LM I (ss = 6) and LM II (ss = 6). The LM Immediate Recall versus Delayed Recall score indicated that delayed recall was consistent with initial levels of recall. On VR, he performed in the low average range on immediate recall (ss = 7) and in the extremely low range on delayed recall (ss = 4). The VR Immediate Recall versus Delayed Recall score (ss = 6) indicated that Mr. Johnson's delayed recall was unexpectedly low controlling for his initial level of recall.

On these two subtests, Mr. Johnson performed below the 10th percentile on three measures. Using multivariate base rate estimates established for the WMS-III (Brooks et al., 2008), three scores below the 10th percentile is observed in approximately 10% of individuals with 16 or more years of education. This number of low scores is unusual and probably indicates an abnormal memory profile. You could report delayed memory as a weakness in the visual domain and that visual and auditory memory functions are equally affected. The overall conclusions are very similar to those reported for the whole battery when only using the primary scores and procedures.

If the recognition trials are also completed, then the clinician would note that for both auditory and visual memory, performance on recognition memory is better than on free recall. Using the contrast scores indicates that memory problems primarily reflect retrieval difficulties; although, in the visual domain both encoding and retrieval problems may be present (i.e., recognition is better than free recall but is still low for his age). This is similar to what was reported for the whole battery except there was no information about specific difficulties with memory for visual details compared to normal memory for spatial location or that visual–motor problems were not confounding results on VR.

The use of select subtests can yield similar generalizations as those obtained from using the whole battery. However, specific information about memory functioning may be lacking, limiting recommendations for accommodating those deficits. Also, important information about functioning within a modality will be missed when there is inconsistency within that modality (e.g., VPA showing more forgetting effects than LM). The overall sensitivity of the battery can be affected by using a shorter battery, so it is not recommended that a partial battery be used in high-stakes testing such as forensic evaluations. Ultimately, you must determine the most effective assessment strategy for a specific patient and select the assessment model that best meets the need of the examinee and referral agent.

≈ TEST YOURSELF ≈

1. **Logical Memory is primarily a measure of**
   (a) Auditory Working Memory
   (b) Memory for Story Details
   (c) Memory for Unrelated Words
   (d) Story Retelling

2. **Verbal Paired Associates is comprised of**
   (a) Semantically related words
   (b) Sequentially related words
   (c) Unrelated words
   (d) Unknown words
   (e) B and C
   (f) A and C

3. **Verbal abilities influence performance on the Designs subtest more than on Visual Reproduction?**
   True/False

4. **There is no way to identify the impact of motor problems on Visual Reproduction.**
   True/False

5. **Which of the following measures uses a scaled score metric?**
   (a) Logical Memory Recognition
   (b) Verbal Paired Associates II Total Intrusions
   (c) Visual Immediate Index
   (d) VR Immediate Recall versus Delayed Recall Contrast

6. **Which of the following statements are true? (Circle all that apply)**
   (a) Index scores are often more reliable than subtest scores.
   (b) Clinicians should always use 1.5 standard deviations below the mean as a cutoff for memory impairment.
   (c) WMS-IV subtests are equally sensitive to memory problems in different clinical samples.
   (d) Low scores are commonly observed in normal controls.

7. **Which subtests are considered working memory subtests?**

    (a) All WMS-IV subtests

    (b) Logical Memory and Visual Reproduction

    (c) Designs and Spatial Addition

    (d) Spatial Addition and Symbol Span

    (e) Verbal Paired Associates and CVLT-II

8. **The entire WMS-IV must be given to obtain a valid assessment of memory.**

    True/False

9. **Visual memory tests can be affected by language functioning?**

    True/False

10. **Which feature makes Designs a unique memory measure?**

    (a) It measures visual memory.

    (b) It uses a memory grid.

    (c) It differentiates spatial memory from memory for details.

    (d) It is correlated with measures of Visual–Perceptual Reasoning.

Answers: 1. b, 2. f, 3. False, 4. False, 5. d, 6. a and d, 7. d, 8. False, 9. True, 10. c

Chapter Five

STRENGTHS AND WEAKNESSES OF THE WMS-IV

OVERVIEW OF STRENGTHS AND WEAKNESSES

Due to its recent publication, few research studies using the Wechsler Memory Scale–Fourth Edition (WMS-IV) currently exist. Therefore, this overview of strengths and weaknesses is based primarily on our clinical experiences with and judgment of the WMS-IV in comparison to other available memory batteries. The major strengths of the WMS-IV include conorming with the WAIS-IV in a large, representative sample covering ages 16–90 and excellent psychometric properties, including strong split-half reliability coefficients and good evidence of construct validity. Weaknesses include substantive changes in subtests and composition of indexes that limit performance comparisons to prior versions of the WMS and little or no evidence of criterion validity for many clinical populations for which memory assessment is crucial, such as neurosurgical candidates (e.g., for epilepsy, deep brain stimulation) and individuals with stroke or neurodegenerative diseases (Loring & Bauer, 2010). However, in many respects, the new edition of the WMS-IV is consistent with the WMS-R with the return of VR as a core subtest, the inclusion of easy items in VPA, and the single presentation of LM stories. Studies employing the WMS-R version of these subtests have continued despite the publication of the WMS-III and provide an additional source of validation for the new edition. Summaries of WMS-IV strengths and weaknesses in test development, administration and scoring, reliability and validity, standardization, and interpretation are presented in Rapid References 5.1–5.5.

CAUTION

Validation studies of the WMS-IV in many relevant clinical samples are limited or nonexistent at present.

≡ *Rapid Reference 5.1*

Strengths and Weaknesses of WMS-IV Test Development

Strengths	Weaknesses
Inclusion of a shorter battery for adults aged 65 and older to lessen the effect of fatigue.	More subtests presented in the visual modality due to the removal of verbal working memory.
Increased score ranges and modified administration and scoring on Logical Memory, Verbal Paired Associates, and Visual Reproduction to reduce floor effects.	Concerns about floor effects for older adults on Visual Reproduction Recognition and Verbal Paired Associates II; Table D.1 of the *WMS-IV Administration and Scoring Manual* shows floor and ceiling effects by age.
Inclusion of a global cognitive screening measure.	Only one subtest with a multitrial learning component (i.e., Verbal Paired Associates) in the primary WMS-IV kit; additional measures using multilearning trials are available in the Advanced Clinical Solutions (ACS) for WAIS-IV/WMS-IV kit.
No overlapping content with the WAIS-IV eliminating discrepant scores under the same index title.	A truncated ceiling on Visual Reproduction I in 18- to 19-year-olds.
Visual working memory tasks require mental manipulation of information.	A truncated floor on Logical Memory II in 85- to 90-year-olds.
Visual memory stimuli are not easily verbalized and do not rely heavily on motor speed or dexterity.	Fewer index scores do not allow further breakdown of memory skills beyond subtest level in the primary WMS-IV kit. Immediate, Delayed, and Recognition indexes are available for auditory and visual modalities in the ACS.
Visual Memory and Visual Working Memory subtests are difficult to verbalize, with the exception of Visual Reproduction, making visual indexes less impacted by verbal abilities.	Visual Reproduction, a visual memory subtest, has many features that are easily verbalized such that poor verbal memory or verbal skills may impact performance on this test.
Simplified index structure resulting in stronger reliability of index scores; the streamlined assessment increases usability and ease of administration.	No alternate forms.

Retention of the two most widely used subtests, Logical Memory and Visual Reproduction.	No effort subtests or embedded effort measures in the primary WMS-IV kit, although these are available in the ACS.
Exclusion of recognition memory scores from immediate and delayed memory indexes.	
Lowered guessing rates on recognition measures resulting in increased reliability and unmasking of floor effects.	
Dropped subtests and scores with poor psychometric properties (e.g., Faces) or no clinical or research support (e.g., Logical Memory Thematic scoring).	

Rapid Reference 5.2

Strengths and Weaknesses of WMS-IV
Administration and Scoring

Strengths	Weaknesses
Administration time for Older Adult battery is shorter than administration time of WMS-III core battery.	Longer administration time for Adult battery; average administration time in patients with traumatic brain injury is 2 hours rather than 83 minutes as indicated in the manual (J. B. Miller, personal communication, May 17, 2010).
Visual Reproduction scoring is faster and easier without a reduction in reliability and clinical sensitivity.	Subtests used as fillers between immediate and delayed subtests do not take up the recommended 20–30 minutes in patients who meet discontinuation criteria quickly (J. B. Miller, personal communication, May 17, 2010).
Ability to substitute CVLT-II scores for VPA scores in deriving index scores.	Instructions for Spatial Addition may be too long and/or complex for more impaired patients requiring simplified instructions for adequate understanding (J. B. Miller, personal communication, May 17, 2010).

(continued)

Interscorer agreement on simple and objective subtests is very high (i.e., 0.98–0.99) and percent agreement rates between scorers on more subjective measures (i.e., clock drawing of the Brief Cognitive Status Exam and Visual Reproduction) is also very high (i.e., 96–97%).	Memory Grid is difficult to use and may fall apart with repeated use.
Better organization of the WMS-IV record form and normative tables makes scoring easier.	Scoring is labor intensive, even with the software.
All norms tables for a single age group are now included in a single table, making scoring easier.	Designs subtest cards are awkward to place back into the card box holder, although it is slightly easier to manage than the WMS-III box.
Contrast scaled scores are included allowing for comparison of results within the examinee's ability level.	Audiotaped administration of Logical Memory and Verbal Paired Associates would have improved standardized administration of these subtests.
Dropped subtests requiring rapid turning of stimulus book pages (e.g., Faces every 2 seconds).	You can still see through the paper used for Visual Reproduction responses. (Note: The response booklet has been updated since the first printing to include gray screens that reduce visibility between pages.)
Training CD is easy to use and improves understanding of administration and scoring issues.	Placing the stimulus book between yourself and the examinee is awkward for examiners who prefer to sit adjacent to rather than opposite of examinees.
Alternate index compositions are provided in the WMS-IV Flexible Approach to allow index scores for briefer batteries; however, the alternate indexes are less comprehensive and reliable.	Calculating Designs content, spatial, and bonus scores by hand is not intuitive and requires practice.
	Use of CVLT-II for substitution requires separate purchase of the CVLT-II kit.

☰ Rapid Reference 5.3

Strengths and Weaknesses of WMS-IV
Reliability and Validity

Strengths	Weaknesses
Average internal consistency reliability coefficients of the index scores in the standardization sample are very strong, ranging from 0.93 to 0.96 for the Adult battery and from 0.92 to 0.97 for the Older Adult battery.	The Designs I and II Content and Spatial scores in the standardization sample have relatively low average internal consistency reliability coefficients ranging from 0.74 to 0.77.
Average internal consistency reliability coefficients of the primary subtest scores are > 0.80 for all but Verbal Paired Associates II in the Older Adult battery (i.e., 0.74).	The average test–retest interval in the standardization sample was 23 days, which is much shorter than the typical test–retest interval in clinical practice.
Average internal consistency reliability coefficients of the index scores in clinical populations are very strong, ranging from 0.93 to 0.98.	Test–retest reliabilities < 0.70 were obtained for Designs I and II Content and Spatial scores and Visual Reproduction I and II in the Adult battery and for Visual Reproduction II and Symbol Span in the Older Adult battery.
Average internal consistency reliability coefficients of the primary subtest scores, as well as Designs I and II Content and Spatial scores, in clinical populations are also strong, ranging from 0.86 to 0.95.	Test–retest reliabilities in clinical populations are unknown.
The primary subtest scores with the strongest average internal consistency reliability coefficients in both the Adult and Older Adult batteries normative and clinical samples are Verbal Paired Associates I and Visual Reproduction I and II (i.e., all ≥ 0.93).	Validation studies in many relevant clinical samples have not been conducted (e.g., stroke, movement disorders, multiple sclerosis, brain tumors, alcohol dependence) or suffer from small sample sizes (e.g., right and left temporal lobectomy, older adults with affective disorders).
Test–retest reliabilities of index scores in both the Adult and Older Adult batteries corrected for variability in the normative sample are strong, ranging from 0.80 to 0.87.	

(continued)

Test–retest reliabilities of most primary subtest scores in both the Adult and Older Adult batteries are > 0.70.

Factor analytic studies in the standardization sample provide strong support for the hypothesized two- (Auditory and Visual Memory) and three-factor (Auditory, Visual, and Visual Working Memory) models.

Good concurrent validity with well-known measures of IQ, memory, academic achievement, executive functioning, daily living skills, and self-report measures of attention-deficit/hyperactivity disorder (ADHD) and depression, is provided in the *WMS-IV Technical and Interpretive Manual.*

Initial validation studies with clinical samples (e.g., Alzheimer's disease, mild cognitive impairment, traumatic brain injury, right and left temporal lobectomy, schizophrenia, affective disorders, learning disorders, ADHD, pervasive developmental disorders, intellectual disability) reveal mostly large effect sizes consistent with established patterns of memory performance.

 *Rapid Reference 5.4*

Strengths and Weaknesses of WMS-IV Standardization

Strengths	Weaknesses
Large U.S. census-based standardization sample (N = 1,400) with 100 participants in each age band (i.e., nine age bands in the Adult battery and five in the Older Adult battery).	Difficulty recruiting minority participants into stratified educational levels, particularly Asian Americans and participants of other ethnicities.

Broad age range (i.e., 16–90 years) with stratification across five education levels.	Language proficiency was not assessed.
Used cognitive screening, functional assessment, and effort measures to exclude persons with possible mild cognitive impairment or early dementia and persons with questionable effort.	
Conormed with the Wechsler Adult Intelligence Scale–Fourth Edition (WAIS-IV), allowing identification of ability–memory discrepancies while correcting for regression effects.	
New norming methodology overcomes simple-difference, regression, and nonlinear model limitations when comparing scores, yielding a contrast score that takes into account variability in base rates at different ability levels and allows direct comparisons.	

≡ *Rapid Reference 5.5*

Strengths and Weaknesses of WMS-IV Interpretation

Strengths	Weaknesses
Contrast scores enhance interpretation of a particular score by controlling for another related score (e.g., determining if delayed recall is high or low given the examinee's immediate recall).	No repetition of Logical Memory story 2 in the Adult battery prevents assessment of multitrial verbal contextual learning and limits comparisons to WMS-III Logical Memory performance.
New Visual Reproduction scoring is more memory oriented, focusing on recall of key visual features and relationships between design elements.	Limited or no criterion validity for new subtests (i.e., Designs, Spatial Addition, Symbol Span) and associated index scores (i.e., Visual Memory and Visual Working Memory) in clinical populations.

(continued)

Process scaled scores allow more in-depth analyses of cognitive processes that may be masked by the total score (e.g., Designs Content and Spatial scaled scores).	Scores on the Designs subtest may be artificially inflated by guessing or random responding (J. B. Miller, personal communication, May 17, 2010).
Discrepancies between WMS-IV and WAIS-IV index scores can be analyzed using three methods, (i.e., simple-difference, predicted-difference, and contrast scores), which are explained clearly in the WMS-IV Technical and Interpretive Manual.	Demographically adjusted norms are not included in the WMS-IV, although they are included in the ACS.
Availability of comparisons with the General Ability Index (GAI) as a measure of Full Scale IQ in cases where working memory and processing speed are affected by the clinical condition in question.	Memory error scores are not provided in the primary WMS-IV, although they are available in the ACS.

AREAS OF MEMORY NOT MEASURED BY WMS-IV

Although the WMS-IV can be viewed as a comprehensive memory battery, several areas of memory are not assessed by the WMS-IV and are listed in the Don't Forget box. Probably the most clinically relevant area is prospective memory or the ability to remember to execute a future intention. For example, remembering to take medication every morning. Prospective memory accounts for a significant proportion of variance in self-reported independence in instrumental activities of daily living such as medication management (Woods et al., 2008). Another clinically important aspect of memory not fully measured by the WMS-IV is implicit or procedural memory, which has shown some promise as a therapeutic target for prolonging independence in individuals with dementia (Harrison, Son, Kim, & Whall, 2007). The diagnostic and treatment relevance of other types of memory not measured by the WMS-IV, such as olfactory memory, emotional memory, kinesthetic memory, and musical memory, are less established in clinical populations, and few validated measures are available for use. Nevertheless, the need to evaluate one or more of these aspects of memory may be important, depending on the referral question or needs of the examinee or evaluator. In these cases, the WMS-IV may be a useful adjunct given the strength of its construct validity.

DON'T FORGET

Types of Memory Assessed by WMS-IV	Types of Memory *Not* Assessed by WMS-IV
Auditory Memory	Prospective Memory
Visual Memory	Implicit or Procedural Memory
Visual Working Memory	Olfactory Memory
Immediate Memory	Emotional Memory
Delayed Memory	Kinesthetic Memory
Recognition Memory	Musical Memory
Incidental Memory (on BCSE)	

TEST YOURSELF

1. **Which type of memory is *not* measured by the WMS-IV?**

    (a) Auditory Memory

    (b) Visual Memory

    (c) Prospective Memory

    (d) Delayed Memory

2. **Concerns about floor effects in older adults were reduced in all of the following subtest scores EXCEPT:**

    (a) Verbal Paired Associates I

    (b) Logical Memory I

    (c) Visual Reproduction I

    (d) Visual Reproduction Recognition

3. **Administration time of the WMS-IV Older Adult battery is shorter compared to the full WMS-III.**

    True/False

4. **Validation studies of the WMS-IV have been conducted in the following clinical populations:**

    (a) Alzheimer's disease, mild cognitive impairment, and traumatic brain injury

    (b) Parkinson's disease, stroke, and multiple sclerosis

    (c) Alcohol dependence, brain tumor, and preneurosurgical candidates

    (d) Alzheimer's disease, Parkinson's disease, and Huntington's disease

5. A strength of WMS-IV standardization is:

(a) Stratification by two education levels

(b) U.S. census-based stratification with 100 individuals per age band

(c) Age range from 20 to 80 years with 100 individuals per age band

(d) Overrepresentation of ethnic minorities

6. The new Visual Reproduction scoring criteria is:

(a) Longer and more involved

(b) More memory-oriented

(c) Significantly more reliable

(d) More sensitive to visual–spatial deficits in right temporal lobectomy patients

Answers: 1. c, 2. d, 3. True, 4. a, 5. b, 6. b

Chapter Six

USING WMS-IV WITH WAIS-IV

The Wechsler Memory Scale–Fourth Edition (WMS-IV) was codeveloped and conormed with the Wechsler Adult Intelligence Scale–Fourth Edition (WAIS-IV). The codevelopment and norming of the tests provides users with expanded construct coverage and flexibility in using these measures. In addition, the conorming of the tests allows direct comparisons of performance across the batteries. The WAIS-IV measures key cognitive processes that may influence performance on WMS-IV memory measures. Specifically, the WAIS-IV measures overall problem solving ability, verbal and perceptual reasoning skills, auditory working memory, and processing speed. Each of these skills can relate to performance on memory tasks.

The concurrent data collection of WAIS-IV with WMS-IV allowed the mean ability level (i.e., General Ability Index [GAI]) to be set at 100 for every WMS-IV normative age band. This was accomplished through oversampling of WMS-IV cases to allow for case replacement rather than through case weighting as was done for the WMS-III. In addition to obtaining a mean ability level of 100, the WMS-IV normative age bands were also matched to the U.S. census demographics. Therefore, the norms for the WMS-IV are not biased by an unexpectedly high or low ability sample or overrepresentation of any demographic group.

Rapid Reference 6.1

Key Concepts

WMS-IV was both conormed and codeveloped with the WAIS-IV.
The average intellectual ability within each WMS-IV normative age band is 100.

The WAIS-IV scores provide a context in which to better understand an examinee's performance on the WMS-IV. For example, the examiner may need to know if a specific memory score is consistent with an examinee's overall intellectual functioning. Or the examiner may wish to know if the examinee's poor verbal problem-solving abilities account for low scores on verbal memory measures. Comparison of memory and ability scores helps determine if an examinee's memory problems are due to poor memory processes or are better explained by poor cognitive abilities.

Various statistical procedures can be applied to compare performance on WAIS-IV and WMS-IV. Each method has relative strengths and weaknesses in providing an estimation of the degree to which scores from each test diverge. Because it is common for healthy individuals to obtain one or more low scores (Brooks, Iverson, Holdnack, & Feldman, 2008) or to have multiple large discrepancies between subtests or indexes (Binder, Iverson, & Brooks, 2009; Matarazzo & Prifitera, 1989), it is critical to base comparisons between scores obtained on the two batteries on clinical hypotheses and not simply a review of all possible comparisons.

As noted previously, there is no such thing as a "pure" memory test. Memory tests measure multiple constructs, one of which is memory. For example, a story memory test measures receptive and expressive language abilities in addition to memory for auditory information. The impact of language ability on memory performance can be reduced but not eliminated.

> ## CAUTION
>
> It is common for healthy adults to have multiple low scores or to have some large discrepancies between ability and memory scores.
>
> Comparisons between ability and memory should be driven by specific hypotheses about memory functioning.

For an examinee with aphasia, verbal memory functions are likely a secondary deficit to the language deficits. While this is an obvious example, more subtle language influences on performance may be observed in individuals with low educational attainment or in ethnic minorities, such that standard American English may be less well learned than other languages or dialectic variations. Language skills are not the only abilities that influence scores on memory tests. Aptitude for visual–spatial information, working memory functioning, attention, and other cognitive abilities may also facilitate aspects of memory performance.

COMPARING WAIS-IV AND WMS-IV SCORES

WAIS-IV/WMS-IV ability–memory comparisons can be derived using three different methods: simple-difference, predicted-difference, and contrast scaled scores. Only those comparisons related to specific clinical hypotheses are included on the record forms and in this chapter. The Advanced Clinical Solutions (ACS) provides additional comparisons between the WAIS-IV and WMS-IV not found in the WMS-IV. Only the simple-difference method is used in the ACS as the scores are considered supplementary and not primary to the interpretation of the test. The additional comparisons enable the examiner to further clarify ability–memory discrepancies. The comparisons included in the WMS-IV and ACS are listed in Rapid Reference 6.2.

DON'T FORGET

Only simple-difference comparisons are available for WAIS-IV versus WMS-IV Additional Index Score (ACS) comparisons.

≡ *Rapid Reference 6.2*

WAIS-IV/WMS-IV Comparisons

WMS-IV Comparisons	ACS Comparisons
General Ability Index versus Auditory Memory Index	General Ability Index versus Auditory Immediate Index
General Ability Index versus Visual Memory Index	General Ability Index versus Auditory Delayed Index
General Ability Index versus Visual Working Memory Index	General Ability Index versus Auditory Recognition Index
General Ability Index versus Immediate Memory Index	General Ability Index versus Visual Immediate Index
General Ability Index versus Delayed Memory Index	General Ability Index versus Visual Delayed Index
Verbal Comprehension Index versus Auditory Memory Index	General Ability Index versus Visual Recognition Index
Perceptual Reasoning Index versus Visual Memory Index	General Ability Index versus Designs Spatial Index
Perceptual Reasoning Index versus Visual Working Memory Index	General Ability Index versus Designs Content Index
Working Memory Index versus Auditory Memory Index	Verbal Comprehension Index versus Auditory Immediate Index
	Verbal Comprehension Index versus Auditory Delayed Index

(*continued*)

WMS-IV Comparisons	ACS Comparisons
Working Memory Index versus Visual Working Memory Index	Verbal Comprehension Index versus Auditory Recognition Index
	Perceptual Reasoning Index versus Visual Immediate Index
	Perceptual Reasoning Index versus Visual Delayed Index
	Perceptual Reasoning Index versus Visual Recognition Index
	Perceptual Reasoning Index versus Designs Spatial Index
	Perceptual Reasoning Index versus Designs Content Index

Simple-Difference Method

The simple-difference method involves the subtraction of a specific WMS-IV index score from a WAIS-IV index score. This method is easy to compute and to interpret. The score difference is identified as a relative strength or weakness, or no difference is observed between the variables. To determine if the scores are different, the difference between the two scores is compared to the established cutoff required for statistical significance. The statistical significance cutoff accounts for measurement error and differentiates between difference scores that are "real" or due to "chance" occurrence. The use of the cutoff minimizes the probability that a difference between scores is related to the imperfect reliability of the measures and not to the examinee's performance. In addition to statistical significance, the frequency of score differences within the general population needs to be considered. Even though a difference is statistically significant, it may occur frequently in normally developing and aging individuals and thus not be clinically meaningful. In order to interpret a significant score difference as clinically meaningful, the difference should be relatively rare in the sample that links the two measures (i.e., the conormative sample of the WAIS-IV and the WMS-IV). The simple-difference method is relatively easy to use and provides information on the statistical and clinical significance of score differences; however, it does not account for any correlation between variables.

Predicted-Difference Method

Shepard (1980) was one of the first to advocate a predicted-difference method based on the correlation between two variables. In this approach to examining discrepancies between ability and memory, the ability score is used in a regression equation to calculate a predicted memory score. The examiner then compares the examinee's actual memory performance to the predicted memory score. For scores that are correlated, such as auditory memory and verbal comprehension, a high score on one variable is "expected" to be associated with a relatively high score on the second score. For example, if an examinee obtains a Verbal Comprehension Index (VCI) of 120, a high score on Auditory Memory Index (AMI) would be expected. Alternately, if the comparison scores are uncorrelated, then the predicted-difference methodology is not as useful because the predicted scores would simply be the mean of the memory scores. Thus, the predicated-difference method is most useful when scores are moderately to highly correlated.

The difference between the actual and predicted scores is evaluated for statistical significance. In the predicted-difference method, both the reliability of each score and the correlation between the scores being compared are used to determine if the score difference reflects a true difference in performance. Just as in the simple-difference method, the base rate of the difference in the linking sample provides an estimate of how frequently a difference occurs in the general population. For scores with a very high correlation, large score differences occur very rarely; however, for scores with low correlations, large score differences will occur more frequently and thus be less clinically meaningful.

≡ Rapid Reference 6.3

Key Concepts

Simple-difference method is easiest to calculate but does not adjust the base rate of the difference by ability level.

Predicted-difference method applies a regression approach to adjust estimates of difference by ability level but may be affected by heterogeneous variance along the prediction line.

Contrast score method uses a linear or nonlinear regression approach that accounts for changes in variance and skew of distribution along the prediction line.

Contrast Scores Method

The contrast score was developed as a statistical, normative model for evaluating performance, controlling for overlapping variance with other cognitive abilities.

If performance on a memory test is also affected by verbal abilities, the contrast score evaluates the distribution of memory scores controlling for verbal ability level. This score is conceptually analogous to image subtraction in neuroimaging research where the brain activation associated with the task of interest (e.g., facial affect recognition) is subtracted from the total brain activation associated with any cognitive functions that are part of the test except for the construct of interest (e.g., face recognition).

The contrast score methodology applies standard norming procedures to adjust a dependent measure by a control variable. These scores answer specific clinical questions, such as, "Is the Auditory Memory Index score considered above or below average given the examinee's verbal comprehension ability?" The independent variable (i.e., control variable) is grouped into ability bands, much like age groups are used for standard norming, and the age-adjusted scaled or index scores (not raw scores) are normed within the ability band. The resulting contrast score provides the examinee's rank order of performance on the dependent measure compared to individuals of similar ability level on the control variable. For all WAIS-IV/WMS-IV contrast scores, the WAIS-IV index score is the control variable and the WMS-IV index score is the dependent measure. The contrast score has the advantage of identifying the infrequency of a score relative to the ability level of the control variable.

The score obtained from the contrast comparison is a contrast scaled score and is interpreted in the same manner as all scaled scores. For example, a scaled score of 6 indicates that an examinee's performance on the dependent variable is at the ninth percentile relative to examinees with a similar level of ability on the control variable. For example, a 53-year-old examinee with a GAI of 87 and a Delayed Memory Index (DMI) of 76 would obtain a contrast scaled score of 6 (ninth percentile). This indicates borderline delayed memory ability given the examinee's general ability. The contrast scaled score has the same meaning regardless of the score on the independent measure. For example, if the GAI in the example was 120 and the DMI was 92, the contrast scaled score is also 6 (ninth percentile). The interpretation of the two scores is the same—the examinee is at the ninth percentile of delayed memory ability compared to examinees with similar general cognitive ability. In the first case, the simple difference is 9 points while in the second case the difference is 28 points; however, the two scores have the same relative standing within the respective ability band. The main advantage of the contrast scaled score is that it accounts for variations in the frequency of score discrepancies between abilities at different levels and places them on the same metric. As observed in the previous example, the magnitude and frequency of score differences can vary widely across ability levels.

The contrast score operates similarly to the regression based predicted-difference methodology with the exception that it can account for any type of nonlinear association between the variables and for systematic variations in the distribution of the scores of the dependent measure along the ability range of the control variable. When the contrast score and predicted-difference methods return very similar results, the estimated regression line (e.g., linear or nonlinear) is a good fit for the data and the variances are reasonably equal along the prediction line. When these conditions are not met, the regression line may systematically under- or overpredict performance at certain points along the regression line, making the contrast scaled scores more precise.

WAIS-IV/WMS-IV COMPARISONS

The WAIS-IV/WMS-IV comparisons focus on clarifying whether observed memory scores are unexpectedly low or high in comparison to relevant scores from the WAIS-IV. As discussed in Chapter Four, cognitive factors that influence memory performance include general intellectual functioning, verbal skills, perceptual skills, and working memory. Comparisons between the WAIS-IV and WMS-IV indicate the degree to which memory functioning is influenced by these overlapping cognitive skills. Not all possible comparisons are provided in the WMS-IV and ACS manuals, only those related to specific hypotheses about memory functioning. For example, the comparison between VCI and AMI tests the hypothesis that verbal comprehension affects verbal memory.

The GAI is used in the WAIS-IV/WMS-IV comparisons instead of the Full Scale IQ (FSIQ). The GAI was not selected because variability in FSIQ, which is common in clinical samples, makes it an invalid predictor of memory functioning (Ryan, Kreiner, & Burton, 2002) or because GAI is a better indicator of intellectual functioning than FSIQ. The GAI was selected for these comparisons because it "holds" better (i.e., the scores are less susceptible to decline due to injury or insult) in the presence of acute and chronic brain dysfunction, primarily due to the sensitivity of processing speed; therefore, GAI scores are consistently higher than FSIQ in clinical samples (Iverson, Lange, Viljoen, & Brink, 2006; Lange, Chelune, & Tulsky, 2006). In addition, GAI versus memory discrepancies were useful in identifying memory deficits in patients with dementia (Lange & Chelune, 2006) and were consistently larger than FSIQ versus memory differences in a mixed clinical sample (Glass, Bartels, & Ryan, 2009). Moreover, in the WAIS-IV and WMS-IV clinical samples, GAI was consistently higher than FSIQ for the clinical samples by 0.5 to 4.6 points, with the highest differences occurring in the Alzheimer's dementia, Asperger's syndrome, traumatic brain injury, right temporal lobectomy, and autism samples. Only left temporal lobectomy patients had higher FSIQ than GAI scores (Wechsler, 2009). Using GAI instead of FSIQ may not yield substantially larger differences in ability versus memory performance, particularly when the predicted difference method is used; however, on a case-by-case basis the use of GAI rather than FSIQ enables the examiner to better identify a relative memory deficit.

GAI Versus Auditory Memory Indexes

The GAI versus Auditory Memory (AMI), Auditory Immediate (AII), Auditory Delayed (ADI), and Auditory Recognition (ARI) index comparisons enable the examiner to clarify if impairments in general cognitive functioning are related to verbal memory impairments or if verbal memory functioning is a relative strength or weakness given the examinee's current intellectual functioning. Specifically, the GAI versus AMI contrast scaled score evaluates the hypothesis that memory for auditory information is unexpectedly low or high in consideration of general cognitive functioning. AMI is the primary, global measure of the examinee's ability to recall verbal information and the GAI versus AMI contrast scaled score is the primary comparison for WMS-IV auditory measures. High scores indicate auditory memory is better than expected for the examinee's general cognitive ability. Low scores indicate auditory memory is lower than expected given general cognitive ability and suggest auditory memory weaknesses. The supplemental simple-difference comparisons of GAI with AII, ADI, and ARI evaluate the hypotheses that general cognitive functioning is relatively better or worse than immediate, delayed, or recognition memory for auditory information, respectively. GAI correlates moderately with all the auditory indexes: AMI (0.54), AII (0.53), ADI (0.49), and ARI (0.50).

GAI Versus Visual Memory Indexes

The GAI versus Visual Memory (VMI), Visual Immediate (VII), Visual Delayed (VDI), and Visual Recognition (VRI) index comparisons enable the examiner to clarify if impairments in general cognitive functioning are related to visual memory impairments or if visual memory functioning is a relative strength or weakness given the examinee's current intellectual functioning. Specifically, the GAI versus VMI contrast scaled score evaluates the hypothesis that memory for visual information is unexpectedly low or high in consideration of general cognitive functioning. VMI is the primary, global measure of the examinee's ability to recall visual details and spatial locations. The GAI versus VMI contrast scaled score is the primary comparison for WMS-IV visual memory measures. High scores indicate visual memory is better than expected for the examinee's general cognitive ability. Low scores indicate visual memory is lower than expected given general cognitive ability and suggest visual memory weaknesses. The supplemental simple-difference comparisons of GAI with VII, VDI, and VRI evaluate the hypotheses that current general cognitive functioning is relatively better or worse than immediate, delayed, or recognition memory for visual information, respectively. GAI correlates moderately with all the visual indexes: VMI (0.58), VII (0.61), VDI (0.51), and VRI (0.50).

GAI Versus Visual Working Memory Index (VWMI)

The comparison between GAI and VWMI evaluates the hypothesis that VWMI is unexpectedly low or high when considering general cognitive functioning. VWMI is a global measure of an examinee's ability to mentally hold and manipulate visual–spatial information. High scores indicate that visual working memory is better than expected for the examinee's general cognitive ability. Low scores indicate visual working memory is lower than expected given general cognitive ability and suggest visual working memory weaknesses. GAI and VWMI are moderately correlated (0.66).

GAI Versus Immediate Memory Index (IMI)

The comparison between GAI and IMI evaluates the hypothesis that IMI is unexpectedly low or high when considering current general cognitive functioning. IMI is a global measure of an examinee's ability to recall information shortly after having seen or heard it. High scores indicate immediate memory is better than expected for the examinee's general cognitive ability. Low scores indicate immediate memory is lower than expected given general cognitive ability and suggest immediate memory weaknesses. GAI and IMI are moderately correlated (0.66).

GAI Versus Delayed Memory Index (DMI)

The comparison between GAI and DMI evaluates the hypothesis that DMI is unexpectedly low or high when considering current general cognitive functioning. DMI is a global measure of an examinee's ability to recall information after a 20- to 30-minute delay. High scores indicate delayed memory is better than expected for the examinee's general cognitive ability. Low scores indicate that delayed memory is lower than expected given general cognitive ability and suggest delayed memory weaknesses. GAI and DMI are moderately correlated (0.58).

GAI Versus Designs Content and Spatial Indexes

The Designs Content Index (DCI) measures the examinee's ability to recall visual details after immediate exposure to the information and after a 20- to 30-minute delay. The Designs Spatial Index (DSI) measures the examinee's ability to recall spatial locations after immediate exposure and after a 20- to 30-minute delay. The comparison with GAI enables the examiner to evaluate if specific memory problems with visual details or spatial information are related to general deficits in intellectual functioning or if memory for visual details or spatial locations is a relative strength or weakness. High scores indicate memory for spatial locations or visual details is better than expected for the examinee's general cognitive ability. Low scores indicate memory for spatial locations or visual details is lower than expected given general cognitive ability and suggest specific visual memory weaknesses. GAI correlates in the moderate range with DCI (0.44) and in the low range with DSI (0.31).

VCI Versus Auditory Memory Indexes

The VCI versus AMI, AII, ADI, and ARI index comparisons enable the examiner to clarify if deficits in language functioning are related to verbal memory impairments or if verbal memory functioning is a relative strength or weakness given the examinee's verbal skills. Specifically, the VCI versus AMI contrast scaled score evaluates the hypothesis that memory for auditory information is unexpectedly low or high when considering general verbal ability. This is the primary comparison for VCI versus WMS-IV auditory memory measures. High scores indicate auditory memory is better than expected for the examinee's verbal reasoning ability. Low scores indicate auditory memory is lower than expected given verbal reasoning ability and suggest auditory memory weaknesses. The supplemental simple-difference comparisons of VCI with AII, ADI, and ARI evaluate the hypotheses that verbal ability is relatively better or worse than immediate, delayed, or recognition memory for auditory information, respectively. GAI correlates moderately with all the auditory indexes: AMI (0.53), AII (0.52), ADI (0.48), and ARI (0.47).

Perceptual Reasoning Index (PRI) Versus Visual Memory Indexes

The PRI versus VMI, VII, VDI, and VRI index comparisons enable the examiner to clarify if impairments in visual–perceptual skills are related to visual memory impairments or if visual memory functioning is a relative strength or weakness given the examinee's visual–perceptual functioning. Specifically, the PRI versus

VMI contrast scaled score evaluates the hypothesis that memory for visual information is unexpectedly low or high when considering visual–perceptual functioning. This is the primary comparison for PRI versus WMS-IV visual memory measures. High scores indicate visual memory is better than expected for the examinee's perceptual reasoning ability. Low scores indicate visual memory is lower than expected given perceptual reasoning ability and suggest visual memory weaknesses. The supplemental simple-difference comparisons of PRI with VII, VDI, and VRI evaluate the hypotheses that current visual–perceptual functioning is relatively better or worse than immediate, delayed, or recognition memory for visual information, respectively. PRI correlates moderately with all the visual indexes: VMI (0.62), VII (0.64), VDI (0.54), and VRI (0.53).

PRI Versus DCI and DSI

The DCI measures the examinee's ability to recall visual details after immediate exposure to the information and after a 20- to 30-minute delay. The DSI measures the examinee's ability to recall spatial locations after immediate exposure and after a 20- to 30-minute delay. The comparison with PRI enables the examiner to evaluate if specific memory problems with visual details or spatial information are related to processing of visual and spatial information in general or if memory for visual details or spatial locations is a relative strength or weakness given the examinee's general ability to process visual and spatial information. High scores indicate visual memory for spatial locations and visual details is better than expected for the examinee's perceptual reasoning ability. Low scores indicate visual memory for spatial locations and visual details is lower than expected given perceptual reasoning ability and suggest visual memory weaknesses. PRI has a low correlation with DSI (0.35) and a moderate correlation with DCI (0.46).

PRI Versus VWMI

The comparison between PRI and VWMI evaluates whether visual working memory deficits are consistent with general visual–perceptual problems or if visual working memory deficits exist beyond the impact of visual–perceptual impairments. High scores indicate visual working memory is better than expected for the examinee's perceptual reasoning ability. Low scores indicate visual working memory is lower than expected given perceptual reasoning ability and suggest visual working memory weaknesses. The correlation between PRI and VWMI is 0.66, which is in the moderate range.

WMI Versus Auditory Memory Index (AMI)

The comparison between WMI and AMI evaluates whether auditory memory deficits are consistent with low auditory working memory ability or if auditory memory deficits exist beyond the impact of auditory working memory deficits. High scores indicate that auditory memory is better than expected for the examinee's verbal working memory ability. Low scores indicate that auditory memory is lower than expected given verbal working memory ability and suggest auditory memory weaknesses. WMI and AMI are moderately correlated (0.50).

WMI Versus VWMI

The comparison between WMI and VWMI evaluates whether there is a modality-specific (i.e., auditory versus visual) deficit in working memory. High scores indicate visual working memory is better than verbal working memory. Low scores indicate visual working memory is lower than expected and suggests a modality-specific visual weakness in working memory. WMI and VWMI are moderately correlated (0.62).

≡ Rapid Reference 6.4

....

Key Concepts

Use GAI versus memory functioning comparisons when an examinee has general impairments in intellectual functioning.

Use VCI and WMI versus memory functioning comparisons when an examinee has a history of or current language or reading difficulties.

Use PRI versus memory functioning when examinee has a history of or current visual–perceptual processing deficits.

APPLYING WAIS-IV/WMS-IV COMPARISONS

In Chapter Four, the interpretation of the WMS-IV at various levels of investigation was presented for a case of possible dementia. This chapter will further elaborate on that case by applying information obtained from WAIS-IV/WMS-IV comparisons.

Mr. Johnson is a 68-year-old white male with 18 years of education. He is currently retired from his job as director of engineering at a machine manufacturer. Mr. Johnson is a widower and lives alone. His adult children visit him frequently but are concerned about his ability to care for himself. Mr. Johnson denies any significant problems with memory or self-care. He reports that he's "just a little depressed and just doesn't feel like doing much." Mr. Johnson denies having problems caring for himself but his family observed that he has not been paying his bills consistently and that he has lost weight. Mr. Johnson was referred for neurological evaluation due to his family's concerns about his forgetfulness, lack of interest in activities he previously enjoyed (e.g., reading, cooking, watching television, participating in social events), and potential problems in managing his finances and weight. Neurological exam was generally unremarkable but indicated decreased mental status; subsequently, further radiological and neuropsychological studies were recommended. Neuropsychological evaluation was performed and included the WAIS-IV and Adult battery of the WMS-IV.

WAIS-IV Results

The WAIS-IV was administered to identify cognitive strengths and weaknesses and to estimate general cognitive and problem solving ability. The results of the WAIS-IV are presented in Figure 6.1. The WAIS-IV scores indicate that Mr. Johnson's overall intellectual functioning is in the average range (FSIQ = 90). His performance on specific index scores shows variability among the skills measured by FSIQ. Specifically, Mr. Johnson has average verbal comprehension (VCI = 100) and perceptual

Figure 6.1 WAIS-IV Index Scores for Mr. Johnson

Composite Score Summary

Scale	Sum of Scaled Score	Composite Score		Percentile Rank	95% Confidence Interval	Qualitative Description
Verbal Comprehension	30	VCI	100	50	94–106	Average
Perceptual Reasoning	30	PRI	100	50	94–106	Average
Working Memory	15	WMI	86	18	80–94	Low Average
Processing Speed	11	PSI	76	5	70–87	Borderline
Full Scale	86	FSIQ	90	25	86–94	Average
General Ability	60	GAI	100	50	95–105	Average

reasoning (PRI = 100) abilities. However, his auditory working memory is in the low average range (WMI = 86) and his processing speed is in the borderline range (PSI = 76). General problem-solving ability is in the average range, as indicated by a GAI of 100.

The index-level comparisons are presented in Figure 6.2. The WAIS-IV index comparisons show that VCI is significantly higher than both WMI and PSI. Similarly, PRI is significantly higher than both WMI and PSI. WMI and PSI do not significantly differ from each other. FSIQ is significantly lower than GAI. The score profile indicates relative weaknesses in both working memory and processing speed. Subsequently, FSIQ is lower than GAI due to the impact of significantly lower processing speed and working memory. While significant index-level variability in performance was observed, there was no significant variability in subtest performance within cognitive domains.

WAIS-IV/WMS-IV Index Comparisons

The WAIS-IV/WMS-IV index comparisons enable the examiner to determine if memory functioning is consistent with general cognitive functioning or if memory functioning is a significant strength or weakness in the overall cognitive profile.

Figure 6.2 WAIS-IV Index Comparisons for Mr. Johnson

Index Level Discrepancy Comparisons

Comparison	Score 1	Score 2	Difference	Critical Value .05	Significant Difference Y/N	Base Rate Overall Sample
VCI–PRI	100	100	0	8.31	N	
VCI–WMI	100	86	14*	8.82	Y	14.1
VCI–PSI	100	76	24*	10.19	Y	7
PRI–WMI	100	86	14*	9.74	Y	13.7
PRI–PSI	100	76	24*	11	Y	5.8
WMI–PSI	86	76	10	11.38	N	24.5
FSIQ–GAI	90	100	–10*	3.08	Y	2.3

Base rate by overall sample.
Statistical significance (critical value) at the 0.05 level.
*Statistically significant difference.

Figure 6.3 displays Mr. Johnson's WAIS-IV/WMS-IV Index comparisons using the predicted-difference method and contrast scores. In Chapter Four, Mr. Johnson's WMS-IV scores were described in detail. His index scores ranged from extremely low (DMI) to low average (VWMI and IMI).

Based on Mr. Johnson's history and score profile, the WAIS-IV/WMS-IV comparisons were obtained to answer the following questions:

- Are immediate and delayed memory scores consistent with general problem solving ability or are memory deficits present separate from general cognitive functioning? (GAI vs. IMI; GAI vs. DMI)
- Are language difficulties producing deficits in auditory memory or do auditory memory deficits exist independent of language functioning? (VCI vs. AMI)
- Are weaknesses in auditory working memory accounting for low scores in auditory memory? (WMI vs. AMI)
- Are visual–perceptual skills producing difficulties with visual memory or do visual memory deficits exist beyond the effects of visual–perceptual functioning? (PRI vs. VMI)
- Are visual working memory deficits present compared to general problem-solving ability? (GAI vs. VWMI)
- Are visual working memory deficits present compared to auditory working memory ability? (WMI vs. VWMI)
- Are visual working memory deficits due to visual–perceptual functioning or are visual working memory deficits present beyond visual–perceptual functioning? (PRI vs. VWMI)

Applying the predicted-difference discrepancy model with GAI as the predictor, significant differences were observed for GAI versus AMI ($p < 0.01$, base rate = 4%), VMI ($p < 0.01$, base rate = 4%), VWMI ($p < 0.01$, base rate = 10%), IMI ($p < 0.01$, base rate = 4%), and DMI ($p < 0.01$, base rate < 1%). These results indicate that memory functioning is significantly lower than expected considering Mr. Johnson's general problem solving ability. Not only are all the scores significantly lower than GAI, but the differences occur infrequently in the standardization sample. His low memory scores are not likely due to low general ability. Without the comparison of the WMS-IV with WAIS-IV, you would have no statistical evidence to support this conclusion.

The contrast scaled scores provide another indication of memory functioning in the context of other cognitive abilities. Controlling for GAI, Mr. Johnson's AMI, VMI, VWMI, IMI, and DMI are all lower than expected. In this case, the contrast scaled scores and the predicted-difference methods yielded similar

Figure 6.3 WAIS-IV/WMS-IV Comparisons for Mr. Johnson

Ability–Memory Analysis
Ability Score Type: GAI
Ability Score: 100

Predicted Difference Method

Index	Predicted WMS-IV Index Score	Actual WMS-IV Index Score	Difference	Critical Value	Significant Difference Y/N	Base Rate
Auditory Memory	100	77	23*	9.98	Y	4%
Visual Memory	100	78	22*	9.3	Y	4%
Visual Working Memory	100	85	15*	11.6	Y	10%
Immediate Memory	100	80	20*	10.99	Y	4%
Delayed Memory	100	67	33*	11.44	Y	<1%

Statistical significance (critical value) at the 0.01 level.
* Statistically significant difference.

Contrast Scaled Scores

Score	Score 1	Score 2	Contrast Scaled Score
General Ability Index versus Auditory Memory Index	100	77	4
General Ability Index versus Visual Memory Index	100	78	4
General Ability Index versus Visual Working Memory Index	100	85	6
General Ability Index versus Immediate Memory Index	100	80	4
General Ability Index versus Delayed Memory Index	100	67	2
Verbal Comprehension Index versus Auditory Memory Index	100	77	5

(*continued*)

Figure 6.3 (Continued)

Perceptual Reasoning Index versus Visual Memory Index	100	78	3
Perceptual Reasoning Index versus Visual Working Memory Index	100	85	6
Working Memory Index versus Auditory Memory Index	86	77	6
Working Memory Index versus Visual Working Memory Index	86	85	8

results. The examiner's conclusions would be the same from either method. In this case, the base rates of the predicted versus actual discrepancies are also similar to the percentile ranks of the contrast scores.

The additional contrast scaled scores can be used to answer the remaining clinical question, are auditory memory deficits present controlling for verbal reasoning ability? The VCI vs. AMI score of 5 indicates that auditory memory functioning is in the borderline range compared to individuals with similar levels of verbal problem solving ability. Therefore, auditory memory skills are lower than expected given Mr. Johnson's performance on VCI. Auditory working memory is a cognitive weakness in comparison to verbal and perceptual skills. Difficulties with auditory working memory may account for low scores on auditory memory. The WMI versus AMI contrast scaled score of 6 indicates that auditory memory skills are lower than expected when compared to individuals with similar levels of auditory working memory. Similarly, the hypothesis "Are visual memory deficits present beyond what would be expected for his visual–perceptual functioning?" is answered by the PRI versus VMI contrast scaled score. The contrast score of 3 indicates that visual memory functioning is in the extremely low range compared to individuals with similar visual–perceptual abilities. Visual memory deficits are present that are not accounted for by low visual–perceptual reasoning skills.

Several hypotheses were proposed regarding visual working memory relative to skills measured on the WAIS-IV. As noted earlier, visual working memory skills were lower than expected compared to general problem-solving ability with both the predicted-difference and contrast score methodology. The additional hypotheses "Are visual working memory deficits present controlling for visual perceptual abilities?" and "Are visual working memory skills better or worse than auditory working memory abilities?" are addressed with the PRI and WMI versus VWMI contrast scaled scores, respectively. The PRI versus VWMI contrast scaled score of 6 indicates that visual working memory skills are lower than expected in comparison to individuals with similar perceptual reasoning ability. The WMI versus VWMI contrast scaled score of 8 indicates that auditory and visual working memory abilities are not different from one another.

Summary

The results obtained on the WAIS-IV and WMS-IV indicate that Mr. Johnson is currently functioning in the average range for general problem solving ability. His verbal and visual-perceptual skills are average and no differences were observed between these skills. Relative to his verbal and visual–perceptual skills, he shows specific weaknesses in auditory and visual working memory, auditory and visual memory, immediate and delayed memory, and processing speed. This cognitive profile is not consistent with overall impairment of cognitive abilities; rather, there are domains of intact and impaired functioning.

Both visual and auditory memory functioning are unexpectedly low in comparison to Mr. Johnson's working memory abilities in the same modality. Therefore, both working memory and memory impairments are present. Auditory and visual memory scores are similar indicating a general memory deficit affecting both immediate and delayed recall although delayed recall is affected to a greater extent. Processing speed performance was in the borderline range and was consistent with deficits in working memory and memory functioning.

In light of the referral question, the examinee is having difficulty with both working memory and immediate and delayed memory functioning. It is not possible to know with the information available if more global intellectual deficits are present; however, the examiner is able to conclude that memory and processing speed deficits are present and may indicate early signs of dementia.

Using WAIS-IV With ACS Index Comparisons

The ACS provides additional WAIS-IV/WMS-IV comparisons for a more refined assessment of memory difficulties relative to general cognitive, verbal, and visual–perceptual functioning. Only simple-difference comparisons are provided for WAIS-IV and ACS additional index scores. Mr. Johnson's comparisons are presented in Figure 6.4. The GAI versus ACS additional index scores clarify if specific memory problems are present compared to general cognitive functioning. Mr. Johnson's results indicate that GAI is significantly higher than Auditory Immediate ($p < 0.01$, base rate = 14.2%), Auditory Delayed ($p < 0.01$, base rate = 3.4%), Visual Immediate ($p < 0.01$, base rate = 10.3%), Visual Delayed ($p < 0.01$, base rate = 4%), and Visual Recognition ($p < 0.01$, base rate = 0.6%). The ACS comparisons confirm deficits in immediate and delayed memory for

Figure 6.4 WAIS-IV/Additional WMS-IV Indexes Comparison for Mr. Johnson

Ability–Memory Analysis

Ability Score Type: GAI
Ability Score: 100

Simple-Difference Method

Index	WAIS-IV GAI Index Score	WMS-IV Index Score	Difference	Critical Value	Significant Difference Y/N	Base Rate
Auditory Immediate	100	83	17*	12.83	Y	14.2%
Auditory Delayed	100	71	29*	14.99	Y	3.4%
Auditory Recognition	100	91	9	21.55	N	30.3%
Visual Immediate	100	83	17*	13.40	Y	10.3%
Visual Delayed	100	72	28*	12.23	Y	4%
Visual Recognition	100	61	39*	23.53	Y	0.6%
Designs Spatial	100	95	5	18.16	N	38.9%
Designs Content	100	84	16	17.74	N	16.1%

Statistical significance (critical value) at the 0.01 level.
* Statistically significant difference.

Ability–Memory Analysis

Ability Score Type: VCI
Ability Score: 100

Simple-Difference Method

Index	WAIS-IV VCI Index Score	WMS-IV Index Score	Difference	Critical Value	Significant Difference Y/N	Base Rate
Auditory Immediate	100	83	17*	13.41	Y	13.9%

(*continued*)

Figure 6.4 (Continued)

Index	WAIS-IV VCI Index Score	WMS-IV Index Score	Difference	Critical Value	Significant Difference Y/N	Base Rate
Auditory Delayed	100	71	29*	15.49	Y	3.5%
Auditory Recognition	100	91	9	21.90	N	30.4%

Statistical significance (critical value) at the 0.01 level.
*Statistically significant difference.

Ability–Memory Analysis
Ability Score Type: PRI
Ability Score: 100

Simple-Difference Method

Index	WAIS-IV PRI Index Score	WMS-IV Index Score	Difference	Critical Value	Significant Difference Y/N	Base Rate
Visual Immediate	100	83	17*	14.98	Y	9.3%
Visual Delayed	100	72	28*	13.94	Y	4.2%
Visual Recognition	100	61	39*	24.46	Y	0.3%
Designs Spatial	100	95	5	19.35	N	38.2%
Designs Content	100	84	16	18.96	N	15.2%

* Statistically significant difference.

both auditory and visual modalities in comparison to Mr. Johnson's current level of general cognitive functioning.

The additional comparisons identified an additional impairment in visual recognition memory; visual recognition memory was significantly lower than the GAI ($p < 0.01$, base rate = 0.6%). Also, the Auditory Recognition and Designs Content and Spatial scores were not different from general ability, suggesting more variability in memory functioning than was observed in the primary

WMS-IV index scores. Mr. Johnson has domains of preserved memory specifically related to recognition memory for auditory information. He is able to remember verbal information when prompted. On the visual memory measures, he does not have specific problems recalling spatial locations or visual details; however, his overall poor visual memory suggests difficulty recalling combined visual and spatial information.

More specific hypotheses relate to comparing memory measures to WAIS-IV measures within the same modality. In Mr. Johnson's case, since GAI, VCI, and PRI are roughly equal, it is not necessary to evaluate modality specific comparisons as they will yield similar results. In instances where VCI and PRI are different from one another, more detailed comparisons would be useful to further examine the relation between memory scores and the underlying cognitive skill in question (e.g., language or visual–perceptual). In Figure 6.4, the results indicate that VCI is significantly higher than the Auditory Immediate ($p < 0.01$, base rate = 13.9%) and Auditory Delayed ($p < 0.01$, base rate = 3.5%) Indexes but not the Auditory Recognition Index. These results are consistent with those reported for GAI. Compared to PRI, Visual Immediate ($p < 0.01$, base rate = 9.3%), Visual Delayed ($p < 0.01$, base rate = 4.2%), and Visual Recognition Indexes ($p < 0.01$, base rate = 0.3%) were significantly lower than PRI; however, Designs Content and Spatial Indexes were consistent with PRI scores. Visual memory functioning is lower than visual–perceptual skills for recall of visual–spatial information and visual details when considered together but individually spatial recall and memory for details are consistent with visual–perceptual functioning.

Summary

The results obtained on the WAIS-IV and WMS-IV indicate that Mr. Johnson is functioning in the average range for general problem-solving ability. His verbal and visual–perceptual skills are average and no differences were observed between these skills. Relative to his verbal and visual–perceptual skills, he shows specific weaknesses in auditory immediate and delayed recall and visual immediate, delayed, and recognition memory. Mr. Johnson shows domains of intact memory functioning including auditory recognition memory and memory for spatial locations and visual details. This cognitive profile is not consistent with overall impairment of cognitive abilities; rather, there are domains of intact and impaired functioning. His intact ability to recognize auditory information suggests that he may have more retrieval than encoding deficits in that modality. The relative preservation of this function might be used to help him with his daily functioning.

The use of the additional indexes does not significantly change the general impression of memory, working memory, and processing speed deficits. However, it yields additional information which might be useful in treatment planning, or in making diagnostic or placement decisions.

CONCEPTS TO CONSIDER WHEN USING WAIS-IV/WMS-IV COMPARISONS

The conorming of the WAIS-IV and WMS-IV provides users with accurate statistical data for comparing performance across the two batteries. In addition, the conormed batteries allow users to expand the constructs they can apply in clinical assessments. Finally, the conorming of the batteries enabled the WMS-IV normative age bands to have an average intellectual ability; as a result, the norms are not biased in favor of higher or lower ability examinees.

The WAIS-IV/WMS-IV comparisons represent a subset of all possible comparisons. However, the available comparisons represent the most common hypotheses about memory functioning. With the exception of the simple-difference method, the direction of the comparison is to partial common variance out of the memory measure to determine if the remaining variance is unexpectedly high or low. This allows for a more pure measure of memory functioning; however, as noted previously some of the common variance may reflect true memory functions (i.e., good memory results in good problem solving). By partialing out common variance between the measures, real memory variance may be lost, which should be considered when interpreting test results. In some cases, significant memory problems could be producing low scores on both memory and nonmemory measures and applying ability–memory discrepancies may mask the severity of the memory deficit.

The use of comparisons between the WAIS-IV and WMS-IV, particularly the contrast scores, does not replace the standard interpretation of the WMS-IV. When using the contrast scores, it is important to report both the standard age-adjusted scores and those adjusted for ability level. These scores represent very different aspects of memory functioning. The application of ability–memory comparisons does not necessarily improve the sensitivity of the memory measures to clinical disorders (Lange & Chelune, 2006) but helps identify whether memory functions are a manifestation of more general cognitive difficulties or are a specific domain of cognitive impairment.

It is also important to consider that by increasing the number of measures used in an evaluation, the probability of finding a low score increases (Brooks, Iverson, Holdnack, & Feldman, 2008). The presence of one or more low scores does not necessarily indicate a loss of functioning or the presence of a specific disorder.

Individual low scores should always be verified with additional information such as self-report, observations, or other test scores. The application of multivariate base rates (Brooks et al., 2008) can aid in determining the number of low scores that is atypical for an examinee based on education and intellectual functioning. Multivariate base rates will be available for the WAIS-IV and WMS-IV in future publications (Brooks, Holdnack, & Iverson, Submitted).

TEST YOURSELF

1. The WAIS-IV and WMS-IV were codeveloped but not conormed, which is why WAIS-IV was published earlier than WMS-IV.
   True/False

2. The WMS-IV used case replication in order to insure that the average ability level of the normative age bands was 100.
   True/False

3. Both the predicted-difference and contrast score methods control for the examinee's ability level when comparing two scores.
   True/False

4. When comparing scores from two tests, it is important to evaluate both statistical significance and base rate of the difference in the general population.
   True/False

5. When comparing scores from two batteries it is important to evaluate all possible combinations of scores so that you don't miss any cognitive deficits.
   True/False

6. When comparing WAIS-IV and WMS-IV scores you are primarily trying to determine if the examinee's memory impairment has lowered their scores on general ability measures.
   True/False

7. Which of the following comparisons would you apply when trying to determine if an examinee with Intellectual Disability (i.e., Mental Retardation) also has deficits in long-term memory?
   (a) Verbal Comprehension Index versus Auditory Immediate Index
   (b) Perceptual Reasoning Index versus Visual Memory Index
   (c) General Ability Index versus Immediate Memory Index
   (d) General Ability Index versus Delayed Memory Index
   (e) Working Memory Index versus Auditory Memory Index
   (f) Perceptual Reasoning Index versus Visual Recognition Index

8. **Which of the following comparisons would you apply when trying to determine if an examinee with a history of language and reading difficulties also has verbal memory deficits? (Circle all that apply)**

   (a) Verbal Comprehension Index versus Auditory Memory Index

   (b) Perceptual Reasoning Index versus Visual Memory Index

   (c) General Ability Index versus Immediate Memory Index

   (d) General Ability Index versus Delayed Memory Index

   (e) Working Memory Index versus Auditory Memory Index

   (f) Perceptual Reasoning Index versus Visual Recognition Index

9. **Which of the following comparisons would you apply when trying to determine if an examinee with impaired visual–perceptual abilities also has a weakness in recognizing information in visual memory?**

   (a) Verbal Comprehension Index versus Auditory Immediate Index

   (b) Perceptual Reasoning Index versus Visual Memory Index

   (c) General Ability Index versus Immediate Memory Index

   (d) General Ability Index versus Delayed Memory Index

   (e) Working Memory Index versus Auditory Memory Index

   (f) Perceptual Reasoning Index versus Visual Recognition Index

10. **Which of the following statements are TRUE when considering WAIS-IV and WMS-IV comparison scores? (Circle all that apply)**

    (a) Ability versus memory scores eliminate the need to report age-adjusted scaled scores.

    (b) It is rare for a healthy person to have a lower memory score than IQ score.

    (c) The frequency of a large discrepancy between IQ and memory can vary depending upon ability level.

    (d) Individuals with a low IQ should not be given memory tests.

    (e) Regression-based comparisons inform the examiner about the patient's memory functioning more than their intellectual functioning.

Answers: 1. False, 2. False, 3. True, 4. True, 5. False, 6. False, 7. d, 8. a and e, 9. f, 10. c and e

Chapter Seven

CLINICAL APPLICATIONS OF THE WMS-IV

Much data on the performance of clinical populations has accumulated since the original Wechsler Memory Scale (WMS) was introduced in 1945. Although the content of the WMS has changed over time, assessment of verbal and visual memory and immediate and delayed memory has remained constant since Russell's addition of a delayed recall component to Logical Memory (LM) and Visual Reproduction (VR) in 1975. The WMS-IV continues this tradition and although research using the WMS-IV in clinical populations is limited at this time, patterns of memory performance can be extrapolated based on prior versions. This chapter reviews the data on WMS performance in commonly assessed populations. It is divided into three sections: individuals with conditions known to affect memory functioning, older adults, and individuals who may be malingering or exhibiting poor effort. In each section, findings from the WMS-IV will be reviewed, when available, as well as findings from the WMS-III. Each review provides information about the typical or expected pattern of WMS-IV performance for that population and serves as a guide until additional research using the WMS-IV becomes available. In all instances, additional studies employing larger and more diverse samples are needed to verify that initial WMS-IV findings can be applied more widely. Due to the focus of this book on memory and the WMS-IV, typical or expected patterns of performance in other cognitive domains will not be discussed in detail, although relevant findings in the context of memory performance patterns may be presented. Readers interested in detailed information about other cognitive domains may wish to consult *Neuropsychological Assessment* (Lezak, Howieson, & Loring, 2004) and/or *A Compendium of Neuropsychological Tests* (Strauss, Sherman, & Spreen, 2006). A detailed review of findings on prior versions of the WMS can be found in *Essentials of WMS-III Assessment* (Lichtenberger, Kaufman, & Lai, 2002).

DON'T FORGET

All the studies reported are based on group mean differences. Scores for specific individuals may vary widely, and multiple scores should be used to obtain evidence of effort or clinical diagnosis.

CAUTION

....

Validation studies of the WMS-IV in relevant clinical samples are limited or non-existent at present.

CONDITIONS KNOWN TO AFFECT MEMORY FUNCTIONING

Traumatic Brain Injury (TBI)

Traumatic brain injury (TBI) is a leading cause of morbidity and disability around the world (cf. Atkinson & Merry, 2001; Centers for Disease Control and Prevention, 2010; Engberg & Teasdale, 2001) and a common reason for neuropsychological evaluation. TBI is typically classified as mild, moderate, or severe depending on injury characteristics such as duration of disturbance in consciousness (if any), the ability to form new, continuous memories (i.e., posttraumatic amnesia), and findings on neuroimaging. Cognitive deficits resulting from TBI, including memory impairment, can vary depending on injury severity, cause of injury (e.g., motor vehicle accident, fall), location and type of neuropathology (e.g., diffuse axonal injury, subdural hematoma affecting the right parietal lobe), and length of time since injury. In general, cognitive deficits are more severe in the acute stages of injury and in the presence of greater neuropathology. Details concerning classification systems, characteristics of injury severity levels, and course and prognosis of TBI are beyond the scope of this chapter. The interested reader is referred to Lezak et al. (2004) for a succinct yet thorough review.

WMS-III Findings

Comparisons of WMS-III performances among 23 mild TBI, 22 moderate-to-severe TBI, and 45 age- and education-matched controls were performed by Fisher, Ledbetter, Cohen, Marmor, and Tulsky (2000). The mild TBI participants were assessed 3 months to 4 years postinjury, and none showed evidence of cognitive or psychiatric exaggeration. Scores for two comparison groups, a moderate-to-severe TBI group assessed 6–18 months postinjury and 45 control participants, were obtained from the WMS-III clinical and normative samples, respectively. In general, controls obtained the highest average WMS-III index scores, followed by the mild TBI group, and then the moderate-to-severe TBI group. Average index scores for mild TBI participants ranged from 87.1 on the Auditory Immediate Index (AII) to 95.6 on the Working Memory Index (WMI), and average index scores for moderate-to-severe TBI participants ranged from 74.3 on the

Visual Delayed Index (VDI) to 93.6 on the Auditory Recognition Index (ARI). Both TBI groups obtained significantly lower index scores than controls on AII and Auditory Delayed Index (ADI), Visual Immediate Index (VII) and VDI, and General Memory Index (GMI). Moderate-to-severe TBI participants also scored significantly lower than controls on the WMI. Mild and moderate-to-severe TBI groups differed significantly from each other on VII and VDI only. There were no significant differences among the three groups on the ARI. Of note, the mild TBI group did not differ significantly from controls on any of the Wechsler Adult Intelligence Scale–Third Edition (WAIS-III) index scores, while the moderate-to-severe TBI group obtained significantly lower scores than both controls and mild TBI participants on all indexes, with the largest difference observed on the Processing Speed Index (PSI; average index score = 73.4). Together, these findings suggest that processing speed and visual memory may be particularly sensitive to moderate-to-severe TBI and may be effective in discriminating between mild and moderate-to-severe TBI.

A similar pattern of findings was reported by Langeluddecke and Lucas (2005) in a sample of 180 TBI litigants with injuries ranging in severity from complicated mild to extremely severe. Only TBI participants more than 6 months postinjury (range 6–140 months) who exhibited adequate effort during testing were included in the study and the group was divided into complicated mild-to-moderate (N = 44), severe (N = 86), and extremely severe (N = 50) groups based on Glasgow Coma Scale scores, duration of posttraumatic amnesia, and/or neuroradiological findings. The three TBI groups were compared to an age-matched control group (N = 50) from the WMS-III normative sample. Results revealed a "dose response" relationship between TBI severity and memory performance, with greater injury severity associated with lower scores on all WMS-III indexes, with the exception of ARI. The complicated mild-to-moderate TBI group obtained average index scores ranging from 88.1 on VDI to 104.2 on WMI, the severe TBI group obtained average index scores ranging from 85.3 on VII to 96.0 on WMI, and the extremely severe TBI group obtained average index scores ranging from 74.9 on VII to 91.8 on WMI. Note that WMI was the highest score for each group. Effect sizes were moderate to large, with VII and VDI showing the largest effect sizes ($d = -1.19$ and -1.08, respectively) and WMI showing the smallest ($d = -0.41$). There were no differences between immediate and delayed performances across auditory and visual modalities leading these researchers to conclude that there is no benefit to administration of delayed recall measures in TBI.

Axelrod, Fichtenberg, Liethen, Czarnota, and Stucky (2001) came to a similar conclusion in their study of 38 mild-to-moderate TBI participants who were, on average, 5 months postinjury. Their participants obtained AII and ADI mean scores of 87.5 and 86.0, respectively, and VII and VDI mean scores of 85.2 and 86.4, respectively. As with the above studies, WMI was the highest (95.7) and PSI was the lowest (79.6) of the WAIS-III Index scores.

In summary, studies of WMS-III performances in TBI samples putting forth adequate effort indicate a "dose response" relationship, with more severely injured individuals performing more poorly across immediate and delayed and auditory and visual indexes. Visual indexes are more sensitive than auditory indexes, in general, and performances on immediate and delayed indexes usually do not differ significantly. The PSI is the most sensitive of the WAIS-III indexes and may be useful in identifying more severe injuries as mild TBI participants perform similarly to controls on this index.

WMS-IV Findings

A sample of 32 individuals with moderate-to-severe TBIs was tested as part of clinical validation of the WMS-IV (see *WMS-IV Technical and Interpretative Manual*, p. 116–118). All were tested within 6 months to 3 years post-injury. Average index scores ranged from 77.8 on the Delayed Memory Index (DMI) to 85.5 on the Visual Working Memory Index (VWMI), and all were significantly lower (i.e., over 1 standard deviation) than those obtained by a matched control group from the WMS-IV standardization sample (see Table 7.1). Similar to findings with the WMS-III, the Auditory Memory Index (AMI) versus Visual Memory Index (VMI) contrast scaled score indicated that visual memory was significantly lower than auditory memory, while the Immediate Memory Index (IMI) versus DMI contrast scaled score was not significantly different, suggesting that when time

Table 7.1 WMS-IV Index Score Means (Standard Deviations) in Traumatic Brain Injury (TBI)

WMS-IV Index	TBI	Matched Controls	Effect Size
Auditory Memory	80.0 (18.5)	101.0 (14.0)	1.25
Visual Memory	82.5 (20.1)	101.2 (14.2)	1.07
Visual Working Memory	85.5 (17.4)	104.6 (12.4)	1.26
Immediate Memory	80.7 (19.0)	102.2 (15.4)	1.24
Delayed Memory	77.8 (21.1)	100.4 (14.9)	1.24

Standardization data from the Wechsler Memory Scale–Fourth Edition (WMS-IV).

and/or the stamina of the individual is limited and there is no question about diagnosis, administration of the delayed memory measures may be omitted without losing too much information. With regard to WAIS-IV performances in this TBI group, the highest average index score was 95.7 on Verbal Comprehension Index (VCI), and the lowest was 80.4 on Processing Speed Index (PSI), which is generally consistent with TBI findings on the WAIS-III of relatively spared verbal abilities and reduced processing speed.

All the additional index scores available on the Advanced Clinical Solutions (ACS) were significantly lower in the moderate-to-severe TBI sample compared to matched controls. The profile of scores within modality (i.e., visual, auditory) was immediate > delayed < delayed recognition memory. Recognition indexes were approximately 7 points higher, on average, in the TBI sample compared to the delayed index in the same modality. On error scores, the TBI sample did not show high rates of intrusions for VR or Verbal Paired Associates (VPA) I; however, significantly more extra-list intrusions were noted on VPA II. The TBI sample had significantly lower scores on VPA I and II Easy and Hard Items, and VPA Recall A and D. Finally, the TBI group was slower than controls in drawing designs on VR I but not on VR II and more frequently required cuing on LM II.

The WMS-IV also was administered to a group of 41 individuals with complicated mild to severe TBI enrolled in the Southeast Michigan Traumatic Brain Injury System (Miller, Holcomb, Bashem, & Rapport, 2010). The sample was primarily men (90%) of mostly African American descent (76%). Average time since injury was 9 years. Average estimated premorbid IQ was in the low average range (i.e., 86.2). All participants demonstrated valid effort on both stand alone and embedded effort measures. Average WMS-IV index scores ranged from 78.7 on IMI to 85.5 on VMI. There were no significant differences between the complicated mild-to-moderate and severe TBI groups on any index score. At the subtest level, the lowest scores, as a group, were obtained on LM I and II (i.e., scaled scores of 6.3 and 6.2, respectively). With regard to differences between complicated mild-to-moderate and severe groups at the subtest level, the severe TBI group performed significantly worse on DE II and VR II. These findings add support to the majority of prior research suggesting that visual memory may be more affected as level of severity of TBI increases.

These individuals also were administered the California Verbal Learning Test–Second Edition (CVLT-II) to investigate comparability of memory indexes if this substitution was employed (Miller et al., 2010). No differences in the AMI or DMI were found, but there was a significant difference on the IMI score. With the substitution, IMI scores were 5–7 points different in 25% of the sample and more than 8 points different in 13% of the sample. Differences ranged from

–9 to 12 points and resulted in meaningful (≥ 1 standard deviation) differences in 14% of the sample, with immediate memory abilities overestimated in 7% of the sample and underestimated in 7%. At the subtest level, VPA I and II differed by more than 1 standard deviation in 41% and 51% of the sample, respectively. On VPA I, the substitution resulted in significantly higher scaled scores (i.e., ≥ 1 standard deviation) in 30% of cases and significantly lower scaled scores in 11% of cases. On VPA II, this substitution resulted in significantly higher scores in 29% of cases and significantly lower scores in 22% of cases.

These data suggest that examiners utilizing the substitution method can feel confident that AMI and DMI scores are not altered significantly while IMI scores should be interpreted more cautiously and VPA subtest equivalent scores interpreted even more cautiously as they tend to overestimate list-learning abilities of individuals with TBI.

≡ *Rapid Reference 7.1*

Expected Performance on WMS-IV in Individuals With TBI

Performance over 1 standard deviation below matched controls in moderate-to-severe TBI

Relatively equivalent auditory and visual memory performance

Relatively equivalent immediate and delayed memory performance

Relatively spared verbal IQ abilities

A "dose response" relationship, with greater severity of TBI associated with poorer performance

Reduced processing speed and visual memory in moderate-to-severe vs. mild TBI

Epilepsy

Epilepsy or seizure disorder is one of the most common chronic neurological disorders (Hirtz et al., 2007; World Health Organization, 2006) and has many underlying causes. Seizures are classified as either partial (focal) or generalized, depending on whether there is a localized area of onset in the brain or large regions of both hemispheres appear to be involved. The most common type of focal epilepsy is temporal lobe epilepsy (TLE). The degree to which cognitive functions are affected in epilepsy depends on multiple factors, including type of epilepsy, age at onset, frequency of seizures, and presence and cause of underlying neuropathology. Treatment of epilepsy, whether with medications or surgery, can also affect cognitive functioning.

WMS-III *Findings*

Most research examining the WMS-III in epilepsy samples evaluated presurgical patients with TLE. TLE patients as a whole perform significantly worse than the normative sample, typically obtaining scores 1 or more standard deviations below the normative mean on all indexes except ARI and WMI, which often are two-thirds to 1 standard deviation lower (Baker, Austin, & Downes, 2003; Harvey et al., 2008; Wilde et al., 2001). In general, individuals with left temporal lobe (LTL) involvement obtain lower scores than individuals with right temporal lobe (RTL) involvement, although the difference is not usually significant, with a few exceptions.

The utility of the WMS-III in determining lateralized dysfunction in individuals with TLE has been investigated by multiple researchers. Wilde and colleagues (2001) were among the first to study the WMS-III in TLE in 102 preoperative TLE patients across three epilepsy centers. The sample was comprised of 55 LTL and 47 RTL patients. The LTL and RTL groups differed significantly on the ADI, with RTL patients obtaining significantly higher mean scores than LTL patients (i.e., 90.91 and 82.64, respectively). No other between group difference was found on WMS-III index scores. Within groups, RTL patients exhibited significant discrepancies between both AII and VII (89.81 and 81.87, respectively) and ADI and VDI (90.91 and 81.63, respectively). The expected difference in the opposite direction was not seen in the LTL group, however, with no significant difference observed between AII and VII (84.29 and 85.91, respectively) or between ADI and VDI (82.64 and 85.43, respectively). Further analyses indicated that although significantly better than chance, classification accuracy rates into LTL and RTL groups were too low to be clinically useful. For the WMS-III, classification accuracy was better for RTL than LTL patients.

The previous findings of RTL patients obtaining significantly lower visual than auditory memory scores while LTL patients obtained similar scores on both auditory and visual memory measures were replicated by subsequent researchers (Baker et al., 2003; Lacritz et al., 2004). The lack of significant differences in LTL suggests the auditory memory indexes of the WMS-III are not sensitive to left hemisphere dysfunction, but this explanation is refuted by LTL patients obtaining significantly lower scores on auditory memory measures than RTL patients and controls (Wilde et al., 2001). An alternate explanation suggests the visual memory measures of the WMS-III can be encoded and/or processed verbally and when LTL patients rely on verbal abilities, performance suffers. There is evidence to support this latter explanation as the Family Pictures subtest of the WMS-III was most strongly related to auditory–verbal abilities in TLE patients (Chapin, Busch, Naugle, & Najm, 2009; Dulay et al., 2002) and thus may be better conceptualized as a general measure of memory rather than as a measure of visual memory specifically. Additionally, Bell, Hermann, and Seidenberg (2004) found left hippocampal volumes of TLE patients correlated significantly with both auditory and visual memory indexes of the WMS-III while right hippocampal volumes correlated significantly with scores on visual memory indexes only. Moreover, a factor analytic study of 254 TLE patients failed to support separate auditory and visual memory factors on the WMS-III (Wilde et al., 2003).

Several researchers have examined the utility of immediate versus delayed memory indexes given evidence that hippocampal volumes were moderately and significantly associated with retention in individuals with TLE (Griffith, Pyzalski, Seidenberg, & Hermann, 2004). Results consistently failed to support significant differences between immediate and delayed memory indexes on the WMS-III in TLE samples (Bell et al., 2004; Wilde et al., 2001), as well as in a general clinical sample (Burton et al., 2003). Moreover, Bell (2006) demonstrated that forgetting on the LM subtest did not differ significantly between TLE patients and healthy controls even after an interval of 2 weeks.

Fewer studies have examined WMS-III performances pre- and postsurgery or just post anterior temporal lobectomy (ATL). Doss, Chelune, and Naugle (2004) investigated the utility of the WMS-III to detect modality specific memory deficits in 56 LTL and 51 RTL patients who had undergone ATL an average of 7–9 months earlier. Results showed the expected pattern of LTL patients performing significantly worse on the auditory versus visual memory indexes, and RTL patients performing significantly worse on the visual versus auditory memory indexes. In both cases, immediate memory measures showed more pronounced difficulties than delayed memory measures. Among individual subtests, VPA I showed the largest effect size in differentiating LTL from RTL patients ($d = 1.17$) with LTL performance worse than RTL. Among visual subtests, Faces I showed the largest effect size ($d = -0.68$) with RTL performance worse than LTL.

Chiaravalloti, Tulsky, and Glosser (2004) studied performance on WMS-III Faces of 10 LTL and 16 RTL patients pre- and post-ATL to determine the ability of Faces to detect lateralized dysfunction. Overall, LTL patients showed improvement from immediate to delayed trials while RTL patients performed similarly across trials. RTL patients performed significantly worse than LTL patients on Faces I both pre- and postsurgery, but Faces II performances in the RTL group were not significantly lower either time. When the revised scoring procedure to correct for response bias (Holdnack & Delis, 2004) was employed, LTL patients showed an overall improvement from preoperative to postoperative performances while RTL patients did not. Moreover, RTL patients performed significantly worse than LTL patients on Faces I and II presurgically but not postsurgically on either test. These researchers concluded that Faces was useful in detecting right temporal lobe dysfunction using either the original or revised scoring procedures, with Faces I more sensitive to dysfunction than Faces II, overall.

In a much larger sample, Harvey and colleagues (2008) examined WMS-III performances 3 months pre-surgery and 6 months post-ATL in 80 LTL and 81 RTL patients. Results revealed that in LTL patients, higher presurgical memory performances were associated with greater decline postsurgery in all areas of memory, while in RTL patients higher presurgical performances were associated with greater losses postsurgery in visual memory only. These findings were consistent with those using prior versions of the WMS, with the exception of the visual memory findings in the RTL patients, which had not been reported previously.

WMS-IV Findings

To investigate whether changes in the WMS-IV are sensitive to lateralized dysfunction, eight LTL and 15 RTL patients were administered the WMS-IV post-ATL as part of the initial clinical validation process (see *WMS-IV Technical and Interpretative Manual*, p. 119–123). Average index scores of the LTL sample ranged from 77.9 for AMI to 98.3 for VMI, while average index scores for the RTL sample ranged from 86.0 for VMI to 94.8 for AMI (see Table 7.2). These findings show the expected pattern of poorer performance on auditory compared to visual memory measures in LTL patients, with the opposite pattern found in RTL patients. In the LTL group, the only significant difference from a matched control group on index scores was found on VWMI ($d = 1.47$), but the 22-point difference between the LTL and control groups on AMI represented a large effect size ($d = 1.18$) and likely did not reach statistical significance due to the small sample size (N = 8). At the subtest level, LM I and II showed the largest effect sizes ($d = 1.56$ and 1.59, respectively) and were the only subtests to reach statistical significance. In the RTL group, VMI, VWMI, and IMI were significantly lower than a matched control group from the standardization sample, while AMI and DMI were not. The largest effect size at the index level was for VMI ($d = 1.49$), and the largest effect size at the subtest level was for DE I ($d = 1.66$).

Table 7.2 WMS-IV Index Score Means (Standard Deviations) in Temporal Lobe Epilepsy

WMS-IV Index	LTL	Matched Controls	Effect Size	RTL	Matched Controls	Effect Size
Auditory Memory	77.9 (20.1)	99.5 (16.4)	1.18	94.8 (17.7)	104.1 (13.6)	0.59
Visual Memory	98.3 (15.8)	103.5 (17.3)	0.32	86.0 (13.0)	107.2 (15.4)	1.49
Visual Working Memory	87.8 (10.9)	102.6 (9.3)	1.47	92.1 (13.2)	106.7 (14.1)	1.07
Immediate Memory	87.8 (13.6)	100.3 (14.9)	0.88	88.4 (14.6)	106.7 (14.2)	1.27
Delayed Memory	85.8 (20.4)	102.5 (17.1)	0.89	90.5 (16.0)	106.0 (16.2)	0.96

Note: LTL = left temporal lobe; RTL = right temporal lobe

Standardization data from the Wechsler Memory Scale–Fourth Edition (WMS-IV).

The LTL group's performance on the ACS additional indexes was consistent with overall WMS-IV performance. The highest index score was VII (100.0) and the lowest was AII (77.8). The error and process scores were generally unremarkable likely due to the small sample size; few measures were significantly different between the LTL sample and the matched controls. The LTL group had lower scores on VPA I Hard Items than on VPA I Easy Items. The RTL group showed a much larger effect size for VII ($d = 1.60$) than on any other measure with the next largest effect size being the Designs Spatial Index (DSI; $d = 1.46$). On the process and error scores, the RTL group was significantly slower than controls in drawing VR I and VR II.

Thus, in spite of small sample sizes, initial findings suggest the WMS-IV has the ability to detect lateralized dysfunction in TLE patients who have undergone ATL. Additional studies are needed to (a) replicate these findings in larger ATL samples, (b) establish similar utility in differentiating presurgical LTL and RTL groups, which tend to be more difficult to lateralize due, in part, to varying levels of unilateral (as well as bilateral) pathology, (c) predict postsurgical changes in memory functioning, and (d) identify specific measures that best differentiate RTL and LTL.

≡ *Rapid Reference 7.2*

Expected Performance on WMS-IV in Individuals With TLE

Auditory memory performance worse than visual memory performance in LTL patients with auditory memory usually more than 1 standard deviation below matched controls

Visual memory performance worse than auditory memory performance in RTL patients with visual memory usually more than 1 standard deviation below matched controls

Performance on the remaining indexes typically 0.5–1.0 standard deviation below matched controls

Relatively equivalent immediate and delayed memory performance

Higher presurgical memory performance associated with greater declines in memory performance post-ATL

Schizophrenia

Although schizophrenia is traditionally classified as a psychiatric disorder characterized by hallucinations, delusions, and disorganized thinking, it is increasingly being conceptualized as a neurodevelopmental disorder with cognitive dysfunction as a central feature that is present prior to the onset of frank psychotic symptoms (Bowie & Harvey, 2005). Attention, working memory, executive functioning, and verbal memory are thought to be the most affected cognitive areas in schizophrenia, with a decline in IQ, as well as global cognitive functioning, noted after the onset of psychosis. Additional declines associated with the aging process, particularly in executive abilities and complex information processing, have been documented (Granholm, Morris, Asarnow, Chock, & Jeste, 2000; Fucetola et al., 2000).

WMS-III Findings

Memory performances of 107 outpatients with an initial diagnosis of schizophrenia spectrum disorder were examined shortly after stabilization of the first psychotic episode (Townsend, Malla, & Norman, 2001). Index scores ranged from 87.8 on VDI to 93.6 on WMI. There was little difference between auditory and visual memory indexes or between immediate and delayed memory indexes. Subtest analyses revealed that the poorest performances were on LM I and II and

Family Pictures I and II, all around 0.75 standard deviations below the normative mean. All other subtest scores were in the average range. WAIS-III Index scores were all in the average range, except for PSI, which was in the low average range (i.e., 85.5); however, scores were still significantly lower (i.e., 4–8 points) in comparison to estimated premorbid IQ. No differences among subtypes of schizophrenia or demographic (e.g., age) or clinical variables (e.g., degree of positive or negative psychotic symptoms) were found. The relatively intact cognitive functioning observed in this group, compared to prior studies of individuals with schizophrenia, may be due to treatment with relatively low-dose atypical antipsychotic medications, outpatient clinical status, and timing of assessment within 3 months of initial diagnosis.

Hawkins (1999) analyzed data from individuals with schizophrenia administered the WMS-III during the standardization process. These individuals obtained index scores generally 1 standard deviation below the normative mean, and, like the first episode patients, there were no differences between auditory and visual or between immediate and delayed memory indexes. A closer analysis of the data revealed that individuals with schizophrenia performed very poorly when asked to repeat material presented just one time (i.e., single-trial learning) but demonstrated a higher learning slope than the normative sample with repeated presentations. Taken together, these findings indicate that memory is generally lower than IQ in individuals with schizophrenia, with particular difficulties in one-trial learning, but there is no significant forgetting of successfully encoded material after a delay. Unlike reports in the prior literature of poorer verbal memory than visual memory, no modality effects were found on the WMS-III. This may be due to the strong auditory–verbal processing component of Family Pictures noted above.

WMS-IV Findings

Fifty-five individuals with schizophrenia were administered the WMS-IV to obtain initial validity data (see *WMS-IV Technical and Interpretative Manual*, pp. 124–126). The average age of this sample was 41 years, 80% were men, and 69% were African American. Index scores ranged from 77.1 on IMI to 81.8 on VMI and all scores were significantly lower than a matched control group (see Table 7.3). The largest effect size was found for IMI ($d = 1.09$), but large effect sizes were apparent on all indexes. LM I and II showed the largest effect sizes at the subtest level ($d = 1.09$ and 1.19, respectively), followed closely by Symbol Span (SSP; $d = 1.01$). These findings are consistent with the broader literature suggesting that some aspects of verbal memory and working memory may be more negatively affected in schizophrenia.

Table 7.3 WMS-IV Index Score Means (Standard Deviations) in Schizophrenia

WMS-IV Index	Schizophrenia	Matched Controls	Effect Size
Auditory Memory	78.8 (15.7)	92.8 (14.8)	0.92
Visual Memory	81.8 (15.3)	94.6 (14.7)	0.86
Visual Working Memory	79.5 (13.1)	93.7 (16.1)	0.96
Immediate Memory	77.1 (13.9)	92.7 (15.1)	1.07
Delayed Memory	78.4 (15.6)	93.6 (16.8)	0.94

Standardization data from the Wechsler Memory Scale–Fourth Edition (WMS-IV). Copyright © 2009 NCS Pearson, Inc. Used with permission. All rights reserved.

 *Rapid Reference 7.3*

Expected Performance on WMS-IV in Individuals With Schizophrenia

Performance about 1 standard deviation below matched controls unless examined shortly after stabilization of the first episode

Relatively equivalent auditory and visual memory performance, with the exception of lower Logical Memory performance

Relatively equivalent immediate and delayed memory performance

Current IQ generally lower than estimated premorbid IQ

OLDER ADULTS

"Normal" Aging and Memory Decline

The importance of differentiating "normal" from pathological memory decline in older adults has risen to the forefront of research and clinical practice due to increased longevity and the associated incidence of cognitive impairment. The population of individuals aged 85 and older is anticipated to reach 10 million in the United States by 2030 (National Institute on Aging, www.nia.nih.gov). In older adults, the prevalence of mild cognitive impairment (MCI), a risk factor for dementia, is approximately 15% (Roberts et al., 2008), and the prevalence of dementia is approximately 14%, increasing with age from 5% in persons aged 71–79 to 37% in persons over age 90 years (Plassman et al., 2007). Thus, it is imperative to have a solid understanding of memory performances of individuals aging normally, as well as those with pathological memory decline, in order to accurately assess memory functioning in older adults.

WMS-III Findings

Interactions between age and performance on the LM and VR subtests have been examined in the WMS-III standardization sample (Haaland, Price, & Larue, 2003; Price, Said, & Haaland, 2004). Findings revealed significant deterioration in immediate and delayed recall raw scores on both LM and VR with age. For LM I, performance was similar for ages 16–49, dropped a little at age 50, held steady through age 79, and then dropped a little again at age 80. The pattern of decline on VR I was slightly different; performance held steady from ages 16–39 and then dropped slightly at each subsequent decade (Haaland et al., 2003). After adjusting for immediate recall, performance on both LM II and VR II was similar across ages 16–49, dropped at age 50, and then held steady (Price et al., 2004). Absolute differences between immediate and delayed recall varied little across the age ranges, however, suggesting that rate of forgetting may be a useful indicator of pathological memory decline, which is consistent with findings on previous versions of these measures (Cullum, Butters, Tröster, & Salmon, 1990). Overall, the findings suggest that the bulk of age-related memory decline is associated with reduced initial encoding and retrieval. Subsequent analyses confirmed that after adjusting for immediate recall, delayed recall and recognition showed minimal age-related declines, suggesting that the ability to store new information remains relatively intact in normally aging adults (Price et al., 2004).

In addition to understanding patterns of age-related changes on memory measures, examiners need to consider the base rate of low scores on any given measure to guard against misclassifying a normally aging adult as one with pathological memory decline. In the WMS-III standardization sample, almost two-thirds of adults aged 55 and older (N = 550) had one or more scores at or below the sixteenth percentile (i.e., 1 standard deviation below the normative mean) and one-fourth had scores at or below the fifth percentile (Brooks et al., 2008). Moreover, scores 2 or more standard deviations below the normative mean were found in 13% of the sample. Individuals with low average intellectual abilities were more likely to have low memory scores, with over 40% obtaining one or more scores at or below the fifth percentile compared to approximately 20% of those with high average intellectual abilities. Education level also was associated with prevalence of low scores with approximately 35–40% of individuals with less than a high school education obtaining one or more scores at or below the fifth percentile. The effects of intellectual functioning and education level were similar across immediate and delayed memory measures. It was uncommon (< 10%), however, for older adults to have three or more scores at or below the fifth percentile. Tables presenting base rates of low memory scores on the WMS-III using age-corrected and demographic-corrected approaches can be found in Brooks and colleagues (2008).

In an effort to assist in clinical decision making when multiple memory measures are administered, Brooks and others (2009) utilized the WMS-III normative sample to develop and cross validate psychometrically derived criteria for "possible" and "probable" memory impairment in older adults. Possible memory impairment was defined as the number of low scores below a specific cutoff in 20% or fewer of the standardization sample (i.e., healthy older adults). Probable memory impairment was defined as the number of low scores below a certain cutoff in 10% or fewer of healthy older adults. When considering the entire sample, *possible* memory impairment is suggested when an examinee obtains four or more index scores at or below the sixteenth percentile or two or more index scores at or below the fifth percentile. *Probable* memory impairment is suggested when an examinee obtains six index scores at or below the sixteenth percentile or three or more index scores at or below the fifth percentile. The criteria were stratified by Full Scale IQ, estimated premorbid intelligence, and level of formal education to allow greater precision. For example, individuals with less than a high school education are likely to have possible memory impairment if two index scores are less than or equal to the fifth percentile and probable memory impairment if three or more scores are at this cutoff. Initial validation of the criteria in 32 individuals with possible or probable Alzheimer's disease indicated good classification accuracy. While these criteria appear promising, additional clinical validation is warranted.

WMS-IV Findings

Aside from a study using the WAIS-IV/WMS-IV normative sample to determine the breadth of age-related influences on cognitive functioning (Salthouse, 2009), the utility of the WMS-IV in healthy older samples has yet to be examined. It is reassuring, though, that previous findings of age-related decrements in speed and some aspects of memory, along with positive effects of age on general verbal abilities were replicated in the WMS-IV normative sample. With regard to memory, after controlling for immediate recall, only LM II showed unique age-related variance, suggesting that healthy adults do not show age-related decline on delayed recall subtests of VPA, Designs (DE), and VR. These findings are consistent with those of Price and colleagues (2004) using the WMS-III and again indicate that rate of forgetting may be helpful in differentiating normal from pathological memory decline. Findings of base rates of low memory performance and the proposed criteria for possible and probable memory impairment (Brooks et al., 2008, 2009) require replication in the WMS-IV, but there is no conceptual reason to believe that findings in the WMS-IV normative sample would vary significantly.

Mild Cognitive Impairment (MCI) and Alzheimer's Disease (AD)

MCI is a term used to refer to individuals who are not demented but who demonstrate decline beyond that expected for age in at least one cognitive domain (e.g., memory, verbal reasoning). Multiple criteria for defining MCI have been proposed, but the criteria developed by a working group convened at an international conference on MCI (Winoblad et al., 2004) have been adopted by the National Institute on Aging (NIA)-sponsored Alzheimer's Disease Centers (ADCs) and Alzheimer's Disease Neuroimaging Initiative (ADNI) and thus have been widely researched. These criteria allow for classification of cognitive phenotypes, including amnestic and nonamnestic MCI and single and multiple domain MCI. Identification of MCI has proven useful in predicting progression to dementia, with approximately 10–15% of MCI cases seen in memory disorders or Alzheimer's disease clinics converting each year and approximately 6–10% of more broadly referred cases converting annually (Petersen et al., 2009).

Alzheimer's disease (AD) is the most common cause of dementia in the United States, with over 5 million Americans affected (NIA, 2008). Symptoms typically manifest after age 60; age is the largest risk factor. Early diagnosis is crucial so appropriate treatments can be initiated sooner and individuals can participate fully in planning for the future. Multiple studies have shown that episodic memory impairment is often one of the first cognitive functions affected, and a promising recent study found that a combination of five factors, verbal memory performance, collateral report of functional impairment, ability to identify smells, and hippocampal and entorhinal cortex volumes on magnetic resonance imaging (MRI), strongly and accurately predicted conversion from MCI to AD over 3 years (Devanand et al., 2008).

WMS-III Findings

Longitudinal studies have been critical in identifying older adults at risk for MCI and dementia. Howieson and colleagues (2008) showed that lack of a practice effect on LM I and II (i.e., no score improvement on retest), as well as category fluency and Block Design, were predictive of which healthy older adults developed MCI over the course of 7 years. Lack of change on LM was the earliest sign of cognitive impairment. Among a variety of verbal memory tests, the combination of LM Recognition and CVLT-II long delayed free recall best predicted conversion from MCI to AD over 4 years with a classification accuracy of 87.5% (Rabin et al., 2009).

Performance of persons with MCI is significantly worse than matched controls on LM and VR I, II and Percent Retention (Griffith et al., 2006). Performances on immediate and delayed recall measures were more than 1 standard deviation lower than matched controls while percent retention ranged from two-thirds to 1 standard deviation below matched controls due to larger variances in the MCI sample. A discriminant function analysis found that baseline VR Percent Retention, along with performance on the Initiation/Perseveration subscale of the Dementia Rating Scale (Mattis, 1988), correctly classified 85.7% of the MCI sample as either AD converters or MCI nonconverters in 2 years. A cutoff of 26% or less on VR Percent Retention yielded sensitivity of 76.9% and specificity of 91.2%, although the false-positive rate was approximately 33%. The addition of a cut score of 36 reduced the false positive rate to 23.1% (Griffith et al., 2006). Likewise, performance of individuals with probable AD is significantly lower than matched controls on IMI, DMI, and GMI, with the AD group performing more than 2 standard deviations below the control group (Lange & Chelune, 2006). Of note, consideration of discrepancies between actual or estimated premorbid IQ and memory indexes did not add useful interpretative information beyond consideration of memory index scores alone in AD, probably due to the severity of memory impairment in this sample (Lange & Chelune, 2006, 2007).

WMS-IV Findings

A group of 50 MCI and 48 probable AD patients were administered the WMS-IV during standardization (see *WMS-IV Technical and Interpretative Manual*, pp. 108–113). In the MCI group, 14 were administered the Adult battery and 36 were administered the Older Adult battery. All 48 probable AD patients were administered the Older Adult battery. Similar to results with the WMS-III, MCI patients generally obtained index scores 1 standard deviation below matched controls and probable AD patients generally obtained index scores >2 standard deviations below matched controls. Index scores for MCI patients ranged from 87.5 on DMI to 91.6 on VWMI. Index scores of probable AD patients ranged from 63.6 on DMI to 71.7 on IMI. It is noteworthy that the lowest index score for both groups was DMI. Index scores by group are presented in Table 7.4. At the subtest level, the largest effect sizes in the MCI group were found on LM I and II ($d = 1.06$ and 1.17, respectively), while in the probable AD group, the largest effect sizes were found on VPA Word Recall and LM II ($d = 2.55$ and 2.20). These findings suggest that verbal memory measures are the most sensitive in

Table 7.4 WMS-IV Index Score Means (Standard Deviations) in Mild Cognitive Impairment (MCI) and Probable Alzheimer's Disease (AD)

WMS-IV Index	MCI	Matched Controls	Effect Size	AD	Matched Controls	Effect Size
Auditory Memory	89.9 (14.9)	105.6 (14.8)	1.05	68.5 (18.2)	107.1 (16.2)	2.24
Visual Memory	89.3 (15.3)	102.1 (13.5)	0.89	69.7 (18.8)	102.5 (13.6)	2.00
Visual Working Memory	91.6 (13.5)	107.2 (12.0)	1.22	NA	NA	NA
Immediate Memory	90.8 (13.7)	105.8 (13.8)	1.09	71.7 (17.4)	107.4 (15.6)	2.16
Delayed Memory	87.5 (17.2)	103.5 (14.2)	1.01	63.6 (18.7)	104.6 (15.5)	2.39

Note: NA = Not administered

Standardization data from the Wechsler Memory Scale–Fourth Edition (WMS-IV).

MCI and probable AD groups, which is consistent with the broader literature in this area. In addition, in the probable AD group, significant forgetting over a delay was evident as indicated by the IMI versus DMI contrast scaled score mean of 4.

WAIS-IV findings in the MCI group, while significantly lower than the matched control group, were in the average range and not clinically noteworthy with the exception of an almost 9-point difference between AMI (i.e., 89.9) and VCI (i.e., 98.5), which resulted in a large effect size ($d = 1.13$). WAIS-IV index scores of the probable AD group were well below those of the matched control group but were not as significantly affected as WMS-IV indices, again indicating that IQ scores do not add useful interpretive information beyond memory scores in probable AD.

The ACS additional indexes confirm general differences in memory functioning between AD and MCI patients and controls. For the MCI group, the lowest scores were observed on the VRI (86.2) and Designs Content Index (DCI; 86.0). The AD patients had high rates of extra-list but not intra-list intrusions on VPA I and II; the MCI group had fewer intrusions than matched controls. Neither group had a high rate of errors on VR I and II. Finally, on LM II, both the AD and MCI samples had more frequent need for prompting on delayed recall compared to matched controls.

CAUTION

Neither individual criteria for determining MCI nor subtypes of MCI were recorded in the MCI clinical sample in the *WMS-IV Technical and Interpretive Manual.*

≡ *Rapid Reference 7.4*

Expected Performance on WMS-IV in Individuals With MCI and Probable AD

Memory indexes generally 1 standard deviation below matched controls for MCI and 2 or more standard deviations below matched controls for probable AD

Relatively equivalent auditory and visual memory performance

Delayed memory index scores typically lower than the other index scores

Logical Memory II is one of the most sensitive indicators of impairment

Auditory Memory Index significantly lower than Verbal Comprehension in MCI patients in the context of relatively spared intellectual functioning

Memory performances significantly lower than intellectual functioning in probable AD patients in spite of declines in overall IQ

MALINGERING/EFFORT

Assessment of malingering or poor effort has become standard practice in neuropsychological evaluations. Both stand-alone effort measures and validity indicators embedded within neuropsychological tests are recommended to detect inadequate effort (Heilbronner et al., 2009). As failure on one effort measure is not uncommon in clinical samples with true cognitive impairment, it is recommended that more than one effort measure be used within a battery of tests with failure on two or more effort indicators suggestive of inadequate effort (Victor, Boone, Serpa, Buehler, & Ziegler, 2009). As one of the most commonly administered memory measures, development of embedded effort measures in the WMS has been a topic of ongoing research.

WMS-III *Findings*

Shortly after publication of the WMS-III, Killgore and DellaPietra (2000) developed the Rarely Missed Index (RMI) as an embedded measure of effort. The

RMI is derived from performance on the LM Recognition subtest and showed an initial classification accuracy rate of 98% in discriminating individuals with true neurological impairment from simulators. Subsequent evaluation of the utility of the RMI revealed high specificity (i.e., ≥75%) in mixed clinical (Miller, Ryan, Carruthers, & Cluff, 2004), mildly to moderately intellectually deficient (Marshall & Happe, 2007), dementia (Dean, Victor, Boone, Philpott, & Hess, 2009), undergraduate simulator (Swihart, Harris, & Hatcher, 2008), and litigant samples (Lange, Sullivan, & Anderson, 2005; Langeluddecke, 2004). However, only moderate positive and negative predictive power was found in litigants, with an unacceptably high number of suspected and borderline exaggerators undetected (Lange et al., 2005). Axelrod, Barlow, and Paradee (2010) were additionally concerned about the effect of random responding and found that only one of the original six rarely missed items was endorsed above chance levels in a mixed clinical sample naïve to the items on LM Recognition, and four different items met this criterion. More than half of this sample was incorrectly classified as giving poor effort by the RMI.

Lange, Iverson, Sullivan, and Anderson (2006) applied the concept of unusual discrepancies between attention/concentration and memory abilities, which had shown promise as an embedded measure of effort within the WMS-R (Mittenberg, Azrin, Millsaps, & Heilbronner, 1993), to the WMS-III by examining the utility of unusual discrepancies between working memory and memory abilities in a sample of 145 litigants. The sample was divided into two groups based on performance on effort measures. Nineteen litigants were suspected of providing poor effort, and 126 were considered to have provided adequate effort. Between group differences were found on AII, ADI, IMI, GMI, and WMI with the adequate effort group outperforming the poor effort group by over 1 standard deviation on all indexes except WMI, which neared 1 standard deviation. Average index scores for the suspected poor effort group ranged from 65.1 on IMI to 83.8 on WMI. Average index scores of the adequate effort group ranged from 90.5 on IMI to 96.9 on WMI. All four memory–working memory discrepancy scores were significantly different as well, with the poor effort group averaging discrepancies ranging from −10.7 to −19.4 compared to the adequate effort group whose average discrepancy scores ranged from −2.2 to −6.4. Subsequent analyses revealed that while all four discrepancy scores demonstrated high specificity (range = 0.95–0.98) and negative predictive power (range = 0.86–0.88), they all showed unacceptably low sensitivity rates (range = 0.00–0.11) and positive predictive power (range = 0.00–0.40). Thus, use of memory–working memory discrepancy scores as indicators of effort was not recommended.

Another approach for detecting exaggerated memory deficits involves comparing performances of individuals strongly suspected of malingering to individuals not suspected of malingering. Langeluddecke and Lucas (2003) used this method in a study of TBI litigants, 75 with mild TBI and 50 with severe TBI. In the mild TBI group, 25 met criteria for probable malingered neurocognitive dysfunction (Slick, Sherman, & Iverson, 1999), and the remaining 50 did not. The severe TBI group also demonstrated adequate effort and was included as a reference group for determining cutoff scores for malingered performance. The probable malingering group performed significantly worse than the nonmalingering mild TBI group on all WMS-III indices and subtests. Average index scores for the probable malingering group ranged from 60.2 on IMI to 82.2 on WMI. Average index scores for nonmalingerers ranged from 88.6 on VII to 100.0 on WMI. The magnitude of the difference between average index scores was even larger, overall, than that observed in the Lange, Iverson, et al. (2006) study, with the probable malingering group obtaining index scores 30 points lower than the nonmalingering mild TBI group on most indexes. Probable malingerers obtained scores at least 13 points below the severe TBI group on all indexes. Recognition memory measures showed the largest between group differences and were the only indicators with acceptable classification accuracy. Of note, memory–working memory discrepancy scores and IQ–memory discrepancy scores were not useful as indicators of malingering.

In a second study utilizing a group of 93 TBI and 115 general clinical patients, Ord, Greve, and Bianchini (2008) examined the utility of WMS-III index scores to correctly differentiate probable malingerers from nonmalingerers. Of the 93 individuals with TBI, 34 were classified as mild TBI nonmalingerers, 28 were classified as moderate-to-severe TBI nonmalingerers, and 31 were classified as mild TBI probable or definite malingerers according to the criteria proposed by Slick and colleagues (1999). None of the general clinical sample had any apparent incentive to perform poorly. The probable malingering mild TBI group performed significantly worse than the nonmalingering mild TBI group on all indexes and significantly worse than the moderate-to-severe TBI group on all indexes except VII and VDI. Average index scores for the probable malingering mild TBI group ranged from 75.87 on GMI to 81.48 on ADI. In contrast, average index scores for the nonmalingering mild TBI group ranged from 97.94 on ARI to 102.79 on WMI, and average index scores for the moderate-to-severe TBI group ranged from 85.57 on VDI to 101.04 on WMI. The mixed clinical group consistently performed in between the moderate-to-severe TBI group and the probable malingering mild TBI group, although differences did not reach statistical significance. After exploring a number of potential methods for discriminating malingerers from nonmalingerers in this sample, Ord and colleagues recommended using an aggregate approach of summing the total number of index scores at or below 75. Using a cutoff of three or more index scores below 75, 58% of mild TBI malingerers were correctly identified without misclassifying any individual from the nonmalingering mild TBI group. A cutoff of two or more index scores at this level correctly identified 65% of mild TBI malingerers but falsely classified 9% of mild TBI nonmalingerers. It was emphasized that classification of mild TBI was the focus of this study; thus, findings may not generalize to more severe TBI groups or other clinical disorders.

WMS-IV Findings

Performances of 19 individuals with TBI failing two or more effort measures were compared to those of 41 TBI patients exhibiting good effort and 41 simulators coached to feign cognitive impairment (Miller, 2010). The suspect effort TBI group obtained average scores significantly lower than the adequate effort TBI group on all indexes and on every subtest except DE I and II. Average index scores of the suspect effort TBI group ranged from 63.1 on IMI to 73.8 on VMI. Average index scores of the adequate effort TBI group ranged from 78.7 on IMI to 85.5 on VMI. Simulators performed significantly worse than the adequate effort TBI group on all indexes except AMI and on all subtests except VPA I and II and DE I. In contrast, no significant differences between simulator and suspect effort TBI groups were found on any index score except AMI. When analyzing subtest performances, this difference was explained by significantly better performances by simulators on VPA I and II. No other subtest scores were significantly different between suspect effort TBI and simulator groups. In summary, these findings are consistent with prior studies indicating global suppressed effort on WMS measures by individuals with TBI and suspected poor effort. The utility of recognition measures and aggregate scoring methods that have been shown to be promising with the WMS-III is worthy of study using the WMS-IV.

The ACS provides initial cutoff scores for identifying poor effort using recognition trials from the WMS-IV, a Word Choice subtest, and Reliable Digit Span from the WAIS-IV. Cut scores based on a large clinical sample are provided at various base rates in the clinical population. Further, the base rates for obtaining multiple scores below clinical cutoffs are provided. The ACS effort assessment can enhance the assessment of memory functioning in cases where secondary gain or suspected insufficient effort may be present. Data for simulators, a no-stimulus condition, and various clinical and demographic groups are presented in the *ACS Technical and Clinical Manual.*

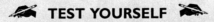 **TEST YOURSELF**

1. **In moderate-to-severe TBI, index scores are likely to be less than 1 standard deviation below matched controls.**

   True/False

2. **Individuals with RTL who underwent ATL showed the largest effect sizes compared to matched controls on the following measures:**

   (a) Visual Memory Index and Logical Memory I

   (b) Auditory Memory Index and Visual Reproduction I

   (c) Auditory Memory Index and Verbal Paired Associates I

   (d) Visual Memory Index and Designs I

3. **Memory performances of individuals assessed shortly after their first episode of psychosis:**

   (a) May be less impaired than those of individuals with more chronic disease

   (b) May be more impaired than those of individuals with more chronic disease

   (c) Are characterized by significant forgetting

   (d) Show steady improvements

4. **A useful indicator for differentiating "normal" from pathological memory decline is:**

   (a) Immediate recall

   (b) Delayed recall

   (c) Rate of forgetting

   (d) Processing speed

5. **MCI and probable AD patients typically perform most poorly on the:**

   (a) Auditory Memory Index

   (b) Visual Memory Index

   (c) Immediate Memory Index

   (d) Delayed Memory Index

6. **Recognition memory measures may be useful indicators of poor effort on the WMS-IV.**

   True/False

Answers: 1. False, 2. d, 3. a, 4. c, 5. d, 6. True

Chapter Eight

ILLUSTRATIVE CASE REPORTS

This chapter provides illustrative examples of the use of WMS-IV as part of a comprehensive neuropsychological evaluation. A detailed case study is presented in Chapters Four and Six with detailed interpretation guidelines. The three case examples included in this chapter were chosen because they cover a range of clinical diagnoses, ages, and referral questions. The first case involves a 47-year-old man with a history of multiple traumatic brain injuries (TBIs) and alcohol dependence. The second case involves a 63-year-old woman with a history of mild cognitive impairment (MCI) and depression who was referred for reevaluation. The final case is a 76-year-old man who was a practicing physician referred for evaluation of memory complaints. In the first two cases, the full Wechsler Memory Scale–Fourth Edition (WMS-IV) was administered. The third case provides an example of how to utilize selected subtests of the WMS-IV rather than the full battery. For each case, information on current complaints and relevant medical and psychosocial histories is provided, along with behavioral observations, test interpretation, summary and impressions, and recommendations. Note that identifying information has been changed to protect confidentiality. Also note that the following report style is not intended to represent the best way to present WMS-IV findings; it is only one possible way to report findings.

> # CAUTION
>
> The reporting style selected for these case examples is not intended to represent the best or only way to communicate WMS-IV findings.

CASE EXAMPLE 1: TBI AND ALCOHOL DEPENDENCE

Reason for Referral

Mr. Harold P. Smith is a 47-year-old, right-handed, divorced, non-Hispanic white male with 9 years of formal education. He was referred for evaluation by his primary care physician to assist in diagnosis of possible dementia due to Mr. Smith's history of multiple TBIs and heavy substance use.

Current Complaints and Relevant History

Mr. Smith was unsure about the purpose of the evaluation. When asked if he had been experiencing memory problems, he related that he noticed memory problems about a year ago. He was prescribed Seroquel shortly after, and he felt that his memory had been getting better. He attributed his improving memory to improved sleep due to "regular use" of Seroquel. He acknowledged that he still sometimes "confuses" appointments and forgets how to do things. He also finds it harder to "get things out," particularly names. He stated that his temper was a bigger problem than his memory. He explained that his temper snaps quickly, as if someone flipped a switch. He said it does not happen often, mostly when he feels overwhelmed, and his anger goes away just as quickly. He began having this problem about 1–2 years ago, and it has been getting worse. With regard to his current mood, he reported feeling "okay," although he admitted to feeling depressed most of his life, manifested primarily as a lack of motivation.

Relevant Medical History

Mr. Smith denied any significant medical problems and reported taking no medications other than Seroquel for sleep. He denied a history of stroke or seizure but reported three TBIs with loss of consciousness (LOC). The first occurred in 1981 while he was in the Navy; he was assaulted upon leaving a bar. He was unsure how long he was unconscious and was "saved" by a taxi driver who chased off his assailants. He was taken to the hospital, and he recalls being "in and out" of consciousness on his way there. The next thing he remembers was being back on the boat the next day. The second TBI occurred in 1989 when he again was assaulted during a fight and he was "knocked out cold." Alcohol use was a factor in the assault. He woke up the next morning with a broken jaw. His third TBI occurred in 2003 when Mr. Smith was assaulted and robbed. He recalls only waking up for a few seconds when an ambulance arrived and took him to the hospital. He remained in the hospital overnight, with a fracture in his neck and a broken nose. He was released the following day, as surgical intervention was not recommended for the type of neck fracture he experienced. Mr. Smith denied any changes in cognition following any of these incidents, but he reports headaches 3–4 times a month, which were not present prior to his most recent TBI. His headaches seem to occur most often when he is fatigued and can be treated adequately with over-the-counter medication. A magnetic resonance imaging (MRI) scan of the brain on 12/9/09 was normal.

Mr. Smith reported two hospitalizations for depression, once in 2006 and once in 2009, and has received outpatient mental health services for substance abuse on two occasions, once in the 1980s and currently. He related using alcohol daily from age 16 until his admission to an outpatient substance use program approximately 4 months ago. He also reported daily recreational drug use, mostly marijuana, cocaine, and heroin, beginning at age 17 until age 40. He admitted using cocaine and heroin less frequently after age 40 and quitting altogether a little over a year ago. He has smoked a pack of cigarettes a day since age 16. Family history is noteworthy for substance dependence in his mother.

Psychosocial History

Mr. Smith was born and raised in Colorado, and English is his only language. He is the product of an uncomplicated pregnancy and birth and met all early developmental milestones within the expected time frames. He denied learning difficulties in school or ever receiving special education services. Although he said he has always been "drifty," meaning his mind often wanders, school was easy for him when he applied himself, and he liked to read. He reported his grades were "up and down" due to absenteeism after he began using substances, and he dropped out of school in the 10th grade. He obtained his GED while in the Navy and achieved a score at the 92nd percentile without studying. He joined the Navy at age 17, serving 2 years. He admitted he got in trouble for substance use while in the Navy. After leaving the Navy, he continued using substances and was incarcerated twice for substance-related reasons. His first incarceration was for roughly 1 year around 21 years of age; his second was for 3 years in the late 1980s. He said he was able to stay out of legal trouble after that because he began trying to "work" the Alcoholics Anonymous program. His primary work over the years has been in unskilled labor positions, and he reports having trouble on the job due to lack of interest and motivation. He was married once for 10 years but has been divorced for approximately 5 years. He has no children.

Behavioral Observations and Mental Status Exam

Mr. Smith presented as a friendly, open man with limited psychological insight. He arrived early for his appointment and was casually dressed with adequate grooming and hygiene. He was thin and appeared his stated age. His gait was unremarkable and no psychomotor abnormalities were apparent. Hearing and vision were adequate for evaluation purposes. He was alert, attentive, and oriented × 4. He made good eye contact and demonstrated appropriate interpersonal skills, although occasionally he was impulsive. Mr. Smith did not appear to have difficulty understanding conversational speech or task instructions; his speech was fluent and goal directed. There was no overt evidence of formal thought disorder, delusions, or hallucinations. Memory for remote and recent events was grossly intact. Judgment was fair. Mood was euthymic with congruent affect. Mr. Smith was pleasant and cooperative throughout the evaluation and appeared to put forth good effort on all tasks. He worked steadily, with occasional cigarette breaks and no lunch break (per his request), until the evaluation was completed. The following results are considered an accurate representation of his current neuropsychological functioning.

Tests Administered

- Test of Memory Malingering
- Wechsler Adult Intelligence Scale–Fourth Edition (WAIS-IV)
- Wechsler Test of Adult Reading (WTAR)
- WMS-IV
- California Verbal Learning Test–Second Edition (CVLT-II)
- Rey Complex Figure (RCF)
- Boston Naming Test
- Controlled Oral Word Association Test (FAS)
- Animal Naming
- Trail Making Test (TMT)
- Stroop Color and Word Test
- Pillbox Test
- Minnesota Multiphasic Personality Inventory–Second Edition (MMPI-2)

Primary index and subtest scores for the WAIS-IV and WMS-IV are presented in Tables 8.1 and 8.2, respectively.

Test Interpretation

Effort

Results of stand-alone and embedded effort measures indicated that Mr. Smith was putting forth adequate effort for valid test interpretation.

Table 8.1 Summary of Mr. Smith's WAIS-IV Scores

Composite Score Summary

Scale	Sum of Scaled Scores	Composite Score	Percentile Rank	95% Confidence Interval	Qualitative Description
Verbal Comprehension	34	VCI 107	68	101–112	Average
Perceptual Reasoning	26	PRI 92	30	86–99	Average
Working Memory	19	WMI 97	42	90–104	Average
Processing Speed	12	PSI 79	8	73–89	Borderline
Full Scale	91	FSIQ 94	34	90–98	Average
General Ability	60	GAI 100	50	95–105	Average

Verbal Comprehension Subtests Summary

Subtest	Raw Score	Scaled Score	Percentile Rank	Reference Group Scaled Score	SEM
Similarities	28	11	63	11	1.04
Vocabulary	50	13	84	15	0.73
Information	14	10	50	11	0.73

Perceptual Reasoning Subtests Summary

Subtest	Raw Score	Scaled Score	Percentile Rank	Reference Group Scaled Score	SEM
Block Design	29	8	25	7	0.95
Matrix Reasoning	17	10	50	9	0.95
Visual Puzzles	11	8	25	7	0.85

(*continued*)

Table 8.1 (Continued)

Working Memory Subtests Summary

Subtest	Raw Score	Scaled Score	Percentile Rank	Reference Group Scaled Score	*SEM*
Digit Span	26	9	37	9	0.73
Arithmetic	14	10	50	10	0.9

Processing Speed Subtests Summary

Subtest	Raw Score	Scaled Score	Percentile Rank	Reference Group Scaled Score	*SEM*
Symbol Search	16	4	2	4	1.56
Coding	56	8	25	7	1.2
(Cancellation)	28	7	16	6	1.62

Table 8.2 Summary of Mr. Smith's WMS-IV Scores

Index Score Summary

Index	Sum of Scaled Scores	Index Score		Percentile Rank	95% Confidence Interval	Qualitative Description
Auditory Memory	31	AMI	87	19	81–94	Low Average
Visual Memory	19	VMI	67	1	63–74	Extremely Low
Visual Working Memory	16	VWMI	88	21	82–96	Low Average
Immediate Memory	23	IMI	72	3	67–80	Borderline
Delayed Memory	27	DMI	78	7	73–86	Borderline

Table 8.2 (Continued)

Primary Subtest Scaled Score Summary

Subtest	Domain	Raw Score	Scaled Score	Percentile Rank
Logical Memory I	AM	20	8	25
Logical Memory II	AM	14	7	16
Verbal Paired Associates I	AM	24	8	25
Verbal Paired Associates II	AM	8	8	25
Designs I	VM	36	2	0.4
Designs II	VM	37	6	9
Visual Reproduction I	VM	26	5	5
Visual Reproduction II	VM	10	6	9
Spatial Addition	VWM	8	7	16
Symbol Span	VWM	21	9	37

WMS-IV Index Level Contrast Scaled Scores

Score	Score 1	Score 2	Contrast Scaled Score
Auditory Memory Index versus Visual Memory Index	87	67	4
Visual Working Memory Index versus Visual Memory Index	88	67	4
Immediate Memory Index versus Delayed Memory Index	72	78	11

Current and Estimated Premorbid Intelligence

Results of intellectual testing revealed overall functioning at the low end of the average range, with significantly stronger verbal compared to nonverbal abilities (see Table 8.1). Of note, his Processing Speed Index (PSI) score was in the borderline range and was significantly lower than his Verbal Comprehension Index (VCI) score at the high end of the average range. This 28-point difference is also rare in the standardization sample with a base rate of 4.2%. The pattern of WAIS-

IV findings is consistent with prior research using the WAIS-III showing that the PSI score is the most sensitive of the WAIS indexes to neurological insult and may be useful in identifying more severe injuries (see Chapter Seven). An estimate of premorbid intellectual functioning based on reading skill was at the high end of the average range (i.e., WTAR standard score = 109) and consistent with his overall verbal abilities.

Language
Mr. Smith performed in the average range on confrontational naming and verbal fluency tasks, including both phonemic and semantic.

Visuoconstruction
Mr. Smith exhibited intact abilities to copy simple geometric designs (i.e., WMS-IV Visual Reproduction [VR] Copy raw score = 43; >75%). In contrast, he performed in the impaired range on the RCF copy trial (i.e., raw score = 28; <1%), primarily due to a disorganized approach to the task.

Attention/Executive Functioning
Mr. Smith demonstrated generally intact basic attention and processing speed, performing in the average range on Part A of the TMT and the Stroop Color and Word subtests. He also performed in the average range on measures of mental set-shifting and inhibition, TMT Part B, and Stroop Color–Word, respectively. However, he exhibited poor attention to detail, resulting in an impaired performance when asked to place a week's worth of pills appropriately in a pillbox.

Learning and Memory
On the WMS-IV, Mr. Smith obtained index scores in the low average range on the Auditory Memory Index (AMI) and Visual Working Memory Index (VWMI), in the borderline range on the Immediate Memory Index (IMI) and Delayed Memory Index (DMI), and in the extremely low range on the Visual Memory Index (VMI; see Table 8.2). When considering his average WAIS-IV General Ability Index (GAI) score (SS = 100), Mr. Smith's VMI, IMI, and DMI scores are significantly below expectations (i.e., GAI versus VMI contrast scaled score = 1, GAI versus IMI contrast scaled score = 2, and GAI versus DMI contrast scaled score = 5).

At the subtest level, he exhibited the most difficulty on Designs (DE) I, performing below the first percentile. He performed at the fifth percentile on VR I, and his VR Copy versus Immediate Recall contrast scaled score was 4, indicating that his poor immediate memory performance was not due to impaired ability to copy the figures. In contrast, he obtained scaled scores in the average range on Logical Memory (LM) I and Verbal Paired Associates (VPA) I. Thus, his borderline IMI score can be attributed to his impaired performances on the visual memory tasks. When considering process scores for DE I, DE Content was at the first percentile, while DE Spatial was at the fifth percentile. The subtest-level contrast scaled score for DE I Spatial versus Content was 3, indicating that immediate memory for details was below expectations when considering his immediate memory for spatial locations.

With regard to delayed memory at the subtest level, Mr. Smith exhibited delayed recall for visual material in the low average range, obtaining a scaled score of 6 on both DE II and VR II, and low average to average delayed recall for verbal material, obtaining scaled scores of 7 on LM II and 8 on VPA II. His process scaled scores for DE II Content and Spatial were both 7, indicating that his ability to retain visual information over a delay was in the low average range and relatively better than his ability to encode the information, and his DE II Spatial versus Content contrast scaled score was 8, indicating average ability to recall content after a delay when accounting for ability to recall spatial locations. Mr. Smith's performances on all recognition tasks were in the average range.

The pattern of subtest findings is made more evident by examining Mr. Smith's index-level contrast scaled scores (see Table 8.2). His AMI versus VMI contrast scaled score was 4, confirming that for someone with Mr. Smith's low average auditory memory abilities, his visual memory performances were well below expectations. He also obtained a contrast scaled score of 4 for VWMI versus VMI, indicating that for someone with Mr. Smith's low average visual working memory abilities, his visual memory again was well below expectations. The contrast scaled score for IMI versus DMI was 11 and not suggestive of significant forgetting. The pattern of WMS-IV findings is generally consistent with those seen in moderate-to-severe TBI samples using the WMS-III. Specifically, his visual indexes are lower than his verbal indexes, working memory is among the highest scores, and immediate and delayed indexes are not significantly different (see Chapter Seven).

Better verbal than visual memory abilities also are observed in Mr. Smith's performances on the CVLT-II and RCF. He demonstrated low average verbal learning, overall, on the CVLT-II while his short and long delayed free recall performances were in the average range. Thus, his CVLT-II performance was consistent with his low average to average auditory memory performances on the WMS-IV. In contrast, on RCF Immediate and Delayed Recall trials, he performed below the first percentile, likely due to poor encoding secondary to his disorganized approach, as well as to relatively weaker nonverbal memory abilities.

Psychological Functioning

On the MMPI-2, validity scales indicated that Mr. Smith's responses were inconsistent and of questionable validity (i.e., Fback = 120, VRIN = 88; TRIN = 72). The pattern of validity indices coupled with his clinical presentation suggest that the most likely reasons for his response style were lack of interest in the test and/or hurrying through the test questions without reading them carefully. Therefore, results of the MMPI-2 were not interpreted.

Summary and Impressions

Mr. Smith reported experiencing memory problems for the past year, which have improved since he began taking Seroquel regularly and sleeping better. He also reported problems with temper outbursts over the past 1–2 years, which he believes are getting worse, and long-standing depressive symptoms. Medical history is significant for recent alcohol detoxification and three TBIs with LOC, the most recent of which was in 2003. Psychosocial history is noteworthy for tendencies to get bored and let his attention wander and substance use beginning in his teenage years, resulting in legal problems during young adulthood. Interview and test data revealed an open, friendly man with limited psychological insight and poor appreciation of his cognitive deficits. While overall IQ, language, working memory, processing speed, and verbal memory were relatively intact, he exhibited impulsivity, poor attention to detail, impaired nonverbal memory, and difficulties attending to and organizing complex nonverbal material. While it is likely that some of Mr. Smith's cognitive inefficiencies are related to long-standing alcohol use and are expected to improve over the next year or two pending continued abstinence, the pattern and severity of his cognitive deficits suggest that some of his neurobehavioral symptoms are sequelae of his multiple TBIs superimposed on long-standing difficulties regulating attention and behavior.

Recommendations

1. Continued emphasis on the need to remain abstinent is recommended. Mr. Smith may benefit from education about how alcohol and other substance use can affect cognitive functioning. Given his level of psychological insight, Mr. Smith will benefit most from concrete, behavioral interventions focused on one or two overt symptoms rather than introspective talk therapy.
2. Because of his nonverbal deficits and related difficulties with novelty and complexity, Mr. Smith may benefit from concrete verbal

explanations whenever instruction involves charts, graphs, or other pictorial material such as maps. He also will need more repetition and review of unfamiliar material and may benefit when novel material or new skills are linked to more familiar information and tasks, so that he can relate what he is learning to established skills.

3. To help cope with impulsivity and inattention to detail, the following strategies may be helpful:
   - Break down complex assignments into smaller steps, completing each one before moving onto the next.
   - Minimize potentially distracting stimuli by working/reading alone or in a quiet room.
   - Check and double-check work.
   - Write down and organize information to be remembered.
   - Utilize a day planner/calendar.
   - Ask for repetition of important information and repeat it back to ensure completeness and accuracy.
   - Take a few extra seconds to make a "mental note" of new information and to repeat it several times to facilitate encoding for later retrieval.
4. Feedback about the results of this evaluation is recommended. Mr. Smith requested that this information be provided by his referring provider.

CASE EXAMPLE 2: MCI AND DEPRESSION

Reason for Referral

Ms. Betty M. Thomas is a 63-year-old, left-handed, divorced, African-American female with 10 years of formal education. She was initially evaluated 2 years prior to this evaluation and diagnosed with depression and MCI, nonamnestic type, as her cognitive deficits were restricted to mild to moderate attention/executive dysfunction, and she displayed average immediate and delayed recall abilities. She was referred by her psychiatrist for reevaluation due to continued memory problems despite improved mood.

Current Complaints and Relevant History

Ms. Thomas reported gradually worsening memory problems over the past 4–5 years. For example, she forgets where she places her keys, cannot remember how to do repetitive tasks, gets lost in unfamiliar places, and has to write things down more often. She also noted that she gets confused, often gets lost in the mall, and can "never remember where I park." She indicated the onset of her memory problems did not coincide with any particular incident, and they have negatively affected her work performance. She explained that she often tries to hide mistakes and makes excuses for tasks not being completed on time or properly. Emotionally, Ms. Thomas reported feeling "okay." She denied any symptoms of depression but admitted that sometimes she stresses about her performance at work. She has been seeing a psychiatrist since her last evaluation and has been receiving antidepressant medication.

Relevant Medical History

Ms. Thomas stated her physical health was "okay." She has high blood pressure and high cholesterol but is otherwise healthy. She takes medication for allergies, cholesterol, and mood. She denied any history of stroke, seizure, or TBI. An MRI scan of the brain 2 years previously noted scattered hyperintensities in the periventricular white matter consistent with subcortical ischemia. She denied using recreational drugs or smoking cigarettes. She reports drinking alcohol only on special occasions and denied any history of alcohol abuse or dependence. Ms. Thomas indicated she has never been hospitalized for psychiatric reasons and had never consulted a mental health professional until recommended after her prior neuropsychological evaluation. She noted that her mother had "problems learning" but denied any other family history of psychiatric or neurological problems.

Psychosocial History

Ms. Thomas was born and raised in Texas. She is the oldest of seven children, with three brothers and three sisters. She is the product of an uncomplicated pregnancy and birth and met all early developmental milestones within the expected time frames. She is right-handed, and English is her only language. She denied problems learning in school, was never held back a grade, and never received special education services. She quit school in the middle of her 11th-grade year to go to work. She worked as a waitress and cashier until the age of 27 and has worked as a medical administrative clerk for the past 19 years. Ms. Thomas has been divorced for 26 years and has one daughter. She reported that her relationship with her daughter is "good."

Behavioral Observations and Mental Status Exam

Ms. Thomas presented as an anxious, disorganized woman with poor psychological insight. She was somewhat overweight and appeared her stated age. She arrived on time for her appointment, unaccompanied. Her vision and hearing were adequate for evaluation purposes. She was casually dressed, and grooming and hygiene were fair; her hair was disheveled but clean. Her gait was within normal limits; no psychomotor abnormalities were apparent. She was alert, attentive, and oriented ×4. She made good eye contact and exhibited good interpersonal skills. She spoke at a normal rate, and her speech was clear but tangential. She appeared to have no difficulty understanding conversational speech or task instructions. There was no overt evidence of formal thought disorder, delusions, or hallucinations. Memory for remote and recent events was grossly intact. Judgment was also intact. Her mood and affect were within normal limits and appropriate to the situation. Ms. Thomas was pleasant and cooperative throughout the evaluation and appeared to put forth good effort on all tasks. Therefore, the following results are considered an accurate representation of her current neuropsychological functioning.

Tests Administered

- Test of Memory Malingering
- Mini-Mental State Examination (MMSE)
- WMS-IV including Brief Cognitive Status Exam (BCSE)
- WAIS-IV selected subtests
- WTAR
- Repeatable Battery for the Assessment of Neuropsychological Status (RBANS)
- Boston Naming Test
- Controlled Oral Word Association Test (FAS)
- Animal Naming
- TMT
- Stroop Color and Word Test
- Wisconsin Card Sorting Test–64-card version (WCST-64)
- Pillbox Test
- Texas Functional Living Scale
- Geriatric Depression Scale–Short Form (GDS-SF; 15 items)
- Geriatric Anxiety Inventory (GAI)

Primary index and subtest scores for the WAIS-IV and WMS-IV are presented in Tables 8.3 and 8.4, respectively.

Test Interpretation

Effort
Results of stand-alone and embedded effort measures indicated that Ms. Thomas was putting forth adequate effort for valid test interpretation.

Table 8.3 Summary of Ms. Thomas's WAIS-IV scores

Scale	Composite Score		Percentile Rank	Qualitative Description
Verbal Comprehension	VCI	85	16	Low Average
Perceptual Reasoning	PRI	94	34	Average
General Ability	GAI	88	21	Low Average

Subtest	Raw Score	Scaled Score	Percentile Rank
Similarities	22	8	25
Vocabulary	26	7	16
Information	9	7	16

Subtest	Raw Score	Scaled Score	Percentile Rank
Block Design	30	8	25
Matrix Reasoning	11	7	16
Visual Puzzles	15	12	75

Table 8.4 Summary of Ms. Thomas's WMS-IV Scores

Index Score Summary

Index	Sum of Scaled Scores	Index Score		Percentile Rank	95% Confidence Interval	Qualitative Description
Auditory Memory	28	AMI	82	12	77–89	Low Average
Visual Memory	35	VMI	92	30	87–98	Average
Visual Working Memory	14	VWMI	83	13	77–91	Low Average
Immediate Memory	34	IMI	89	23	83–96	Low Average
Delayed Memory	29	DMI	81	10	75–89	Low Average

Table 8.4 (Continued)

Primary Subtest Scaled Score Summary

Subtest	Domain	Raw Score	Scaled Score	Percentile Rank
Logical Memory I	AM	19	7	16
Logical Memory II	AM	10	5	5
Verbal Paired Associates I	AM	22	8	25
Verbal Paired Associates II	AM	7	8	25
Designs I	VM	58	9	37
Designs II	VM	47	9	37
Visual Reproduction I	VM	33	10	50
Visual Reproduction II	VM	11	7	16
Spatial Addition	VWM	6	6	9
Symbol Span	VWM	16	8	25

WMS-IV Indexes

Score	Score 1	Score 2	Contrast Scaled Score
Auditory Memory Index versus Visual Memory Index	82	92	10
Visual Working Memory Index versus Visual Memory Index	83	92	11
Immediate Memory Index versus Delayed Memory Index	89	81	7

General Cognitive Functioning
She obtained an MMSE raw score of 27, which is in the average range for persons of her age and education level. On the BCSE, she also performed in the average range.

Estimated Current and Premorbid Intelligence
Results of intellectual testing revealed overall functioning at the high end of the low average range, with significantly stronger nonverbal compared to verbal

abilities (see Table 8.3), similar to her performance 2 years earlier. An estimate of premorbid intellectual functioning based on reading skill was in the average range (i.e., WTAR standard score = 96), suggesting a slight decline in intellectual functioning, particularly in verbal abilities.

Language

Ms. Thomas performed in the low average range on confrontation naming and on two out of three verbal fluency tasks. Animal Naming was in the average range. Her performance on these measures was generally consistent with her performance 2 years ago.

Visuospatial/Constructional Skills

Ms. Thomas exhibited intact ability to copy the RBANS figure (i.e., T score = 49) but performed below expectations when asked to copy the WMS-IV designs (i.e., raw score = 36; third to ninth percentile). She also performed in the moderately impaired range when asked to judge visuospatial relationships in the context of angles, which represented a slight decline from her prior evaluation when she performed in the low average range.

Attention/Executive Functioning

Ms. Thomas demonstrated generally intact basic attention as measured by RBANS Digit Span, and her performances on Parts A and B of the TMT were in the average and low average range, respectively. She demonstrated impaired verbal processing speed on the Stroop Color and Word subtests, while performing in the average range on the Color–Word subtest. She also performed within normal limits on the WCST-64 and Pillbox Test. In general, Ms. Thomas performed similarly to her prior evaluation when accounting for practice effects on TMT Part B, Stroop Color–Word, and WCST-64, which resulted in scores improving from the impaired range to within normal limits on TMT Part B and Stroop Color–Word.

Learning and Memory

On the WMS-IV, Ms. Thomas obtained index scores in the low average range for AMI, VWMI, IMI, and DMI. Her VMI score was in the average range (see Table 8.4). There were no significant differences between Ms. Thomas's GAI and any WMS-IV memory indexes.

At the subtest level, she exhibited the most difficulty on LM II, performing at the fifth percentile. LM I, VR II, and SA were in the low average range, while all other performances were in the average range. Subtest-level contrast scaled scores indicated significant difficulty recalling stories after a delay when considering initial encoding of those stories (i.e., LM Immediate Recall versus Delayed Recall contrast scaled score = 5). Relative difficulties were also noted in delayed recall of stories when taking into account recognition performance (i.e., LM II Recognition versus Delayed Recall contrast scaled score = 6) and in delayed recall of figures when considering initial encoding (i.e., VR Immediate Recall versus Delayed recall contrast scaled score = 6). Contrast scaled scores at the index level also reveal this pattern, with the IMI versus DMI contrast scaled score of 7 suggesting overall low average delayed recall abilities when considering immediate recall performance (see Table 8.4).

On the RBANS, Ms. Thomas obtained an IMI score in the low average range and a DMI score in the average range. However, a closer look at her subtest performances revealed that delayed story and figure recall were in the mildly and moderately impaired ranges, respectively, representing a significant decline from prior performances 2 years ago. Her List Recall and List Recognition subtest scores were in the average range, although her List Recall raw score dropped from 9 out of 10 possible to 5.

Functional Abilities

Ms. Thomas obtained an overall functional abilities score in the mildly impaired range. While she demonstrated average abilities to use a calendar and monitor time and low average memory functional skills, her ability to calculate and make change and to describe events in sequence was poorer than expected (i.e., third to ninth percentile), resulting in a total functional abilities score in the mildly impaired range.

Psychological Functioning

Ms. Thomas's responses on the GDS-SF were not indicative of significant depressive symptoms and reflected improvements compared to her prior evaluation. However, her responses on the GAI suggested a severe level of generalized anxiety.

Summary and Impressions

Ms. Thomas reported worsening memory problems over the past 4–5 years and was diagnosed with MCI, nonamnestic type, and depression 2 years prior to this evaluation. Despite treatment for depression, she reported continued memory problems that interfere with her work. On cognitive tasks, Ms. Thomas demonstrated impairment in judgment of angles, verbal processing speed, and delayed recall of short stories and figures. On functional measures, she exhibited difficulties in calculations and sequencing of everyday tasks. Her performances on measures of intellect, language, and attention/executive functioning were similar to her previous testing when considering practice effects, but she showed declines in visuospatial/constructional skills and memory. Results suggest Ms. Thomas is in the early stages of a neurodegenerative disease process, most likely Alzheimer's disease with a vascular component, given her medical history and disease progression. In addition, anxiety may further negatively impact her cognitive functioning.

Recommendations

1. Consider referral to Neurology for further evaluation and possible treatment of neurodegenerative disease process.
2. Continued treatment and monitoring of mood will be important, as Ms. Thomas is at risk for developing more severe psychiatric symptoms as her cognitive abilities decline and her difficulties at work increase. She may also benefit from help in determining when to retire, as well as instruction in stress management techniques.
3. Ms. Thomas is encouraged to continue all activities, as tolerated. At least 1 hour of cognitively stimulating activity per day is recommended. Continuation of physical activity is also important if approved by her medical providers.
4. Ms. Thomas is encouraged to use compensatory techniques such as taking notes and reviewing material more than once. In addition, the following strategies may be helpful:
   • Break down large pieces of information into smaller, more meaningful bits before attempting to commit them to memory.
   • Use memory aids, such as lists, notebooks, calendars, and audio tapes, whenever possible.
   • Ask for repetition of information and repeat it back to ensure completeness and accuracy.
   • Take a few extra seconds to make a "mental note" of new information and repeat it several times.
   • Establish a "memory place" where important information, such as keys and telephone numbers, is kept routinely.
   • Break down complex tasks into smaller steps, completing each one before moving onto the next.
   • Minimize potentially distracting stimuli by working/reading alone or in a quiet room.

- Allow extra time to complete projects (i.e., double or triple the time expected for completion).
- Check and double-check work.

5. Family, friends, and health care providers are encouraged to provide information to Ms. Thomas in written form.

6. If not already addressed, Ms. Thomas and her family are encouraged to discuss legal issues such as guardianship and/or power of attorney to assist in future financial and health care decisions.

7. Feedback concerning the results of this evaluation is recommended, and Ms. Thomas will be provided this information by phone per her request.

CASE EXAMPLE 3: MEMORY COMPLAINTS IN HIGH-FUNCTIONING OLDER ADULT

Reason for Referral

Dr. Geraldo Martin is a 76-year-old, left-handed, married Hispanic male with 20 years of formal education. He was referred by Psychiatry for an evaluation of memory complaints.

Current Complaints and Relevant History

Dr. Martin reported mild progressive memory problems since 2005. For instance, he misplaces common objects, has problems with word- and name-finding, and sometimes forgets conversations. He stated that his wife has also noticed these problems. However, he asserted that these problems have only a minimal impact on his daily functioning; he continues to work part time as a psychiatrist without difficulty. In terms of psychological functioning, he reported an increased "temper" within the past few years; this results in very brief outbursts of anger that are typically directed toward his wife. However, he reported that he generally has a "good" mood.

Relevant Medical History

Dr. Martin's reported medical problems were "minimal" sleep apnea, hypertension, hypercholesterolemia, heart disease, diabetes, irritable bowel syndrome, gastroesophageal reflux disease (GERD), hiatal hernia, sinusitis, nephritis, and color blindness. He denied sleep problems but noted that he takes Ativan as a sleep aid. He also takes medication for hypertension, high cholesterol, irritable bowel syndrome, and GERD, and various over-the-counter medicines for sinusitis. He denied significant psychiatric history and reported minimal alcohol use, only occasional beer and wine consumption. Dr. Martin smoked cigarettes from ages 15 to 70, averaging approximately one-half pack per day. Family history is remarkable for a brother with lupus, maternal aunt and cousin with possible Tourette's disorder, mother with cancer, and father with heart disease.

Psychosocial History

Dr. Martin was born prematurely, although he reported that he was early to progress through developmental milestones. He denied any history of emotional, sexual, or physical abuse. English is his only language. He stated that he was scholastically talented and was placed in an accelerated curriculum beginning in junior high. He also reported that he only took 3 years to complete his undergraduate degree and then completed an MD. He denied ever failing a grade or class and denied receiving special education services. Despite his good academic performance overall, he reported earning a D in trigonometry. He reported no behavioral problems as a child and was involved in extracurricular activities. He served in the Air Force from 1956 to 1964 and obtained the rank of major. Prior to serving in the military, he held several jobs, demonstrating a consistent work history. Following the military, he worked as a psychiatrist specializing in adolescent mental health. He continues to work about 20 hours per week and is engaged in several hobbies and interests. Dr. Martin indicated that he has a regular exercise regimen. He lives in Ohio with his second wife of 45 years. The couple has three children and four grandchildren.

Behavioral Observations and Mental Status Exam

Dr. Martin arrived on time for his appointment, unaccompanied. He appeared his stated age, was slender, and was casually dressed with good grooming and hygiene. Posture was upright, ambulation and gait were within normal limits, and no psychomotor abnormalities were noted. His hearing (with hearing aids) and vision were adequate for evaluation purposes. He was alert, attentive, and oriented ×4. Speech was within normal limits for articulation, pace, tone, volume, and prosody. The quality and content of his speech was appropriate, logical, and goal directed, and he generated spontaneous conversation. Comprehension of simple and complex instructions and directions was largely within normal limits. Rapport was easily established, and he was cooperative during the session.

Dr. Martin's eye contact and interpersonal skills were good. His mood was euthymic with broad, appropriate affect. No suicidal ideation was present. There was no evidence of delusions, preoccupations/obsessions, or hallucinations. He appeared to put forth good effort on all tasks; the following results are considered an accurate representation of his current neuropsychological functioning.

Tests Administered

- Test of Memory Malingering
- MMSE
- WMS-IV (Older Adult battery) including BCSE
- WAIS-IV selected subtests
- WTAR
- Boston Naming Test
- Controlled Oral Word Association Test (FAS)
- Animal Naming
- RBANS Line Orientation
- RCF Copy Trial
- Conners' Continuous Performance Test (CPT)
- TMT
- Stroop Color and Word Test
- WCST-64
- Pillbox Test
- CVLT-II
- Finger Tapping Test
- Grooved Pegboard
- Grip Strength
- Texas Functional Living Scale
- GDS-SF (15 items)
- GAI

Primary index and subtest scores for the WAIS-IV and WMS-IV are presented in Tables 8.5 and 8.6, respectively.

Test Interpretation

Effort
Results of stand-alone and embedded effort measures indicated that Dr. Martin was putting forth adequate effort for valid test interpretation.

Table 8.5 Summary of Dr. Martin's WAIS-IV Scores

Composite Score Summary

Scale	Sum of Scaled Scores	Composite Score		Percentile Rank	95% Confidence Interval	Qualitative Description
Verbal Comprehension	40	VCI	118	88	112–123	High Average
Perceptual Reasoning	36	PRI	111	77	104–117	High Average
Working Memory	33	WMI	136	99	127–141	Very Superior
Processing Speed	35	PSI	140	99.6	128–144	Very Superior
Full Scale	144	FSIQ	132	98	127–135	Very Superior
General Ability	76	GAI	117	87	112–121	High Average

Verbal Comprehension Subtests Summary

Subtest	Raw Score	Scaled Score	Percentile Rank	Reference Group Scaled Score	SEM
Similarities	27	12	75	11	1.12
Vocabulary	53	15	95	16	0.73
Information	19	13	84	14	0.73

Perceptual Reasoning Subtests Summary

Subtest	Raw Score	Scaled Score	Percentile Rank	Reference Group Scaled Score	SEM
Block Design	28	10	50	6	1.27
Matrix Reasoning	22	17	99	13	0.73
Visual Puzzles	9	9	37	6	0.99
(Picture Completion)	12	12	75	9	1.12

Table 8.5 (Continued)

Working Memory Subtests Summary

Subtest	Raw Score	Scaled Score	Percentile Rank	Reference Group Scaled Score	SEM
Digit Span	36	16	98	14	0.79
Arithmetic	20	17	99	15	0.95

Processing Speed Subtests Summary

Subtest	Raw Score	Scaled Score	Percentile Rank	Reference Group Scaled Score	SEM
Symbol Search	42	19	99.9	13	1.12
Coding	76	16	98	11	1.12

General Cognitive Functioning

Dr. Martin obtained an MMSE raw score of 30 out of 30. On the BCSE, he performed in the average range, obtaining a raw score of 57 out of 58.

Estimated Current and Premorbid Intelligence

Results of intellectual testing revealed overall functioning in the very superior range, with relatively equivalent verbal and nonverbal abilities, both in the high average range (see Table 8.5). Working Memory Index (WMI) and PSI were also in the very superior range. An estimate of premorbid intellectual functioning based on reading skill was in the superior range (i.e., WTAR standard score = 121) and consistent with his overall verbal abilities.

Language

Dr. Martin performed in the low average range for his age and education level on a confrontation naming task but performed in the superior to very superior ranges on verbal fluency tasks.

Visuospatial/Constructional Abilities

Dr. Martin exhibited average abilities to judge visuospatial relationships on RBANS Line Orientation (i.e., T score = 49), but he performed in the borderline

Table 8.6 Summary of Dr. Martin's WMS-IV scores

Index Score Summary

Index	Sum of Scaled Scores	Index Score		Percentile Rank	95% Confidence Interval	Qualitative Description
Auditory Memory	46	AMI	109	73	102–115	Average
Visual Memory	26	VMI	116	86	111–120	High Average
Immediate Memory	38	IMI	117	87	110–122	High Average
Delayed Memory	34	DMI	108	70	100–115	Average

Primary Subtest Scaled Score Summary

Subtest	Domain	Raw Score	Scaled Score	Percentile Rank
Logical Memory I	AM	36	12	75
Logical Memory II	AM	14	9	37
Verbal Paired Associates I	AM	28	13	84
Verbal Paired Associates II	AM	7	12	75
Visual Reproduction I	VM	34	13	84
Visual Reproduction II	VM	25	13	84
Symbol Span	VWM	26	15	95

WMS-IV Indexes

Score	Score 1	Score 2	Contrast Scaled Score
Auditory Memory Index versus Visual Memory Index	109	116	13
Immediate Memory Index versus Delayed Memory Index	117	108	7

to low average ranges when asked to copy a complex figure (i.e., RCF raw score = 26.5; 6th–10th percentile).

Attention/Executive Functioning

Dr. Martin demonstrated intact attention and processing speed as measured by the CPT, and his performances on the TMT and Stroop Color and Word Test ranged from high average to very superior. He performed nearly flawlessly on the WCST-64, completing four categories while making only seven total errors, and he had no difficulties on the Pillbox Test.

Learning and Memory

On the WMS-IV, Dr. Martin's AMI and DMI scores were in the average range, and his VMI and IMI scores were in the high average range (see Table 8.6). There were no significant differences between his overall intellectual functioning as measured by the GAI and his WMS-IV memory indexes. At the subtest level, he performed in the high average range on all subtests except LM II, on which he performed in the average range. Subtest-level contrast scaled scores indicated that when considering his immediate memory for stories, his delayed memory was mildly impaired (LM Immediate Recall versus Delayed Recall contrast scaled score = 5). This finding was reflected in the index-level contrast scaled score as a relative weakness in overall delayed recall abilities when taking into account immediate memory abilities (i.e., IMI versus DMI contrast scaled score = 7). On the CVLT-II, Dr. Martin performed in the superior to very superior ranges on measures of total learning and short and long delayed free recall. He made a significant number of repetitions (i.e., 25) but showed good recognition discriminability.

Psychomotor Functioning

Dr. Martin demonstrated average fine motor coordination with his dominant (left) hand but performed in the moderately impaired range with his nondominant hand. His performance on a task of manual dexterity was mildly impaired with his dominant hand and moderately impaired with his nondominant hand. Grip strength was in the average range bilaterally.

Functional Abilities

Dr. Martin obtained an overall functional abilities score in the low average range. He demonstrated high average abilities to use a calendar and monitor time, average ability to perform calculations, and average functional memory skills. His score on the Communications subscale was poorer than expected (i.e., third to ninth percentile) due to difficulties simulating the use of a microwave, even though he was provided multiple cues.

Psychological Functioning

Dr. Martin's responses on the GDS-SF and GAI were not indicative of significant depressive or anxious symptoms.

Summary and Impressions

Dr. Martin reported mild progressive memory problems of minimal functional impact since 2005 and no significant psychiatric distress. Relevant medical history includes essential hypertension, hypercholesterolemia, nephritis, heart disease, and diabetes. Neuropsychological test results revealed high functioning across measures of intelligence, verbal fluency, attention/executive functioning, and learning. However, confrontational naming abilities were below expectations, and his visuospatial processing of a complex figure, delayed recall of verbally complex material, and nondominant (right) hand psychomotor speed and coordination were impaired. In sum, his performance suggests possible mild impairment. In addition, the early stages of a neurodegenerative disease process cannot be ruled out at this time.

Recommendations

1. A referral to Neurology is recommended for additional assessment, including possible imaging and/or electrophysiological studies. Neuropsychological reevaluation in 12–18 months is suggested to monitor cognitive functioning. The current evaluation can serve as a baseline against which future performance is compared.
2. Given a high number of cardiovascular risk factors, it is recommended that Dr. Martin continue regular follow-up with his primary care physician.
3. Dr. Martin should continue to use memory and organizational aids, such as lists and calendars. He may also find it beneficial to break down information to be remembered into smaller units to facilitate learning and recall.
4. Dr. Martin is encouraged to continue his high activity level, including work, social, and recreational activities.
5. Feedback concerning the results of this evaluation is recommended and an appointment for this purpose has been scheduled.

References

Anastasi, A., & Urbina, S. (1997). *Psychological testing* (7th ed.). Upper Saddle River, NJ: Prentice Hall.

Atkinson, L., & Merry, G. (2001). Advances in neurotrauma in Australia 1970–2000. *World Journal of Surgery, 25*, 1224–1229.

Atkinson, R. C., & Shiffrin, R. M. (1968). A proposed system and its control processes. In K. W. Spence & J. T. Spence (Eds.), *The psychology of learning and motivation: Advances in research and theory* (Vol. 2, pp. 82–90). New York, NY: Academic Press.

Attix, D. K., & Welsh-Bohmer, K. A. (Eds.) (2006). *Geriatric neuropsychology: Assessment and intervention*. New York, NY: Guilford Press.

Axelrod, B. N. (2001). Administration duration for the Wechsler Adult Intelligence Scale–III and Wechsler Memory Scale–III. *Archives of Clinical Neuropsychology, 16*, 293–301.

Axelrod, B. N., Barlow, A., & Paradee, C. (2010). Evaluation of the WMS-III Rarely Missed Index in a naïve clinical sample. *Clinical Neuropsychologist, 24*, 96–102.

Axelrod, B. N., Fichtenberg, N. L., Liethen, P. C., Czarnota, M. A., & Stucky, K. (2001). Performance characteristics of postacute traumatic brain injury patients on the WAIS-III and WMS-III. *Clinical Neuropsychologist, 15*(4), 516–520.

Baddeley, A. D. (2000). The episodic buffer: A new component of working memory? *Trends in Cognitive Sciences, 4*, 417–423.

Baddeley, A. D. (2003). Working memory: Looking back and looking forward. *Nature Reviews: Neuroscience, 4*, 829–839.

Baddeley, A., & Hitch, G. (1974). Working memory. In G. H. Bower (Ed.), *The psychology of learning and motivation: Advances in research and theory* (Vol. 8, pp. 47–90). San Diego, CA: Academic Press.

Baker, G. A., Austin, N. A., & Downes, J. J. (2003). Validation of the Wechsler Memory Scale–III in a population of people with intractable temporal lobe epilepsy. *Epilepsy Research, 53*(3), 201–206.

Bauer, R. M. (2008). The three amnesias. In J. E. Morgan, & J. H. Ricker (Eds.), *Textbook of Clinical Neuropsychology*. New York, NY: Taylor & Francis.

Bell, B. D. (2006). WMS-III Logical Memory performance after a two-week delay in temporal lobe epilepsy and control groups. *Journal of Clinical & Experimental Neuropsychology, 28*(8), 1435–1443.

Bell, B. D., Hermann, B. P., & Seidenberg, M. (2004). Significant discrepancies between immediate and delayed WMS-III indices are rare in temporal lobe epilepsy patients. *Clinical Neuropsychologist, 18*(2), 303–311.

Binder, L. M., Iverson, G. L., & Brooks, B. L. (2009). To err is human: "Abnormal" neuropsychological scores and variability are common in healthy adults. *Archives of Clinical Neuropsychology, 24*, 31–46.

Bowie, C. R., & Harvey, P. D. (2005). Cognition in schizophrenia: Impairments, determinants, and functional importance. *Psychiatric Clinics of North America, 28*, 613–633.

Brinkman, S. D., Largen, J. W., Gerganoff, S., & Pomara, N. (1983). Russell's revised Wechsler Memory Scale in the evaluation of dementia. *Journal of Clinical Psychology, 39*, 989–993.

Brooks, B. L., Holdnack, J. A., & Iverson, G. L. (in press). Advanced clinical interpretation of the WAIS-IV and WMS-IV: Prevalence of low scores varies by level of intelligence and years of education. *Assessment.*

Brooks, B. L., Iverson, G. L., Feldman, H. H., & Holdnack, J. A. (2009). Minimizing misdiagnosis: Psychometric criteria for possible or probable memory impairment. *Dementia & Geriatric Cognitive Disorders, 27*(5), 439–450.

Brooks, B. L., Iverson, G. L., Holdnack, J. A., & Feldman, H. H. (2008). Potential for misclassification of mild cognitive impairment: a study of memory scores on the Wechsler Memory Scale–III in healthy older adults. *Journal of the International Neuropsychological Society, 14*(3), 463–478.

Buchsbaum, B. R., & D'Esposito, M. (2008). Short-term and working memory systems. In J. H. Byrne, & H. Eichenbaum (Eds.), *Learning and memory: A comprehensive reference: Memory systems* (Vol. 3, pp. 237–257). San Diego, CA: Elsevier Science.

Buckner, R. L. (2003). Functional–anatomic correlates of processes in memory. *Journal of Neuroscience, 10,* 3999–4004.

Buckner, R. L., & Koutstaal, W. (1998). Functional neuroimaging studies of encoding, priming, and explicit memory retrieval. *Proceedings of the National Academy of Sciences of the United States of America, 95,* 891–898.

Burton, D. B., Ryan, J. J., Axelrod, B. N., Schellenberger, T., & Richards, H. M. (2003). A confirmatory factor analysis of the WMS-III in a clinical sample with cross validation in the standardization sample. *Archives of Clinical Neuropsychology, 18,* 629–641.

Bush, S. S., Ruff, R. M., Troster, A. I., Barth, J. T., Koffler, S. P., Pliskin, N. H., . . . Silver, C. H. (2005). Symptom validity assessment: Practice issues and medical necessity. *Archives of Clinical Neuropsychology, 20,* 419–426.

Carstensen, L. L., Edelstein, B. A., & Dornbrand, L. (Eds.) (1997). *The practical handbook of clinical gerontology.* Thousand Oaks, CA: Sage.

Centers for Disease Control and Prevention. (2010). *Traumatic brain injury in the United States: emergency department visits, hospitalizations and deaths 2002–2006.* Retrieved from www.cdc.gov/TraumaticBrainInjury

Chapin, J. S., Busch, R. M., Naugle, R. I., & Najm, I. M. (2009). The Family Pictures subtest of the WMS-III: relationship to verbal and visual memory following temporal lobectomy for intractable epilepsy. *Journal of Clinical & Experimental Neuropsychology, 31*(4), 498–504.

Chiaravalloti, N. D., Tulsky, D. S., & Glosser, G. (2004). Validation of the WMS-III Facial Memory subtest with the Graduate Hospital Facial Memory Test in a sample of right and left anterior temporal lobectomy patients. *Journal of Clinical & Experimental Neuropsychology, 26*(4), 484–497.

Chlopan, B. E., Hagen, R. L., & Russell, E. W. (1990). Lateralized anterior and posterior lesions and performance on digit span and Russell's revision of the Wechsler Memory Scale. *Journal of Consulting and Clinical Psychology, 58,* 855–861.

Cohen, J. (1988). *Statistical power analysis for the behavioral sciences* (2nd ed.). Hillsdale, NJ: Erlbaum.

Crosson, B., Hughes, C. W., Roth, D. L., & Monkowski, P. G. (1984). Review of Russell's (1975) norms for the Logical Memory and Visual Reproduction subtests of the Wechsler Memory Scale. *Journal of Consulting and Clinical Psychology, 52,* 635–641.

Cullum, C. M., Butters, N., Tröster, A., & Salmon, D. (1990). Normal aging and forgetting rates on the Wechsler Memory Scale–Revised. *Archives of Clinical Neuropsychology, 5,* 23–30.

Cummings, J. L., & Mega, M. S. (2003). *Neuropsychiatry and behavioral neuroscience.* New York, NY: Oxford University Press.

Curry, J. F., Logue, P. E., & Butler, B. (1986). Child and adolescent norms for Russell's revision of the Wechsler Memory Scale. *Journal of Clinical and Child Psychology, 15,* 214–220.

Dean, A. C., Victor, T. L., Boone, K. B., Philpott, L. M., & Hess, R. A. (2009). Dementia and effort test performance. *Clinical Neuropsychologist, 23*(1), 133–152.

Delis, D. C., Kaplan, E., & Kramer, J. H. (2001). *Delis–Kaplan executive function system*. San Antonio, TX: Pearson NCS.

Delis, D. C., Kramer, J. H., Kaplan, E., & Ober, B. A. (2000). *California verbal learning test* (2nd ed.). San Antonio, TX: Pearson NCS.

Devanand, D. P., Liu, X., Tabert, M. H., Pradhaban, G., Cuasay, K., Bell, K., . . . Pelton, G. H. (2008). Combining early markers strongly predicts conversion from mild cognitive impairment to Alzheimer's disease. *Biological Psychiatry, 64*(10), 871–879; www.ncbi.nlm. nih.gov/pubmed/18723162

Doss, R. C., Chelune, G. J., & Naugle, R. I. (2000). Comparability of the expanded WMS–III standardization protocol to the published WMS-III among right and left temporal lobectomy patients. *Clinical Neuropsychologist, 14*, 468–473.

Doss, R. C., Chelune, G. J., & Naugle, R. I. (2004). WMS-III performance in epilepsy patients following temporal lobectomy. *Journal of the International Neuropsychological Society, 10*(2), 173–179.

Dulay, M. F., Schefft, B. K., Testa, S. M., Fargo, J. D., Privitera, M., & Yeh, H. (2002). What does the Family Pictures subtest of the Wechsler Memory Scale–III measure? Insight gained from patients evaluated for epilepsy surgery. *Clinical Neuropsychologist, 16*(4), 452–462.

Eichenbaum, H. (2008). *Learning and memory*. New York, NY: Norton.

Engberg, A. W., & Teasdale, T. W. (2001). Traumatic brain injury in Denmark 1979–1996. A national study of incidence and mortality. *European Journal of Epidemiology, 17*, 437–442.

Erickson, R. C., & Scott, M. L. (1977). Clinical memory testing: A review. *Psychological Bulletin, 84*, 1130–1149.

Fisher, D. C., Ledbetter, M. F., Cohen, N. J., Marmor, D., & Tulsky, D. S. (2000). WAIS-III and WMS-III profiles of mildly to severely brain-injured patients. *Applied Neuropsychology, 7*(3), 126–132.

Flanagan, D. P., McGrew, K. S., & Ortiz, S. O. (2000). *The Wechsler Intelligence Scales and Gf-Gc theory: A contemporary approach to interpretation*. Boston, MA: Allyn & Bacon.

Folstein M. F., Folstein S. E., & McHugh, P. R. (1975). Mini-mental state: A practical method for grading the cognitive state of patients for the clinician. *Journal of Psychiatric Research, 12*(3), 189–298.

Fucetola R., Seidman L. J., Kremen, W. S., Faraone, S. V., Goldstein, J. M., & Tsuang, M. T. (2000). Age and neuropsychologic function in schizophrenia: A decline in executive abilities beyond that observed in healthy volunteers. *Biological Psychiatry, 48*(2), 137–146.

Glass, L. A., Bartels, J. M., & Ryan, J. J. (2009). WAIS-III FSIQ and GAI in ability–memory discrepancy analysis. *Applied Neuropsychology, 16*, 19–22.

Glassmire, D. M., Bierley, R. A., Wisniewski, A., M., Greene, R. L., Kennedy, J. E., & Date, E. (2003). Using the WMS-III faces subtest to detect malingered memory impairment. *Journal of Clinical and Experimental Neuropsychology, 25*, 465–481.

Gorsuch, R. L. (2003, August). *Update on continuous norming*. Paper presented at the annual meeting of the American Psychological Association, Toronto, Canada.

Granholm, E., Morris, S., Asarnow, R. F., Chock, D., & Jeste, D. V. (2000). Accelerated age-related decline in processing resources in schizophrenia: Evidence from pupillary responses recorded during the span of apprehension task. *Journal of the International Neuropsychological Society, 6*(1), 30–43.

Griffith, H. R., Netson, K. L., Harrell, L. E., Zamrini, E. Y., Brockington, J. C., & Marson, D. C. (2006). Amnestic mild cognitive impairment: Diagnostic outcomes and clinical prediction over a two-year time period. *Journal of the International Neuropsychological Society, 12*(2), 166–175.

Griffith, H. R., Pyzalski, R. W., Seidenberg, M., & Hermann, B. P. (2004). Memory relationships between MRI volumes and resting PET metabolism of medial temporal lobe structures. *Epilepsy & Behavior, 5*(5), 669–676.

Groth-Marnat, G. (2009). *Handbook of Psychological Assessment* (5th ed.). Hoboken, NJ: John Wiley & Sons.

Haaland, K. Y., Linn, R. T., Hunt, W. C., & Goodwin, J. S. (1983). A normative study of Russell's variant of the Wechsler Memory Scale in a healthy elderly population. *Journal of Consulting and Clinical Psychology, 51*, 878–881.

Haaland, K. Y., Price, L., & Larue, A. (2003). What does the WMS-III tell us about memory changes with normal aging? *Journal of the International Neuropsychological Society, 9*(1), 89–96.

Hambleton, R. K., Merenda, P. F., & Spielberger, C. D. (2005). *Adapting educational and psychological tests for cross-cultural assessment.* Mahwah, NJ: Erlbaum.

Harrison, B. E., Son, G.-R., Kim, J., & Whall, A. L. (2007). Preserved implicit memory in dementia: A potential model for care. *American Journal of Alzheimer's Disease & Other Dementias, 22*(4), 286–293.

Harvey, D. J., Naugle, R. I., Magleby, J., Chapin, J. S., Najm, I. M., Bingaman, W., & Busch, R. M. (2008). Relationship between presurgical memory performance on the Wechsler Memory Scale–III and memory change following temporal resection for treatment of intractable epilepsy. *Epilepsy & Behavior, 13*(2), 372–375.

Hawkins, K. A. (1999). Memory deficits in patients with schizophrenia: Preliminary data from the Wechsler Memory Scale–Third Edition support earlier findings. *Journal of Psychiatry & Neuroscience, 24*(4), 341–347.

Heilbronner, R. L. (1992). The search for a "pure" visual memory test: Pursuit of perfection? *The Clinical Neuropsychologist, 6*, 105–112.

Heilbronner, R. L., Sweet, J. J., Morgan, J. E., Larrabee, G. J., Millis, S. R., & Conference Participants. (2009). American Academy of Clinical Neuropsychology Consensus Conference Statement on the neuropsychological assessment of effort, response bias, and malingering. *Clinical Neuropsychologist, 23*(7), 1093–1129.

Hirtz, D., Thurman, D. J., Gwinn-Hardy, K., Mohammed, M., Chaudhuri, A. R., & Zalutsky, R. (2007). How common are the "common" neurological disorders? *Neurology, 68*, 326–337.

Holdnack, J. A., & Delis, D. C. (2004). Parsing the recognition memory components of the WMS-III Face Memory Subtest: Normative data and clinical findings in dementia groups. *Journal of Clinical and Experimental Neuropsychology, 26*, 459–483.

Holdnack, J. A., & Drozdick, L. W. (2010). Using WAIS-IV with WMS-IV. In L. G. Weiss, D. H. Saklofske, D. Coalson, & S. E. Raiford (2010). *WAIS-IV clinical use and interpretation: Scientist–practitioner perspectives.* Burlington, MA: Academic Press.

Howieson, D. B., Carlson, N. E., Moore, M. M., Wasserman, D., Abendroth, C. D., Payne-Murphy, J., & Kaye, J. A. (2008). Trajectory of mild cognitive impairment onset. *Journal of the International Neuropsychological Society, 14*, 192–198.

Iverson, G. L., Brooks, B. L., & Holdnack, J. A. (2008). Misdiagnosis of cognitive impairment in forensic neuropsychology. In R. L. Heilbronner (Ed.), *Neuropsychology in the courtroom: Expert analysis of reports and testimony.* New York, NY: Guilford Press.

Iverson, G. L., Lange, R. T., Viljoen, H., & Brink, J. (2006). WAIS-III General Ability Index in neuropsychiatry and forensic psychiatry inpatient samples. *Archives of Clinical Neuropsychology, 21*, 77–82.

Judd, T., Capetillo, D., Carrión-Baralt, J., Mármol, L. M., San Miguel-Montes, L., Navarrete, M. G., . . . Valdés, J. (2009). Professional considerations for improving the neuropsychological evaluation of Hispanics: A national academy of neuropsychology education paper. *Archives of Clinical Neuropsychology, 24*, 127–135; doi: 10.1093/arclin.acp016.

Kaplan, E. (1988). A process approach to neuropsychological assessment. In T. J. Boll & B. K. Bryant (Eds.), *Clinical neuropsychology and brain function: Research, measurement, and practice* (pp. 129–167). Washington, DC: American Psychological Association.

Kaufman, A. S., & Kaufman, N. L. (1993). *Kaufman adolescent and adult intelligence test.* Circle Pines, MN: American Guidance Service.

Killgore, W. D., & DellaPietra, L. (2000). Using the WMS-III to detect malingering: Empirical validation of the rarely missed index (RMI). *Journal of Clinical & Experimental Neuropsychology, 22*(6), 761–771.

Korkman, M., Kirk, U., & Kemp, S. (2007). *NEPSY-II.* San Antonio, TX: Pearson.

Kozora, E., Kongs, S., Hampton, M., & Zhang, L. (2008). Effects of examiner error on neuropsychological test results in a multi-site study. *Clinical Neuropsychologist, 22,* 977–988; doi: 10.1080/13854040701679025

Kryukov, V. I. (2008). The role of the hippocampus in long-term memory: Is it memory store or comparator? *Journal of Integrative Neuroscience, 7,* 117–184.

Lacritz, L. H., Barnard, H. D., Van Ness, P., Agostini, M., Diaz-Arrastia, R., & Cullum, C. M. (2004). Qualitative analysis of WMS-III Logical Memory and Visual Reproduction in temporal lobe epilepsy. *Journal of Clinical & Experimental Neuropsychology, 26*(4), 521–530.

Lange, R. T., & Chelune, G. J. (2006). Application of new WAIS-III/WMS-III discrepancy scores for evaluating memory functioning: relationship between intellectual and memory ability. *Journal of Clinical & Experimental Neuropsychology, 28*(4), 592–604.

Lange, R. T., & Chelune, G. J. (2007). Examining the relationship between WAIS-III premorbid intellectual functioning and WMS-III memory ability to evaluate memory impairment. *Applied Neuropsychology, 14*(3), 171–177.

Lange, R. T., Chelune, G. J., & Tulsky, D. S. (2006). Development of WAIS-III General Ability Index minus WMS-III memory discrepancy scores. *Clinical Neuropsychologist, 20,* 382–395.

Lange, R. T., Iverson, G. L., Sullivan, K., & Anderson, D. (2006). Suppressed working memory on the WMS-III as a marker for poor effort. *Journal of Clinical & Experimental Neuropsychology, 28*(3), 294–305.

Lange, R. T., Sullivan, K., & Anderson, D. (2005). Ecological validity of the WMS-III rarely missed index in personal injury litigation. *Journal of Clinical & Experimental Neuropsychology, 27*(4), 412–424.

Langeluddecke, P. M. (2004). Validation of the Rarely Missed Index (RMI) in detecting memory malingering in mild head injury litigants. *Journal of Forensic Neuropsychology, 4,* 49–64.

Langeluddecke, P. M., & Lucas, S. K. (2003). Quantitative measures of memory malingering on the Wechsler Memory Scale–Third Edition in mild head injury litigants. *Archives of Clinical Neuropsychology, 18*(2), 181–197.

Langeluddecke, P. M., & Lucas, S. K. (2005). WMS-III findings in litigants following moderate to extremely severe brain trauma. *Journal of Clinical & Experimental Neuropsychology, 27*(5), 576–590.

Levy, B. (2006). Increasing the power for detecting impairment in older adults with the faces subtest from Wechsler Memory Scale–III: An empirical trial. *Archives of Clinical Neuropsychology, 21,* 687–692.

Lezak, M. D., Howieson, D. B., & Loring, D. W. (with Hannay, H. J., & Fischer, J. S.). (2004). *Neuropsychological assessment* (4th ed.). New York, NY: Oxford University Press.

Lichtenberg, P. (2010). *Handbook of assessment in clinical gerontology* (2nd ed.). Hoboken, NJ: John Wiley & Sons, Inc.

Lichtenberger, E. O., Kaufman, A. S., & Lai, Z. C. (2002). *Essentials of WMS-III Assessment.* Hoboken, NJ: Wiley.

Loring, D. W., & Bauer, R. M. (2010). Testing the limits: Cautions and concerns regarding the new Wechsler IQ and memory scales. *Neurology, 74*, 685–690.

Marshall, P., & Happe, M. (2007). The performance of individuals with mental retardation on cognitive tests assessing effort and motivation. *Clinical Neuropsychologist, 21*(5), 826–840.

Matarazzo, J. D., & Prifitera, A. (1989). Subtest scatter and pre-morbid intelligence: Lessons from the WAIS-R standardization sample. *Psychological Assessment, 1*, 186–191.

Mattis, S. (1988). *Dementia Rating Scale (DRS)*. Odessa, FL: Psychological Assessment Resources.

McDowell, B. D., Bayless, J. D., Moser, D. J., Meyers, J. E., & Paulsen, J. S. (2004). Concordance between the CVLT and the WMS-III word lists test. *Archives of Clinical Neuropsychology, 19*, 319–324.

Miller, J. B. (2010). *Assessment of memory functioning and effort on the Wechsler Memory Scale–Fourth Edition* (unpublished doctoral dissertation). Wayne State University, Detroit, MI.

Miller, J. B., Holcomb, E. M., Bashem, J. R., & Rapport, L. J. (2010, February). *Substitution of the CVLT-II for Verbal Paired Associates on the Wechsler Memory Scale–Fourth Edition: Relationship between scaled scores in a traumatic brain injury sample.* Poster presented at the 38th Annual Meeting of the International Neuropsychological Society, Acapulco, Mexico.

Miller, L. J., Ryan, J. J., Carruthers, C. A., & Cluff, R. B. (2004). Brief screening indexes for malingering: A confirmation of Vocabulary minus Digit Span from the WAIS-III and the Rarely Missed Index from the WMS-III. *Clinical Neuropsychologist, 18*(2), 327–333.

Millis, S. R., Malina, A. C., Bowers, D. A., & Ricker, J. H. (1999). Confirmatory factor analysis of the WMS-III. *Journal of Clinical and Experimental Neuropsychology, 21*, 87–93.

Mitrushina, M., Boone, K. B., Razani, J., & D'Elia, L. F. (2005). *Handbook of normative data for neuropsychological assessment* (2nd ed.). New York, NY: Oxford University Press.

Mittenberg, W., Azrin, R. L., Millsaps, C., & Heilbronner, R. L. (1993). Identification of malingered head injury on the Wechsler Memory Scale–Revised. *Psychological Assessment, 5*, 34–40.

Morris, F., Leach, L., Kaplan, E., Winocur, G., Shulman, K., & Delis, D. (1994). *Clock Drawing: A Neuropsychological Analysis.* New York, NY: Oxford University Press.

Nadel, L., & Moscovitch, M. (1997). Memory consolidation, retrograde amnesia and the hippocampal complex. *Current Opinion in Neurobiology, 7*, 217–227.

National Institute on Aging. (2008). National Institute on Aging. (2008). Progress report on Alzheimer's disease: moving discovery forward. Retrieved from www.nia.nih.gov/Alzheimers/Publications/ADProgress2008/

Nyberg, L. (2008). Structural basis of episodic memory. In J. H. Byrne & H. Eichenbaum (Eds.), *Learning and memory: A comprehensive reference: Memory systems* (Vol. 3, pp. 99–109). San Diego, CA: Elsevier Science.

Ord, J. S., Greve, K. W., & Bianchini, K. J. (2008). Using the Wechsler Memory Scale–III to detect malingering in mild traumatic brain injury. *Clinical Neuropsychologist, 22*(4), 689–704.

Packard, M. G., & Knowlton, B. J. (2002). Learning and memory functions of the basal ganglia. *Annual Review of Neurosciences, 25*, 563–593; doi: 10.1146/annurev.neuro.25.112701.142937

Pearson. (2000). *Wechsler Abbreviated Scales of Intelligence (WASI)*. San Antonio, TX: Author.

Pearson. (2009). *Advanced Clinical Solutions for WAIS-IV and WMS-IV*. San Antonio, TX: Author.

Pearson. (2010). *WMS-IV Flexible Approach Manual*. San Antonio, TX: Author.

Petersen, R. C., Roberts, R. O., Knopman, D. S., Boeve, B. F., Geda, Y. E., Ivnik, R. J., . . . Jack, C. R. (2009). Mild cognitive impairment: Ten years later. *Archives of Neurology, 66*(12), 1447–1455.

Plassman, B. L., Langa, K. M., Fisher, G. G., Heeringa, S. G., Weir, D. R., Ofstedal, M., . . . Wallace, R. B. (2007). Prevalence of dementia in the United States: The aging, demographics, and memory study. *Neuroepidemiology, 29*(1–2), 125–132.

Postle, B. R., Druzgal, T. J., & D'Esposito, M. (2003). Seeking the neural substrates of visual working memory storage. *Cortex, 39*, 927–946.

Price, L., Said, K., & Haaland, K. Y. (2004). Age-associated memory impairment of Logical Memory and Visual Reproduction. *Journal of Clinical & Experimental Neuropsychology, 26*(4), 531–538.

Price, L., Tulsky, D., Millis, S., & Weiss, L. (2002). Redefining the factor structure of the Wechsler Memory Scale–III: Confirmatory factor analysis with cross-validation. *Journal of Clinical and Experimental Neuropsychology, 56*, 1133–1142.

Rabin, L. A., Barr, W. B., & Burton, L. A. (2005). Assessment practices of clinical neuropsychologists in the United States and Canada: A survey of INS, NAN, and APA division 40 members. *Archives of Clinical Neuropsychology, 20*, 33–65.

Rabin, L. A., Pare, N., Saykin, A. J., Brown, M. J., Wishart, H. A., Flashman, L. A., & Santulli, R. B. (2009). Differential memory test sensitivity for diagnosing amnestic mild cognitive impairment and predicting conversion to Alzheimer's disease. *Aging Neuropsychology & Cognition, 16*(3), 357–376.

Ranganath, C., & Blumenfeld, R. S. (2008). Prefrontal cortex and memory. In J. H. Byrne & H. Eichenbaum (Eds.), *Learning and memory: A comprehensive reference: Memory systems* (Vol. 3, pp. 261–279). San Diego, CA: Elsevier Science.

Roberts, R. O., Geda, Y. E., Knopman, D., Cha, R. H., Pankratz, V. S., Boeve, B. F., . . . Rocca, W. A. (2008). The Mayo Clinic study of aging: Design and sampling, participation, baseline measures and sample characteristics. *Neuroepidemiology, 30*(1), 58–69.

Rockey, L. S. (1997). Memory assessment of the older adult. In P. D. Nussbaum (Ed.), *Handbook of Neuropsychology and Aging (Critical Issues in Neuropsychology)* (pp. 385–393). New York, NY: Plenum Press.

Russell, E. W. (1975). A multiple scoring method for the assessment of complex memory functions. *Journal of Consulting and Clinical Psychology, 43*, 800–809.

Russell, E. W. (1981). The pathology and clinical examination of memory. In S. B. Filskov & T. J. Boll (Eds.), *Handbook of clinical neuropsychology* (pp. 287–319). New York, NY: John Wiley & Sons.

Russell, E. W. (1988). Renorming Russell's version of the Wechsler Memory Scale. *Journal of Clinical and Experimental Neuropsychology, 10*, 235–249.

Ryan, J. J., Kreiner, D. S., & Burton, D. B. (2002). Does high scatter affect the predictive validity of WAIS–III IQs? *Applied Neuropsychology, 9*, 173–178.

Salthouse, T. A. (2009). Decomposing age correlations on neuropsychological and cognitive variables. *Journal of the International Neuropsychological Society, 15*, 650–661.

Sattler, J. (2008). *Assessment of Children: Cognitive Foundations* (5th ed.). San Diego, CA: Author.

Scoville, W. B., & Milner, B. (1957). Loss of memory after bilateral hippocampal lesions. *Journal of Neurology, Neurosurgery, and Psychiatry, 20*, 11–21.

Shepard, L. (1980). An evaluation of the regression discrepancy method for identifying children with learning disabilities. *Journal of Special Education, 14*(1), 79–91.

Shimamura, A. P. (2002). Relational binding theory and the role of consolidation in memory retrieval. In L. R. Squire & D. L. Schacter (Eds.), *The neuropsychology of memory* (3rd ed., pp. 61–72). New York, NY: Guilford Press.

Shimamura, A. P., & Wickens, T. D. (2009). Superadditive memory strength for item and source recognition: The role of hierarchical relational binding in the medial temporal lobe. *Psychological Review, 116*, 1–19; doi:10.1037/a0014500

Simeonsson, R. J., & Rosenthal, S. L. (2001). *Psychological and developmental assessment: Children with disabilities and chronic conditions.* New York, NY: Guilford Press.

Slick, D. J., Sherman, E. M., & Iverson, G. L. (1999). Diagnostic criteria for malingered neurocognitive dysfunction: Proposed standards for clinical practice and research. *Clinical Neuropsychologist, 13*(4), 545–561.

Slick, D. J., Tan, J. E., Strauss, E. H., & Hultsch, D. F. (2004). Detecting malingering: A survey of experts' practices. *Archives of Clinical Neuropsychology, 19*, 465–473.

Smith, G., & Rush, B. K. (2006). Normal aging and mild cognitive impairment. In D. K. Attix & K. A. Welsh–Bohmer (Eds.), *Geriatric neuropsychology: Assessment and intervention* (pp. 27–55). New York, NY: Guilford Press.

Squire, L. R. (1987). *Memory and brain.* New York: Oxford University Press.

Squire, L. R., Cohen, N. J., & Nadel, L. (1984). The medial temporal region and memory consolidation: A new hypothesis. In H. Weingartner & E. S. Parker (Eds.), *Memory consolidation: Psychobiology of cognition* (pp. 185–210). Hillsdale, NJ: Erlbaum.

Squire, L. R., & Schacter, D. L. (2002). *Neuropsychology of memory* (3rd ed.). New York, NY: Guilford Press.

Strauss, E., Sherman, E. M. S., & Spreen, O. (2006). *A compendium of neuropsychological tests: Administration, norms, and commentary* (3rd ed.). New York, NY: Oxford University Press.

Sullivan, K. (2000). Examiners' errors on the Wechsler Memory Scale–Revised. *Psychological Reports, 87*, 234–240.

Swihart, A. A, Harris, K. M., & Hatcher, L. L. (2008). Inability of the Rarely Missed Index to identify simulated malingering under more realistic assessment conditions. *Journal of Clinical and Experimental Neuropsychology, 30*, 120–126.

Takashima, A., Nieuwenhuis, I. L. C., Jensen, O., Talamini, L. M., Rijpkema, M., & Fernández, G. (2009). Shift from hippocampal to neocortical centered retrieval network with consolidation. *Journal of Neuroscience, 32*, 10087–10093.

Tombaugh, T. N. (1997). The Test of Memory Malingering (TOMM): Normative data from cognitively intact and cognitively impaired individuals. *Psychological Assessment, 9*, 260–268.

Townsend, L. A., Malla, A. K., & Norman, R. M. (2001). Cognitive functioning in stabilized first-episode psychosis patients. *Psychiatry Research, 104*(2), 119–131.

Tulsky, D. S., Saklofske, D. H., Chelune, G. J., Heaton, R. K., Ivnik, R. J., Bornstein, R., . . . Ledbetter, M. F. (Eds.). (2003). *Clinical interpretation of the WAIS-III and WMS-III.* New York,: Academic Press.

Victor, T. L., Boone, K. B., Serpa, J. G., Buehler, J., & Ziegler, E. A. (2009). Interpreting the meaning of multiple symptom validity test failure. *Clinical Neuropsychologist, 23*(2), 297–313.

Wang, S.-H., & Morris, R. G. M. (2010). Hippocampal–neocortical interactions in memory formation, consolidation, and reconsolidation. *Annual Review of Psychology, 61*, 49–79.

Wechsler, D. (1945). A standardized memory scale for clinical use. *Journal of Psychology, 19*, 87–95.

Wechsler, D. (1955). *Wechsler Adult Intelligence Scale.* New York: Psychological Corporation.

Wechsler, D. (1987). *Wechsler Memory Scale–Revised.* San Antonio, TX: Psychological Corporation.

Wechsler, D. (1997a) *Wechsler Adult Intelligence Scale–Third Edition.* San Antonio, TX: Psychological Corporation.

Wechsler, D. (1997b). *Wechsler Memory Scale–Third Edition.* San Antonio, TX: Psychological Corporation.

Wechsler, D. (2001). *Wechsler Test of Adult Reading.* San Antonio, TX: Pearson.

Wechsler, D. (2002a). *WAIS-III/WMS-III technical manual, updated.* San Antonio, TX: Psychological Corporation.

Wechsler, D. (2002b). *Wechsler Memory Scale–Third Edition, Abbreviated.* San Antonio, TX: Psychological Corporation.

Wechsler, D. (2008). *Wechsler Adult Intelligence Scale–Fourth Edition.* San Antonio, TX: Pearson.

Wechsler, D. (2009) *Wechsler Memory Scale–Fourth Edition.* San Antonio, TX: Pearson.

Weiss, L. G., Saklofske, D. H., Coalson, D. L., & Raiford, S. E. (2010). *WAIS-IV clinical use and interpretation.* New York, NY: Elsevier.

Weiss, L. G., Saklofske, D. H., Prifitera, A., & Holdnack, J. A. (2006). *WISC-IV advanced clinical interpretation.* San Diego, CA: Academic Press.

Werner, H. (1937). Process and achievement: A basic problem of education and developmental psychology. *Harvard Educational Review, 7,* 353–368.

Wilde, N. J., Strauss, E., Chelune, G. J., Hermann, B. P., Hunter, M., Loring, D. W., . . . Sherman, E. M. S. (2003). Confirmatory factor analysis of the WMS-III in patients with temporal lobe epilepsy. *Psychological Assessment, 15*(1), 56–63.

Wilde, N., Strauss, E., Chelune, G. J., Loring, D. W., Martin, R. C., Hermann, B. P., . . . Hunter, M. (2001). WMS-III performance in patients with temporal lobe epilepsy: Group differences and individual classification. *Journal of the International Neuropsychological Society, 7*(7), 881–891.

Winoblad, B., Palmer, K., Kivipelto, M., Jelic, V., Fratiglioni, L., Wahlund, L., . . . Petersen, R. C. (2004). Mild cognitive impairment–beyond controversies, towards a consensus: Report of the international working group on mild cognitive impairment. *Journal of Internal Medicine, 256,* 240–246.

Woodcock, R. W., McGrew, K. S., & Mather, N. (2000). *Woodcock–Johnson Psychoeducational Battery, Third Edition (WJ-3).* Chicago, IL: Riverside.

Woods, S. P., Iudicello, J. E., Moran, L. M., Carey, C. L., Dawson, M. S., & Grant, I. (HIV Neurobehavioral Research Center Group). (2008). HIV-associated prospective memory impairment increases risk of dependence in everyday functioning. *Neuropsychology, 22*(1),110–117.

World Health Organization. (2006). Neurological disorders: Public health challenges. Retrieved from www.who.int/mental_health/neurology/neurodiso/en/index/html

Zhu, J., & Tulsky, D. S. (2000). Co-norming of the WAIS-III and WMS-III: Is there a test-order effect on IQ and memory scores? *Clinical Neuropsychologist, 14*(1), 1.

Appendix

ADMINISTRATIVE AND SCORING CHECKLIST FOR THE WMS-IV (ALL RESPONSES SHOULD BE "YES")

Developed with André C. Lane, MA, Jayme Lyon, MA, and Elsa Tijerina, MA

Brief Cognitive Status Exam

1. Reads directions verbatim?	Yes	No
2. Starts with item 1?	Yes	No
3. Orientation questions read verbatim?	Yes	No
4. If the examinee's response was unclear, asks for clarification?	Yes	No
5. Responses recorded verbatim for items 1–6?	Yes	No
6. Records actual time on record form for item 6?	Yes	No
7. Difference in minutes calculated correctly for item 6?	Yes	No
8. Presents naming stimuli one at a time without providing hints?	Yes	No
9. Records errors (skipped responses, additional words, or sequencing errors) on items 7 and 8 as the examinee responded?	Yes	No
10. Does not count self-corrections as errors?	Yes	No
11. Begins timing for items 7 and 8 after presenting item and stopped timing once the examinee finished responding?	Yes	No
12. Records completion times for items 7 and 8?	Yes	No
13. Calculates the total number of errors correctly for items 7 and 8?	Yes	No
14. For item 9, records the sequence in which the examinee drew numbers on the clock face?	Yes	No
15. Presents the response booklet correctly?	Yes	No
16. Uses a pencil without an eraser?	Yes	No
17. If the examinee attempts to erase or restart the clock drawing, says "Do not start over, just do your best"?	Yes	No

18. Scores clock-drawing elements correctly?   Yes   No
19. Records responses to incidental recall verbatim?   Yes   No
20. Administers the sample inhibition item prior to item 11?   Yes   No
21. Records errors (skipped shapes, incorrect shapes, or self-corrections) on item 11 as the examinee responded?   Yes   No
22. Counts self-corrections as errors?   Yes   No
23. Begins timing for item 11 after reading the instructions and stopped timing once the examinee finished responding?   Yes   No
24. Records completion time for item 11?   Yes   No
25. Calculates commission and omission errors correctly?   Yes   No
26. Records examinee's response verbatim on item 12?   Yes   No
27. Begins timing after reading the instructions for item 12 and stops the examinee after 30 seconds?   Yes   No
28. Calculates weighted raw scores correctly?   Yes   No
29. Sums the BCSE total raw score correctly?   Yes   No
30. Obtains the correct classification level based on the examinee's age and education?   Yes   No

Visual Reproduction I

1. Reads directions verbatim?   Yes   No
2. Presents response booklet correctly?   Yes   No
3. Presents each design for 10 seconds?   Yes   No
4. Does not allow the examinee to draw during exposure of the items?   Yes   No
5. Uses pencils with erasers?   Yes   No
6. Allows examinee time to complete designs?   Yes   No
7. Records a completion time for each item (optional)?   Yes   No
8. Provides encouragement by saying "Don't worry about your artistic ability; just draw it as best you can" if the examinee is reluctant to draw?   Yes   No
9. States, "Well, just draw it as well as you remember," if the examinee says he or she cannot remember?   Yes   No
10. Allows the examinee to erase and make corrections?   Yes   No
11. Records the subtest stop time?   Yes   No
12. Scores item criteria correctly after WMS-IV administration is completed?   Yes   No
13. Sums the item scores correctly to obtain the VR I total raw score?   Yes   No

Logical Memory I

1. Reads directions verbatim?	Yes	No
2. Presents the correct stories for the battery administered?	Yes	No
3. Records responses verbatim for later scoring?	Yes	No
4. Allows an appropriate amount of time for the examinee to respond?	Yes	No
5. Records the subtest stop time?	Yes	No
6. Scores each story detail correctly?	Yes	No
7. Sums the item scores correctly to obtain the LM I total raw score?	Yes	No

Spatial Addition

1. Does not administer to individuals taking the Older Adult battery?	Yes	No
2. Reads directions verbatim?	Yes	No
3. Administers the Card Placement Sample, Demonstration item, and Sample Items A and B prior to test items?	Yes	No
4. Starts at the age-appropriate start point?	Yes	No
5. Follows the reverse rule correctly, if appropriate?	Yes	No
6. Presents the memory grid in the correct orientation?	Yes	No
7. Presents all the cards in a stack, design side up for each item?	Yes	No
8. Assists the examinee with placing the cards in the grid, if needed?	Yes	No
9. Says "Do not touch the grid until I tell you to do so" if the examinee attempts to mark places in the grid during presentation of the stimulus cards?	Yes	No
10. Records responses or scores for each item administered?	Yes	No
11. Records responses from the correct perspective?	Yes	No
12. Removes the cards from the grid following each item?	Yes	No
13. Removes cards by pushing fingers through holes in the grid?	Yes	No
14. Provides the correct prompts during the card placement and demonstration items?	Yes	No
15. Repeats the demonstration item if the examinee does not understand the task?	Yes	No
16. Provides corrective feedback during the sample items?	Yes	No
17. Presents each stimulus grid for 5 seconds?	Yes	No
18. Provides no feedback during test items?	Yes	No

19. Discontinues administration after three consecutive scores of 0?   Yes   No
20. Scores each item correctly?   Yes   No
21. Sums the item scores correctly to obtain the SA total raw score?   Yes   No

Visual Reproduction II

1. Calculates elapsed time correctly?   Yes   No
2. Begins administration 20–30 minutes after completing VR I? Yes   No
3. Reads directions verbatim?   Yes   No
4. Presents response booklet correctly for recall and optional copy items without revealing previously drawn items?   Yes   No
5. Uses pencils with erasers?   Yes   No
6. Records a completion time for each recall item (optional)? Yes   No
7. Provides encouragement but does not provide specific cues about the designs?   Yes   No
8. For recall, states, "Each page had one or more designs on it" or "Just try to remember one of them" if the examinee says he or she cannot remember?   Yes   No
9. Allows the examinee to erase and make corrections?   Yes   No
10. Allows examinee time to complete designs?   Yes   No
11. Administers all recognition items?   Yes   No
12. For recognition items, circles one response for each item? Yes   No
13. For copy, presents the stimulus throughout the item and response?   Yes   No
14. Scores item criteria correctly following completion of WMS-IV?   Yes   No
15. Sums the item scores correctly to obtain the VR II total raw score?   Yes   No
16. Sums the item scores correctly to obtain the VR II recognition total raw score (optional)?   Yes   No
17. Sums the item scores correctly to obtain the VR II copy total raw score (optional)?   Yes   No

Logical Memory II

1. Calculates elapsed time correctly?   Yes   No
2. Begins administration 20–30 minutes after completing LM I? Yes   No

3. Reads directions verbatim?   Yes   No

4. Presents the correct stories for the battery administered?   Yes   No

5. Allows the examinee to recall the stories out of order?   Yes   No

6. Provides appropriate cue and marks cue given box if examinee does not recall anything from a story?   Yes   No

7. Records responses verbatim for later scoring?   Yes   No

8. Allows an appropriate amount of time for the examinee to respond?   Yes   No

9. Scores each story detail correctly?   Yes   No

10. Circles a response for each recognition item (optional)?   Yes   No

11. Administers all recognition items (optional)?   Yes   No

12. Repeats recognition items if needed?   Yes   No

13. Sums the item scores correctly to obtain the LM II total raw score?   Yes   No

14. Sums the item scores correctly to obtain the LM II Recognition total raw score (optional)?   Yes   No

Verbal Paired Associates I

1. Reads directions verbatim?   Yes   No

2. Repeats instructions if the examinee does not understand the task?   Yes   No

3. Presents the correct word pairs for the battery administered?   Yes   No

4. Presents the word pairs with 1 second between words and 2 seconds between pairs?   Yes   No

5. Allows 5 seconds for the examinee to respond to each item?   Yes   No

6. Records a checkmark or verbatim incorrect response for each item?   Yes   No

7. Provides corrective feedback for each incorrect response?   Yes   No

8. Records the subtest stop time?   Yes   No

9. Scores each item correctly?   Yes   No

10. Sums the item scores correctly to obtain the VPA I total raw score?   Yes   No

Designs I

1. Does not administer to individuals taking the Older Adult battery?   Yes   No

2. Reads directions verbatim?   Yes   No

3. Administers the Demonstration item prior to test items?   Yes   No

4. Presents the memory grid in the correct orientation?   Yes   No

5. Shuffles the cards before placing them in front of the examinee?   Yes   No

6. Presents the correct cards in a stack, design side up for each item?   Yes   No

7. Assists the examinee with placing the cards in the grid, if needed?   Yes   No

8. Administers all four items?   Yes   No

9. If the examinee places more than the correct number of cards in the grid, gives the prompt to not place more than (insert appropriate number) cards in the grid?   Yes   No

10. Does not prompt if there are too few cards in the grid for an item?   Yes   No

11. Records responses for each item?   Yes   No

12. Records responses from the correct perspective?   Yes   No

13. Removes the cards from the grid following each item?   Yes   No

14. Removes cards by pushing fingers through holes in the grid?   Yes   No

15. Presents each stimulus grid for 10 seconds?   Yes   No

16. Redirects the examinee if he or she is not attending to the task?   Yes   No

17. If the examinee places the cards in a manner that suggests he or she is placing the cards from the orientation of the examiner, reorients him or her as directed?   Yes   No

18. Does not count rotations as incorrect?   Yes   No

19. Records rule violations by placing a checkmark in the rule violations box?   Yes   No

20. Does not record a rule violation if the examinee places fewer than the correct number of cards in the grid for an item?   Yes   No

21. Records the subtest stop time?   Yes   No

22. Scores each item correctly?   Yes   No

23. Sums the item scores correctly to obtain the DE I total raw score?   Yes   No

Symbol Span

1. If subtests are reordered, does not administer between VR I and VR II?   Yes   No

2. Reads directions verbatim?   Yes   No

3. Repeats the sample item if the examinee does not understand
the task? Yes No
4. Provides specific feedback during the sample items? Yes No
5. Presents each stimulus page for 5 seconds? Yes No
6. Provides specific feedback during items 3 and 4? Yes No
7. Provides no feedback during remaining test items? Yes No
8. Records response or score for each item administered? Yes No
9. Discontinues administration after four imperfect scores? Yes No
10. Scores each item correctly? Yes No
11. Sums the item scores correctly to obtain the SSP total
raw score? Yes No

Verbal Paired Associates II

1. Calculates elapsed time correctly? Yes No
2. Begins administration 20–30 minutes after completing
VPA I? Yes No
3. Reads directions verbatim? Yes No
4. Presents the correct word pairs for the battery administered? Yes No
5. Allows 10 seconds for the examinee to respond to each
delayed recall item? Yes No
6. Records a checkmark or verbatim incorrect response for
each delayed recall item? Yes No
7. Does not provide feedback or correct responses on
delayed recall? Yes No
8. Scores each item correctly? Yes No
9. Sums the item scores correctly to obtain the VPA II total
raw score? Yes No
10. Presents the recognition word pairs with 1 second
between words? Yes No
11. Circles a response for each recognition item (optional)? Yes No
12. Administers every recognition item (optional)? Yes No
13. Repeats recognition instructions if needed (optional)? Yes No
14. Sums the item scores correctly to obtain the VPA II
Recognition total raw score (optional)? Yes No
15. Records all word recall responses verbatim (optional)? Yes No
16. Scores each word correctly? Yes No
17. Sums the words correctly to obtain the VPA II word
recall total raw score? Yes No

Designs II

1. Does not administer to individuals taking the Older Adult battery?   Yes   No
2. Calculates elapsed time correctly?   Yes   No
3. Begins administration 20–30 minutes after completing DE I?   Yes   No
4. Reads directions verbatim?   Yes   No
5. Presents the memory grid in the correct orientation?   Yes   No
6. Shuffles the cards before placing them in front of the examinee?   Yes   No
7. Presents all the cards in a stack, design side up for each item?   Yes   No
8. Assists the examinee with placing the cards in the grid, if needed?   Yes   No
9. Administers all four items?   Yes   No
10. If the examinee places more than the correct number of cards in the grid, gives the prompt to not place more than (insert appropriate number) cards in the grid?   Yes   No
11. Does not prompt if there are too few cards in the grid for an item?   Yes   No
12. Records responses for each item?   Yes   No
13. Records responses from the correct perspective?   Yes   No
14. Removes the cards from the grid following each item?   Yes   No
15. Removes cards by pushing fingers through holes in the grid?   Yes   No
16. Does not count rotations as incorrect?   Yes   No
17. Records rule violations by placing a checkmark in the rule violations box?   Yes   No
18. Does not record a rule violation if examinee places fewer than the correct number of cards in the grid for an item?   Yes   No
19. Scores each item correctly?   Yes   No
20. Sums the item scores correctly to obtain the DE II total raw score?   Yes   No
21. Circles two responses for each recognition item (optional)?   Yes   No
22. Administers all recognition items (optional)?   Yes   No
23. Sums the item scores correctly to obtain the DE II Recognition total raw score (optional)?   Yes   No

Summary Pages

1.	Correctly transfers scores to the summary pages?	Yes	No
2.	Correctly derives the scaled scores from the raw scores?	Yes	No
3.	Correctly derives CVLT-II equivalent scores, if needed?	Yes	No
4.	Correctly sums the scaled scores?	Yes	No
5.	Correctly derives the index scores from the sum of scaled scores?	Yes	No
6.	Correctly completes the percentile ranks and confidence intervals for the index scores?	Yes	No
7.	Correctly transfers the scaled scores and index scores to the score profiles?	Yes	No
8.	Correctly places scores on the profiles?	Yes	No
9.	Correctly derives the process scaled scores and cumulative percentages from the raw scores?	Yes	No
10.	Correctly transfers scaled scores to the within index comparisons table?	Yes	No
11.	Correctly computes the subtest mean scores within each index, if appropriate?	Yes	No
12.	Correctly computes the differences from the mean for each score, if appropriate?	Yes	No
13.	Identifies which differences are statistically significant?	Yes	No
14.	Supplies the appropriate base rate for each significant difference?	Yes	No
15.	Transfers SA and SSP scaled scores to the subtest discrepancy table?	Yes	No
16.	Subtracts SSP from SA correctly?	Yes	No
17.	Identifies whether the difference is statistically significant?	Yes	No
18.	Supplies the appropriate base rate for the difference?	Yes	No
19.	Correctly transfers the appropriate scores to the subtest-level and index-level contrast scaled scores tables?	Yes	No
20.	Derives the contrast scaled scores correctly?	Yes	No

Annotated Bibliography

Blumenfeld, H. (2002). *Neuroanatomy through clinical cases.* Sunderland, MA: Sinauer Associates, Inc.

This text provides detailed descriptions of neuroanatomy and neurological evaluation with the use of clinical case studies, including MRI and CT scans, to reinforce the connection between the brain and test results.

Byrne, J. H. (2008). *Learning and memory: The editor's selection.* San Diego, CA: Elsevier Science.

The top 30 chapters from the four-volume *Learning and Memory: A Comprehensive Reference* series. This is a comprehensive overview of the state of research on memory.

Eichenbaum, H. (2008). *Learning and memory.* New York, NY: Norton.

A comprehensive overview of the current theories of memory. This book integrates research using animal learning, human memory, and neuroscience.

Lezak, M. D., Howieson, D. B., & Loring, D. W. (with Hannay, H. J., & Fischer, J. S.). (2004). *Neuropsychological assessment* (4th ed.). New York, NY: Oxford University Press.

The fourth edition of the classic text on neuropsychological assessment. Along with an overview of memory assessment, this book provides an overview of neuropsychology, neuropsychological assessment, and instruments used to assess a variety of cognitive abilities.

Lichtenberg, P. (2010). *Handbook of assessment in clinical gerontology* (2nd ed.). New York, NY: John Wiley & Sons.

This text provides an overview of assessment in older adults. Along with detailed descriptions of disorders commonly experienced by older adults, it provides information on assessment instruments, and clinical case studies.

Morgan, J. E., & Ricker, J. H. (2008) *Textbook of clinical neuropsychology.* New York, NY: Taylor & Francis.

A basic, comprehensive book on the neuropsychological assessment of clinical disorders. Chapters are organized around specific disorders and include detailed research on the disorder, neuropsychological findings in the disorder, and clinical case studies.

Pearson. (2009). *Advanced clinical solutions for WAIS-IV and WMS-IV clinical and interpretive manual.* San Antonio, TX: Author.

The ACS manual provides detailed information on the interpretation of the ACS scores described. In addition, it includes information on effort assessment, reliable change, demographically adjusted norms, and premorbid functioning using the WAIS-IV and WMS-IV.

Squire, L. R., & Schacter, D. L. (2002). *Neuropsychology of memory* (3rd ed.). New York, NY: Guilford Press.

The third edition of the classic reference provides detailed information on the current state of the field in memory research, including animal research, cognitive neuroscience, and imaging.

Strauss, E., Sherman, E. M. S., & Spreen, O. (2006). *A compendium of neuropsychological tests: Administration, norms, and commentary* (3rd ed.). New York, NY: Oxford University Press.

A detailed review of instruments used in neuropsychological evaluation. Chapters are organized around cognitive ability and include detailed information on each available assessment, including references on available normative data.

Tulsky, D. S., Saklofske, D. H., Chelune, G. J., Heaton, R. K., Ivnik, R. J., Bornstein, R., ...Ledbetter, M. F. (Eds.). (2003). *Clinical interpretation of the WAIS-III and WMS-III.* New York: Academic Press.

A comprehensive overview of the history, development, clinical research, and clinical use of the WAIS-III and WMS-III. Many of the chapters are relevant to the revised editions of the products.

Wechsler, D. (2009). *Wechsler Memory Scale–Fourth Edition administration and scoring manual.* San Antonio, TX: Pearson.

The comprehensive guide to the administration and scoring of the WMS-IV.

Wechsler, D. (2009). *Wechsler Memory Scale–Fourth Edition technical and interpretive manual.* San Antonio, TX: Pearson.

The comprehensive guide to the technical aspects of the WMS-IV and an introduction to interpretation.

Weiss, L. G., Saklofske, D. H., Coalson, D. L., & Raiford, S. E. (2010). *WAIS-IV clinical use and interpretation.* New York, NY: Elsevier.

Although the main focus of this text is the WAIS-IV, use of the WMS-IV in a variety of clinical evaluations is discussed.

About the Authors

Lisa Whipple Drozdick is a research director on the neuropsychology team for Pearson. She earned her PhD in 2003 from West Virginia University, with a special focus in geropsychology. She has developed and codeveloped several assessment instruments, including the WMS-IV, Texas Functional Living Scale, Advanced Clinical Solutions for WAIS-IV and WMS-IV, NEPSY-II, and Form B of Wechsler Fundamentals. She has published and presented on assessment and geropsychology topics. She is a licensed psychologist in the state of Texas.

James A. Holdnack, PhD, is a senior research director for Pearson. As manager of the neuropsychology team, he has developed neuropsychological tests including WMS-IV, Advanced Clinical Solutions for the Wechsler Scales, NEPSY-II and D-KEFS. He has published book chapters and research articles and provided professional presentations on the Wechsler Scales and other neuropsychological topics. Dr. Holdnack is a licensed psychologist in Pennsylvania and Delaware.

Robin C. Hilsabeck earned her PhD in clinical psychology from Louisiana State University in 1999, with a specialty focus in neuropsychology. She completed an internship in neuropsychology at the University of Oklahoma Health Science Center and a 2-year postdoctoral fellowship in neuropsychology at University of California, San Diego Medical Center. Dr. Hilsabeck currently is Director of Neuropsychology Postdoctoral Residency Training at South Texas Veterans Health Care System, Associate Professor of Psychiatry at University of Texas Health Science Center at San Antonio, and Assistant Clinical Professor of Psychiatry at University of California, San Diego. She became board certified in clinical neuropsychology through the American Board of Professional Psychology in 2003.

Author Index

Subject Index

CPSIA information can be obtained
at www.ICGtesting.com
Printed in the USA
EDOW040956260613